Artificial Intelligence in Information and Communication Technologies, Healthcare and Education

Artificial Intelligence in Information and Communication Technologies, Healthcare and Education: A Roadmap Ahead is designed as a reference text and discusses inter-dependability, communication and effective control for the betterment of services through artificial intelligence (AI), as well as the challenges and path ahead for AI in computing and control across different domains of business and human life. The book accommodates technologies and application domains including backbone hardware, systems and methods for deployment, which help in incorporating intelligence through different supervised and probabilistic learning approaches.

Features

- The book attempts to establish a connection between hardware, software technologies and algorithmic intelligence for data analysis and decision support in domains such as healthcare, education and other aspects of business and mobility.
- It presents various recent applications of artificial intelligence in information and communication technologies such as search and optimization methods, machine learning, data representation and ontologies and multi-agent systems.
- The book provides a collection of different case studies with experimentation results than mere theoretical and generalized approaches.
- This book covers most of the applications using the current technologies like AI, machine learning (ML), data science (DS), Internet of Things (IoT), and underlying information and communication technologies.

The book is aimed primarily at advanced undergraduates and postgraduate students studying computer science, computer applications and information technology. Researchers and professionals will also find this book useful.

T0293117

Artificial Intelligence in Information and Communication Technologies, Healthcare and Education

A Roadmap Ahead

Edited by
Parikshit N. Mahalle
Rajendra S. Talware
Ganesh C. Patil
Sachin R. Sakhare
Yogesh H. Dandawate
Pravin R. Futane

CRC Press
Taylor & Francis Group
Boca Raton London New York

CRC Press is an imprint of the
Taylor & Francis Group, an **informa** business

A CHAPMAN & HALL BOOK

First edition published 2023
by CRC Press
6000 Broken Sound Parkway NW, Suite 300, Boca Raton, FL 33487-2742

and by CRC Press
4 Park Square, Milton Park, Abingdon, Oxon, OX14 4RN

CRC Press is an imprint of Taylor & Francis Group, LLC

Library of Congress Cataloging-in-Publication Data
Names: Mahalle, Parikshit N., editor.
Title: Artificial intelligence in information and communication technologies,
healthcare and education : a roadmap ahead / edited by Parikshit N Mahalle [and 5 others].
Description: First edition. | Boca Raton, FL : Chapman & Hall/CRC Press, 2023. |
Includes bibliographical references and index. |
Summary: "Artificial Intelligence in Information and Communication Technologies, Healthcare and Education: A Roadmap Ahead is designed as a reference text and discusses inter-dependability, communication and effective control for the betterment of services through artificial intelligence, as well as the challenges and path ahead for AI in computing and control across different domains of business and human life. The book accommodates technologies and application domains including backbone hardware, systems and methods for deployment, which help incorporating intelligence through different supervised and probabilistic learning approaches"–
Provided by publisher.
Identifiers: LCCN 2022036469 (print) | LCCN 2022036470 (ebook) |
ISBN 9781032374598 (hbk) | ISBN 9781032379562 (pbk) | ISBN 9781003342755 (ebk)
Subjects: LCSH: Artificial intelligence.
Classification: LCC TA347.A78 A835 2023 (print) | LCC TA347.A78 (ebook) |
DDC 006.3–dc23/eng/20221024
LC record available at https://lccn.loc.gov/2022036469
LC ebook record available at https://lccn.loc.gov/2022036470

ISBN: 9781032374598 (hbk)
ISBN: 9781032379562 (pbk)
ISBN: 9781003342755 (ebk)

DOI: 10.1201/9781003342755

Typeset in Palatino
by Newgen Publishing UK

Contents

Section I   Convergence of AI, IoT, and Communication Technologies for Futuristic Innovations

Section II   Advances in Sensor and Chip Design, Controls, Communication, and Signal Processing

Section III Data Science and Analysis for Intelligence and Enterprise

Contributors

Vijaya N. Aher Vishwakarma Institute of Information Technology, Pune, Maharashtra, India

Prathamesh Akole Vishwakarma Institute of Information Technology, Pune, Maharashtra, India

S. Ananthakumaran VIT Bhopal University, Bhopal, Madhya Pradesh, India

Deepali Arun Bhanage Symbiosis International (Deemed University), Pune, Maharashtra, India

Rohan Awale Vishwakarma Institute of Information Technology, Pune, Maharashtra, India

Arti Bang Vishwakarma Institute of Information Technology, Pune, Maharashtra, India

Ambar Bidkar Vishwakarma Institute of Information Technology Pune, Maharashtra, India

Hridyesh Singh Bisht Symbiosis International (Deemed University), Pune, Maharashtra, India

Rohini Chavan Vishwakarma Institute of Information Technology, Pune, Maharashtra, India

Priya Yuvaraj Chougale Vishwakarma Institute of Information Technology, Pune, Maharashtra, India

Kale Navnath Dattatraya Koneru Lakshmaiah Education Foundation, Vaddeswaram, Andhra Pradesh, India

R.R. Deshmukh Dr. Babasheb Ambedkar Marathwada University, Aurangabad, Maharashtra, India

Pallavi Deshpande Vishwakarma Institute of Information Technology, Pune, Maharashtra, India

Sarita Deshpande PES's Modern College of Engineering, Savitribai Phule Pune University, Pune, Maharashtra, India

Animesh D. Dolas Vishwakarma Institute of Information Technology, Pune, Maharashtra, India

Dhananjay R. Dolas MGM'S JNEC, Aurangabad, Maharashtra, India

Chandrashekhar B. Dongre Vishwakarma Institute of Information Technology, Pune, Maharashtra, India

Rushikesh Dudhate Vishwakarma Institute of Information Technology, Pune, Maharashtra, India

Pravin R. Futane Vishwakarma Institute of Information Technology, Pune, Maharashtra, India

Gauri Ghule Vishwakarma Institute of Information Technology, Pune, Maharashtra, India

Shraddha Habbu Vishwakarma Institute of Information Technology, Pune, Maharashtra, India

Ajinkya Hapase Vishwakarma Institute of Information Technology, Pune, Maharashtra, India

Swapnil Jadhav Vishwakarma Institute of Information Technology, Pune, Maharashtra, India

Varsha D. Jadhav Vishwakarma Institute of Information Technology, Pune, Maharashtra, India

Mrudul Jain Vishwakarma Institute of Information Technology, Pune, Maharashtra, India

Kalpesh Joshi Vishwakarma Institute of Information Technology, Pune, Maharashtra, India

Rupesh Kapse Vishwakarma Institute of Information Technology, Pune, Maharashtra, India

K.V.D. Kiran Koneru Lakshmaiah Education Foundation, Vaddeswaram, Andhra Pradesh, India

Ketki P. Kshirsagar Vishwakarma Institute of Information Technology, Pune, Maharashtra, India

Kalpana A. Kumbhar Vishwakarma Institute of Information Technology, Pune, Maharashtra, India

Suyog Mahagaonkar Vishwakarma Institute of Information Technology, Pune, Maharashtra, India

Prachi Mukherji Cummins College of Engineering, Savitribai Phule Pune University, Pune, India

Pradip Mukundrao Paithane VPKBIET Baramati, Pune, Maharashtra, India

Yashkumar Mundada Vishwakarma Institute of Information Technology, Pune, Maharashtra, India

Yash Navin Agarwal Vishwakarma Institute of Information Technology, Pune, Maharashtra, India

Shaikh Naziya Sultana Dr. Babasheb Ambedkar Marathwada University Aurangabad, India

Deepali Nilesh Naik Pimpri Chinchwad College of Engineering, Pune, Maharashtra, India

Pratik Patil PES's Modern College of Engineering, Savitribai Phule Pune University, Pune, Maharashtra, India

Rutuja Patil Vishwakarma Institute of Information Technology, Pune, Maharashtra, India

Sanmit Patil Vishwakarma Institute of Information Technology, Pune, Maharashtra, India

Suvarna Pawar School of Engineering, MITADT University, Pune, Maharashtra India

Vishal Phulmante Vishwakarma Institute of Information Technology, Pune, Maharashtra, India

Vipul Pisal Vishwakarma Institute of Information Technology, Pune, Maharashtra, India

Rahul Pol Vishwakarma Institute of Information Technology, Pune, Maharashtra, India

Radhika Purandare Vishwakarma Institute of Information Technology, Pune, Maharashtra, India

Sarfraz Ali Quadri MGM'S JNEC, Aurangabad, Maharashtra, India

Archana Ratnaparkhi Vishwakarma Institute of Information Technology, Pune, Maharashtra, India

Ganesh S. Sable M.I.T. Aurangabad, Pune, Maharashtra, India

Nitin N. Sakhare Vishwakarma Institute of Information Technology, Pune, Maharashtra, India

Amit Samgir Vishwakarma Institute of Information Technology, Pune, Maharashtra, India

Ajinkya Sawadkar Vishwakarma Institute of Information Technology Pune, Maharashtra, India

Sachin S. Sawant Vishwakarma Institute of Information Technology, Pune, Maharashtra, India

Jay Shimpi Student, Department of Information Technology, Vishwakarma Institute of Information Technology, Pune, Maharashtra, India

Sejal Shrestha Symbiosis International (Deemed University), Pune, Maharashtra, India

Kavya Suthar Symbiosis International (Deemed University), Pune, Maharashtra, India.

Rushikesh S. Tanksale Vishwakarma Institute of Information Technology, Pune, Maharashtra, India

Rudra Tarte Vishwakarma Institute of Information Technology, Pune, Maharashtra, India

Ashish Tathod Vishwakarma Institute of Information Technology, Pune, Maharashtra, India

Ambika Vishal Pawar Symbiosis International (Deemed University), Pune, Maharashtra, India.

Pranav Wagh Vishwakarma Institute of Information Technology, Pune, Maharashtra, India

Ajay Yadav Vishwakarma Institute of Information Technology, Pune, Maharashtra, India

Preface

Education is the process of performing one's own duties for the attainment of peace, joy, satisfaction and salvation being rid of three wraths (lust, anger, fear) with steady mind and wisdom.

- Bhagvad Gita, a sacred Indian text

With advancements in broadband technology and semiconductor industry, the cost of internet and sensory devices is decreasing at a faster rate. The internet is getting cheaper and faster with each passing day, resulting in the reduction in cost of internet connectivity. Due to this transformation, more number of devices are connected to the Internet, which is causing data overflow, that is, big data. Fortunately, database management systems, that is, extracting, transformation and loading of the data, are mature and the main challenge today is how to make sense out of this big data. All information technology leaders and researchers are facing the main challenge of drawing meaningful insights from this big data and extending these insights for business intelligence. In addition to this, there are more efforts being applied in smart automation and digitization where human efforts and thinking are being replaced by machines. Consequently, majority of the use cases in information and communication technologies, education and healthcare are driven by artificial intelligence (AI). The main objective of this book is to guide beginners and experts about the application of AI in these areas of engineering. The text is divided into three parts: concepts and foundations, applications and research areas.

The convergence of AI, IoT and Blockchain aims at delivering features such as scalability, security and privacy to high-level intellectual functions that are beneficial to the new era of digital information. In recent times, the IoT has touched major milestones by overcoming the challenges faced in realizing the full potential of projects in various fields such as smart homes, agriculture, smart cities, healthcare and education. However, IoT faces many challenges in many areas such as security (attacks and threats), analysis of large amount of data, connectivity issues and many more. AI and deep learning are good decision-making tools used in our day-to-day activities/services such as healthcare, finances, mobility, biometrics and games.

The challenges faced in AI are determining or choosing the right data set, data storage and security, the integration of AI into the existing system, integration of AI with Cloud, poor data quality and high computing power. Communication, computing and control play a vital role in all the social development projects by providing a backbone in terms of energy supply and control, computing power and chip design, intelligent sensors, transmission and storage of data, and communication in heterogeneous networks. Signal processing in 1-D to 3-D resides at the core of most of the healthcare and security applications.

This book is an attempt to discuss inter-dependability, communication and effective control for the betterment of services through AI, keeping the backbone of hardware and software co-design, challenges and path ahead for AI in computing and control for different domains of business and human life.

The main characteristics of this book are as follows:

- Collection of different case studies with experimentation results
- Provides a strong foundation for the readers regarding the basics of AI and analytics, its relevance and need especially for the beginners
- Equips the readers with the ability to identify and categorize the problem at hand using a detailed review of the state of the art and future directions
- Provides and in-depth understanding on the various categories/classes of problems in AI

This book is specifically designed for beginners who want to get acquainted with the emerging field of AI and its application in information and communication technologies, healthcare and education for better business intelligence. A focus on the identification of the category of problem and the application of appropriate AI technique is a key highlight in this book. The book is useful for undergraduates, postgraduates, industry, researchers, teachers and research scholars in engineering and we are sure that this book will be well-received by all stakeholders.

Parikshit N. Mahalle
Rajendra S. Talware
Ganesh C. Patil
Sachin R. Sakhare
Yogesh H. Dandawate
Pravin R. Futane

Editor Biographies

Parikshit N. Mahalle is a senior member of IEEE and is Professor and Head of the Department of Artificial Intelligence and Data Science at Vishwakarma Institute of Information Technology, Pune, India. He completed his Ph.D. from Aalborg University, Denmark, and continued as a post-doctoral researcher at CMI, Copenhagen, Denmark. He has 23+ years of teaching and research experience. He is a member of the Board of Studies in Computer Engineering, Ex-Chairman of Information Technology, SPPU and various universities and autonomous colleges across India. He has 9 patents, 200 plus research publications (Google Scholar citations – 2,250 plus, H-index – 22 and Scopus citations are 1,190 plus with H index – 16) and authored/edited 42+ books with Springer, CRC Press, Cambridge University Press, etc. He is editor in chief for IGI Global – *International Journal of Rough Sets and Data Analysis*, Associate Editor for IGI Global – *International Journal of Synthetic Emotions, Inter-science International Journal of Grid and Utility Computing*, member of the Editorial Review Board for IGI Global – *International Journal of Ambient Computing and Intelligence*. His research interests are machine learning, data science, algorithms, Internet of Things, identity management and security. He is a recognized Ph.D. guide of SSPU, Pune, guiding seven Ph.D. students in the area of IoT and machine learning. Recently, five students have successfully defended their Ph.D. He is also the recipient of "Best Faculty Award" by Sinhgad Institutes and Cognizant Technology Solutions. He has delivered 200 plus lectures at the national and international levels. He is also the recipient of the best faculty award by Cognizant Technology Solutions.

Rajendra S. Talware completed his Doctoral studies from the College of Engineering Pune (COEP) under the Pune University, Pune, in Electronics and Telecommunication (E&TC) engineering. He has varied experience encompassing industry, software consultancy, teaching and university administration. He is currently working as a Professor in E&TC and looks after research and development as Dean (Research) of Vishwakarma Institute of Info Technology (VIIT), Pune. He is a member and Chartered Engineer of the Institute of Engineers, India. He is the recipient of various research grants from the Defense Research and Development Organization (DRDO), Konkan Railway, S. P. Pune University and industry consultancy. He has published 18 research communications in referred journal and international conferences. He has authored a book on broadband communication. He has filed and published three patents and three copyrights. He is invited as a member of technical and advisory committee for various international conferences and symposiums and as a resource person. Dr. Rajendra Talware is associated with industry and universities in teaching and administrative capacities.

Ganesh C. Patil received a bachelor's degree in electronics and telecommunication engineering from the University of Pune and M.Tech degree from the College of Engineering Pune (COEP) in 2002 and 2007, respectively. After M.Tech, he completed Ph.D. in the area of microelectronics and VLSI from the Indian Institute of Technology Kanpur, India, in January 2014. Dr. Patil bagged the Best Student Award at 4th International Student Workshop on Electrical Engineering, at Kyushu University, Fukuoka, Japan, and also received Cash Award (INR 20,000) twice by IIT Kanpur for publishing the papers in reputed journals. He is a reviewer of various SCI-listed journals and also worked as Technical Program Chair for various IEEE international conferences. The areas of his research work are device physics and modeling, novel nanoscale MOSFETs, analog/digital CMOS circuits, VLSI system design and organic electronics. Dr. Patil has published several research papers in various reputed journals and more than 30 research papers in peer-reviewed international conferences held at the United States, Japan, Egypt, Singapore, India and China. He has a total teaching experience of 18 years and currently working as an associate professor at the Center for VLSI and Nanotechnology at Visvesvaraya National Institute of Technology, Nagpur.

Sachin R. Sakhare obtained his doctorate in computer science and engineering in 2014. He has 25 years of experience and currently he is working as a professor in computer engineering at VIIT, Pune, India. He is a member of Computer Society of India and ISTE. He has availed the research workshop grants from BCUD, Pune University. He has published 32 research communications in web of Science and Scopus-indexed journals and presented papers in national and international conferences, He has 200 citations and H-index of 4. He has authored four books. He has filed and published four patents and three copyrights. He is and currently guiding four Ph.D. scholars at Savitribai Phule Pune University. He worked as a reviewer of *Applied Soft Computing Journal* from Elsevier, *The Journal of Soft Computing* from Springer, IEEE-ICCUBEA-2018 and 2019. IEEE-INDICON, Springer and ACM conferences. Dr. Sachin has delivered invited talks at various conferences, Faculty Development Programs and Short term training Programs as well as to PG students. Dr. Sachin is associated with international universities including the Amsterdam University of Applied Sciences (AUAS), Netherlands, Aalborg University, Copenhagen, Denmark, and RWTH Aachen University, Germany, for academic collaboration and content delivery on specialized fields.

Yogesh H. Dandawate received his bachelor of engineering from University of Pune (India) in 1991, masters of engineering from Gulbarga University (India) in 1998 and Ph.D. in electronics and telecommunications engineering in 2009 University of Pune (India). Presently, he is working as Professor in Electronics and Telecommunications Engineering Department at Vishwakarma Institute of Information Technology, Pune. He has 30 years of teaching experience and has published more than 102 papers in reputed national and international conferences/ referred journals and one copyright . He has worked on several research projects funded by BCUD, RPS (AICTE), Rajiv Gandhi Science and Technology Commission, Maharashtra Government. He has authored two books, namely, *Microcontroller Techniques* and *Image and Video Compression: Techniques and Fundamentals* published by the renowned CRC press. He has contributed a book chapter "Computer Vision and Recognition Systems using Machine and Deep Learning" published by IET (UK). He has three patents granted, two patents published and one copyright granted on his account. He is on the editorial board of two reputed Indian journals and reviewer of 10 journals published by IET(UK), Elsevier and Springer. His areas of interests are computer vision and deep machine learning, signal and image processing, embedded systems and pattern recognition. He is a senior member of IEEE and fellow member of IETE, India. He has served as Treasurer, Secretary of IEEE Pune Section and IEEE Signal Processing Pune Chapter and presently member of the Executive Committee of IEEE Pune Section and IETE, Pune Chapter. He was Chairman, Board of Studies, Electrical and Electronics Engineering, Faculty of Technology, Savitribai Phule Pune University and currently Member of the Board of Studies, Electronics and Telecommunications Engineering, Savitribai Phule Pune University and Government College of Engineering, Pune and Karad. He is invited Board of Studies Member in Electronics at Bharati Vidyapeeth, Solapur University and Symbiosis International University.

Pravin R. Futane obtained his Ph.D. in computer science and engineering from Amravati University. He is currently associated with VIIT, Pune, as Professor in Computer Engineering and heading the Department of Information Technology. In his 24 years of experience, he has spent majorly in teaching with some industry experience and expertise. He reviewed and examined scholars for Ph.D. thesis. His research interest domain is sign language, artificial intelligence, computer and databases. He has published more than 63 research papers in international journals (31 papers) and conferences (32 papers). His Google Scholar paper citation is 126, H-Index is 5 and i10 index is 5. He is a member of many professional bodies, viz. ISTE, IAMG and ISC. He has also received a research grant or QIP funding for around three programs. He has played a role in various capacities as a reviewer, session chair, invited talk, editorial board member and organizer of conferences supported by funding organizations. He has filed three patents and received one Australian patent granted to his credit.

Section I

Convergence of AI, IoT, and Communication Technologies for Futuristic Innovations

1

Convergence of Blockchain Technology and Artificial Intelligence

Yash Navin Agarwal, Priya Yuvaraj Chougale, and Varsha D. Jadhav

CONTENTS

1.1 Introduction

AI is now being integrated with blockchain solutions to facilitate smooth operations, especially in the supply chain and financial transactions. This integration is the need of the future as this convergence deals with both sharing of data and its secure storage. Blockchain is a disruptive software technology that is giving an edge to different business sectors. In this chapter, we review the applications of convergence of blockchain technology with AI and its future merits. Most of the research efforts are aimed at converging AI with blockchain to overcome the privacy vulnerabilities of AI. On the other hand, AI is also being used to overcome the challenges in blockchain such as in operational maintenance and quality assurance of smart contracts. AI depends on three key elements, that is, algorithms, computing power and data whereas blockchain can break this barrier and realize these three elements based on its inherent characteristics such as immutability and anonymization. Blockchain also promises the decision-making capability of AI, hence making it more trustworthy and transparent. When these two technologies are combined, they can be used tackle many challenges faced by companies and industries to provide various solutions for them. On one hand, AI algorithms help in perceiving deceit or work under very subtle data; on the other hand, blockchain will assist in improving the same data or will ensure that the data is secure using its cryptocurrency encryption process. It

DOI: 10.1201/9781003342755-2

simply means that the intersection of AI and blockchain offers you opportunities to safe-guard the data against cyber attacks.

1.1.1 Blockchain Technology

Blockchain technology offers utilitarian benefit for the world because it can be used in different systems in different industries and companies but hasn't been used to its fullest capability as it has not been explored much [1–3]. The biggest IT companies have been using blockchain technology for enhancing system quality and its working. Blockchain technology first became widely known in 2009 when Bitcoin was launched. Blockchain owes its name to its vast use in modern cryptocurrencies [4–6]. Blockchain relies on three concepts: peer-to-peer networks, cryptography and distributed consensus using the resolution of a randomized mathematical riddle. A blockchain stores its data in digital containers called blocks. Each block is linked to its parent block using unique digital fingerprints known as hashes [7–9]. Despite the recent development in blockchain technology, it has faced many issues due to poor scalability and difficulties in operational maintenance.

1.1.2 Artificial Intelligence

AI belongs to the realm of human intelligence and has emerged from various attempts to reduce human reasoning to a logical formalism. In recent years, AI has gained attention of many as a key or way of growth in many developed and developing countries. AI is a general-purpose technology (GPT), which represents a core set of capabilities that can accomplish a wide variety of tasks. The term AI is widely used by technologists, academicians, journalists and venture capitalists [10,11].

1.2 Blockchain Applications Using AI

1.2.1 Data Protection

Recent increase in security breaches highlight the need for improved security and privacy pertaining to users' personal data. Blockchain technology provides fresh and new opportunities to protect user data using different privacy mechanisms. The adaptability of blockchain for reforming data protection can be considered as an innovative way to research and discover or develop new techniques. Blockchain technology provides a creative way of collaboration, especially in cross-organizational workflows. Blockchain technology not only helps the owners of the organization to maintain control over their respective activities but also enables them to establish a "shared and persistent truth" on the state of the workflow [11,12]. The data stored in blockchain would be broadcasted into the whole peer-to-peer (P2P) network to be verified by a central algorithm. After receiving the content of all nodes, the new block containing the objective data is added to the blockchain. Hence it is almost impossible for hackers to modify block's information since they must gain access over multiple systems to overcome concord mechanisms.

Currently, companies and enterprises working with AI are facing difficulties due to structural issues such as invasion of user privacy, lack of dataset transparency, biased AI programs and altered datasets [13]. Blockchain includes properties such as self-sovereign ownership, decentralization and transparency, which makes it possible for both AI and blockchain to be combined together. AI consists of datasets that need to be accurate, immutable and adequate; hence blockchain-based technology can be used, which ensures that data need not be saved until it goes through a consensus mechanism [14,15]. Moreover, data records are not only time-stamped, unhackable and cryptographically signed, but they also provide the ability for private and public entities to enhance their data. This utilization of blockchain can enhance datasets completely. Blockchain's data record provides an understanding about the framework behind AI and the fount of the data it has been using. The use of blockchain to store and distribute AI models provides an audit trial as to how data can be more secured. By providing access to large volumes of data, blockchain helps AI to manage data usage, thus creating a data economy that is both trustworthy and

FIGURE 1.1

transparent. The security of data and shareholders can be further strengthened through AI tools, which can take the help of blockchain technology to open new methods for learning from data without taking ownership of data. AI can be used along with blockchain technology to combine personal data from users of blockchain and their stakeholders in a way that helps to protect security and personal data privacy [16].

1.2.2 Resource Optimization

Resource optimization is a collection of processes and methods that match the available resources with the needs of the company. It is a process of using minimum resources in order to achieve desired outcomes in a shorter time span. The need for optimization arises when the demands tend to exceed the number of resources available. It can also be described as a process of ensuring that both labor and non-labor resources are matched to the schedule.

The increasing complexity of AI models and the explosive growth of AI models are extensively outpacing the current development in computer resources and memory capacity available on a device. Field system software embedded with AI helps to deliver knowledge efficiently by processing solutions of complex data sets and helps in automating repetitive activities to allow human workers to focus on personalized service. AI is already revolutionizing the process through which resources are optimized, opening a way for predictive scheduling and enabling organizations to constantly meet service level agreements by enhancing outcomes. A database built for AI should be such that it should support popular language use, natural language querying and blockchain technology [17]. It should also be powered by AI to optimize data management for greater effectual results and performance. Blockchain-based systems suggest a consolidated system for distribution of different tasks to support decorousness among clients in the systems. Client's computational program participation will be maintained in the open record of blockchain as exchanges and every client's credit equalization can be easily available for the client to access [18]. For complex networks, traditional resource optimization algorithms may bring computational complexity of considerable importance [19]. Their AI-based resource optimization has gained intense interest. AI-based resource allocation algorithms can make predictions from historical data much more accurately compared to conventional resource optimization schemes.

1.2.3 Data Monetization

Data monetization refers to the method of generating economic benefits from available data resources to get significant economic benefit. Data monetization leverages data generated through business operations as well as data associated with individual sources such as those collected through electronic devices. As the trajectory of blockchain technology moves at a rapid pace and with the rapid worldwide development, most companies are in search of most organizations and companies are in search of massive amounts of data. Deciding how to profit from data spate can give companies an advantage in the market because data has the potential to add tremendous value to different aspects of business [20]. The market has already had a glimpse of monetization across various domains in the form of layering connected devices with a variety of software as a service (SaaS) choices such as subscriptions plans or smart device insights. The recent emergence of technological advances has opened new avenues of competitions where data is used strategically to unleash new revenue opportunities for monetization. Such growth has made room for the development of new tools, platforms and marketplaces that enable organizations to successfully monetize data.

Generally, organizations can monetize data by (1) monopolizing it to make superior business decisions or alter processes, (2) encircling flagship services or products with data and (3) vending information to current or new markets [21]. Blockchain not only provides an environment in which data is processed responsibly but also provides an encrypted, immutable distributed ledger to facilitate transactions smoothly. It enables the transaction to be transparent and validated, enabling digital marketers to calculate the size of marketing efforts. The main goal of blockchain technology is to make transactions secure and transparent. Breakthroughs in AI and blockchain have led to new ways to make money off personal information that most people generally give away at liberty. AI accelerates monetization by optimizing the matching of sellers and buyers [22].

1.2.4 Improved AI User Experience

Imagine opening a food delivery app. First, you will be shown the home page, which consists of all the food you have previously ordered and recommends you some dishes which have been chosen by the algorithm that works on AI. It not only gives you recommendations but also divides food into different categories to help you choose which cuisine you want to try out. After you have chosen your dish, it directs you to the payment page where the app also helps you choose all the applicable coupons that can be redeemed. After making the payment through your preferred payment mode, your food gets ordered. The app not only shows you the details of the food ordered but also helps you track your food through real-time updates. Once your food gets delivered to your location, you receive an email to rate the delivery and provide a review for the restaurant from which you had ordered the food. This whole experience right from choosing your dish to giving reviews is a great example of AI user experience. A bad user experience is like a maze; you keep figuring your way out only to reach no desired results.

Blockchain, along with its decentralized capabilities, has the potential to revolutionize the digital and industrial landscape in ways that have never been thought before [23]. Custom software development services are using blockchain for improving the security of data, software, and applications. Many giant e-commerce websites request their customers to make transactions online for which blockchain technology is important to help preserve security [24]. It ensures the transparency of transactions and also reduces the friction within the ecosystem of business.

The businesses that sell or offer services on mobile apps can save a lot of time and storage space by using blockchain technology for ensuring safe communication among all its users and clients.

For example, take the example of a blockchain analyst who has got too much data on his fingertips and needs the help of some tools to tell him where to focus attention first. This is the scenario where AI lends its hand; blockchain has been utilizing AI to predict service outages for companies.AI tools classify the state of repair and prioritize maintenance by showing what equipment and machinery are most likely to cause an outage.

1.2.5 Cloud Computing

Cloud computing is the process through which services like databases, servers, software and analytics are offered over the internet. It can also be defined as a process of storing and accessing the data over the internet rather than accessing it from a physical device. In a bid to improve user experience, several cloud services providers have begun leveraging data to provide smart solutions. The role of cloud computing is to make data storage easier and more data accessible for corporate and individual organizations. The use of blockchain technology in this field will ensure that the data stored in the cloud won't be tampered with [25]. The role of AI is to make sure that the large amount of big data is smartly utilized to provide the services more efficiently. The scope of expansion with fruitful results is enormous if these three technologies, namely, AI, blockchain and cloud computing are combined together. AI will enable the organizations to solve problems and queries in a smarter way and create intelligent services whereas blockchain will ensure that more layers of security is added for securing the data [26,27]. We can term their integrations as follows:

1. Cloud computing: data storage
2. Blockchain technology: data privacy
3. AI: maximizing data intelligence

Hence by combining all these three technologies, a network can be created where all the aspects such as storage, its safety and its efficient outcomes can be ensured.

1.3 Challenges

The concept behind both the technologies (AI and blockchain) is very different and the idea of combining these technologies is relatively new. A large amount of money is required to explore these particular fields. Blockchain provides a publicly distributed and encrypted database and for AI to access data, the data has to be decrypted, which results in data hacking [28–30]. Both these technologies require high computing power and if this requirement is not met, it's tough to maintain the speed at which results are obtained [31,32].

1.4 Conclusion

From this chapter, we can conclude that on the convergence of AI and blockchain, many possibilities arise, which provide a new ray of light for the future. A lot is yet to be achieved in these particular domains, which will open new vistas for the computing world. Blockchain technology is scaling new heights with each passing day. Data integrity, which is one of the main aspects of blockchain technology, is the reason as to why most computer enthusiasts are taking interest in it. Hence it has the full potential to revolutionize digital privacy, trust, and the relationship with an individual related to individual information on the internet. AI, on the other hand, has its own identity and can be clubbed in different domains so as to make decisions faster due to its capability of generating new algorithms. We can name this integration of blockchain and AI as blockchain intelligence. We explained how the different characteristics of blockchain and AI can be used in supporting data protection, monetization, resource optimization, cloud computing and in AI user experience.

References

1. J. Golosova and A. Romanovs (2018). "The Advantages and Disadvantages of the Blockchain Technology," 2018 IEEE 6th Workshop on Advances in Information, Electronic and Electrical Engineering (AIEEE), pp. 1–6, doi: 10.1109/AIEEE.2018.8592253.
2. D. Yaga, P. Mell, N. Roby, and K. Scarfone (2019). "Blockchain Technology Overview". arXiv preprint arXiv:1906.11078, arxiv.org
3. V. Madisetti Bahga (2016). "Blockchain Platform for Industrial Internet of Things", *Journal of Software Engineering and Applications*, 9 (10), 533–546.
4. J. Golosova and A. Romanovs (2018). "Overview of the Blockchain Technology Cases". In Proceedings of the 59th International Scientific Conference on Information Technology and Management Science of Riga Technical University (ITMS), October 10–12, 2018, Riga, Latvia, IEEE, pp. 1–6. ISBN 978-1-7281-0098-2
5. Lisk, "Government" [online]. Available from: https://lisk.io/academy/blockchain-basics/use-cases/decentralizationin-governments
6. M. Pilkington (2016). "Blockchain Technology: Principles and Applications". In *Research Handbook on Digital Transformations*, edited by F. Xavier Olleros and Majlinda Zhegu. Edward Elgar, Cheltenham, UK.
7. S. Nakamoto, "Bitcoin: A Peer-to-Peer Electronic Cash System Bitcoin: A Peer-to-Peer Electronic Cash System."
8. D. Tapscott and A. Tapscott (2016). *Blockchain Revolution: How the Technology Behind Bitcoin Is Changing Money, Business, and the World*. Penguin, London.
9. S. Dick (2019). Artificial Intelligence. *Harvard Data Science Review*, 1(1). https://doi.org/10.1162/99608f92.92fe150c
10. H. Lu, , Y. Li, M. Chen, et al. (2018). "Brain Intelligence: Go beyond Artificial Intelligence." *Mobile Network Applications* 23, 368–375. https://doi.org/10.1007/s11036-017-0932-8
11. F. Shawudzicz, T. Jamieson, and A. Goldfarb (2019). "Artificial Intelligence and the Implementation Challenge", *Journal of Medical Internet Research* 21(7), e13659. doi: 10.2196/13659PMID: 31293245PMCID: 6652121
12. S. Schwerin (2018). "Blockchain and Privacy Protection in the Case of the European General Data Protection Regulation (GDPR): a Delphi Study." *The Journal of the British Blockchain Association* 1(1), 3554.
13. C. Kuner, F.H. Cate, O. Lynskey, C. Millard, N. Ni Loideain, D. Jerker, and B Svantesson (2018). "Expanding the Artificial Intelligence-data Protection Debate", *International Data Privacy Law*, 8(4), 289–292, https://doi.org/10.1093/idpl/ipy024
14. A. Rieger, et al. (2019). "Building a Blockchain Application that Complies with the EU General Data Protection Regulation." *MIS Quarterly Executive* 18(4), 263–279.
15. Phan The Duy, Do Thi Thu Hien, and Van-Hau Pham (2020). "A Survey on Blockchain-based Applications for Reforming Data Protection, Privacy and Security." arXiv preprint arXiv:2009.00530.
16. Stanton Heister and Kristi Yuthas (2021). How Blockchain and AI Enable Personal Data Privacy and Support Cybersecurity. 10.5772/intechopen.96999.
17. Dorri Ali, Salil S. Kanhere, and Raja Jurdak (2017). "Towards an Optimized Blockchain for IoT." *2017 IEEE/ACM Second International Conference on Internet-of-Things Design and Implementation (IoTDI)*. IEEE.
18. Bhanuka Rathnayaka (2019). Resource Sharing and Optimizing using Blockchain Technology. 10.13140/RG.2.2.34572.13443
19. Min Zhao and Lu Wang (2021). "Classroom Resource Optimization of the English Four-Step Model Based on Deep Learning." *Security and Communication Networks* 2021.
20. Firouzi, F., B. Farahani, M. Barzegari and M. Daneshmand, "AI-Driven Data Monetization: The Other Face of Data in IoT-based Smart and Connected Health," *IEEE Internet of Things Journal*. doi: 10.1109/JIOT.2020.3027971.

21. A. Javaid, N. Javaid, and M. Imran (2019). *Ensuring Analyzing and Monetization of Data Using Data Science and Blockchain in IoT Devices.* Dissertation, MS thesis, COMSATS University Islamabad (CUI), Islamabad, Pakistan,.

22. Thang N. Dinh and My T. Thai (2018). "AI and Blockchain: A Disruptive Integration." *Computer* 51(9), 48–53.

23. Sushil Kumar Singh, Shailendra Rathore, and Jong Hyuk Park (2020). "Blockiotintelligence: A Blockchain-enabled Intelligent IoT Architecture with Artificial Intelligence." *Future Generation Computer Systems* 110, 721–743.

24. Meikang Qiu, et al. (2020). "AI Enhanced Blockchain (II)." 2020 3rd International Conference on Smart BlockChain (SmartBlock). IEEE, 2020.

25. Uttam Kumar Roy and Weining Tang (2021). "Transformation the Business of eCommerce Through Blockchain." *International Conference on Human-Computer Interaction.* Springer, Cham.

26. Abhineet Anand and Achintya Jha (2019). "Application and Usability of Blockchain in Cloud Computing." *i-manager's Journal on Cloud Computing* 6(2), 26.

27. Hecai Han, et al. (2021). "Research of the Relations Among Cloud Computing, Internet of Things, Big Data, Artificial Intelligence, Block Chain and Their Application in Maritime Field." *Journal of Physics: Conference Series.* 1927(1), 1–11.

28. Inbaraj, X. Alphonse, and T. Rama Chaitanya (2020). "Need to Know about Combined Technologies of Blockchain and Machine Learning." In *Handbook of Research on Blockchain Technology.* Academic Press, London, pp. 417–432.

29. Rui Wang, Kejiang Ye, and Cheng-Zhong Xu (2019). "Performance Benchmarking and Optimization for Blockchain Systems: A Survey." *International Conference on Blockchain.* Springer, Cham.

30. N. Herbaut and N. Negru (2017). "A Model for Collaborative Blockchain-Based Video Delivery Relying on Advanced Network Services Chains." *IEEE Communication Magazine* 55, 70–76 [CrossRef].

31. B. Nour, A. Ksentini, N. Herbaut, P.A. Frangoudis, and H. Moungla (2019). "A Blockchain-Based Network Slice Broker for 5G Services." *IEEE Network Letters* 1, 99–102 [CrossRef].

32. Quoc Khanh Nguyen and Quang Vang Dang (2018). "Blockchain Technology for the Advancement of the Future." *2018 4th International Conference on Green Technology and Sustainable Development (GTSD).* IEEE.

2

Low-Cost Single-Phase Smart Energy Meter Using GSM Module

Rushikesh S. Tanksale, Swapnil Jadhav, Amit Samgir, and Nitin N. Sakhare

CONTENTS

2.1 Introduction

In the present era, for the survival and progress of human society, electricity has become an absolute necessity. Presently, the human society can be said to be living in a 'machine society' where technology has been playing a pivotal role in the day-to-day activity of humans where almost all of our modern conveniences are powered electrically. Due to this, electricity is an essential part of modern society and has become one of the basic requirements of humanity becoming widely deployed for domestic, industrial and agricultural use and also for medical purposes. Despite a number of many well-developed sources of electricity in our country, there are many problems with transmission, distribution, metering, billing and consumption of electrical power. Our distribution policies are also partly responsible for the incorrect estimation of our exact requirements. Another major problem is electricity theft. Globally, the cost of electricity theft was estimated at $89.3 billion every year [1]. Moreover, the consumers are also dissatisfied with the power utility due to low reliability and bad quality of energy supply even though the bills are paid regularly and frequently

DOI: 10.1201/9781003342755-3

consumers complain about errors in their monthly bills. The solution to all the mentioned problems is to regularly and periodically monitor and keep track of the consumers' load and to remotely control the energy meter. This will lead to accurate billing, tracking maximum demand, detecting threshold value and preventing energy theft. This chapter introduces us to the project of "Smart Energy Meter using GSM Module", which meets all the above-mentioned requirements. This project helps accurately measure the energy consumption of consumers, which will be received periodically and directly without human effort. Till now, meter readings are recorded by power utility staff who visit each house individually. This practice has shown to result in human error and also is time-consuming. The details of the average expenditure of electricity in a locality can be gathered from the consumption data accurately using smart meters so that the power can be supplied according to the available data. The electricity supply can also be remotely controlled through the installed smart meters. In case of energy theft, the direct supply to the particular unit could be cut out immediately and remotely through the control centre.

In the current metering system, to measure electricity consumption in an area, the electricity distribution board sends personnel to visit each house individually in the area to manually record the meter reading, which is used for billing. Then the calculated bill is sent to each consumer by manual delivery or by post. This process can be simply stated as too laborious and it also causes human error with the power utility having no control over it. A large amount of revenue loss is being incurred in the country due to energy theft, which has become a major problem. People try to manipulate the meter readings by various corrupt methods such as bypassing meter, current reversal and magnetic interference. Our project helps to overcome this problem by offering a definite solution, which allows the electricity distribution board to have a complete control over the energy meters and can provide a monitoring system that can gather real-time information from individual meters from remote locations, which can be obtained with less than no human effort and also any interference with the energy meter can be detected at much reduced cost compared to the current methods.

The purpose of this project is to monitor and remotely control the single-phase energy meter. Its aim includes designing a simple circuit of GSM-based single-phase smart energy meter, which will continuously monitor the energy meter readings and would send real-time data to the electricity distribution board and the consumers, to program GSM modem with AT (Attention) Command Sequence, to interface the programmable chip with energy meter and GSM modem and to control the device remotely. Low-cost single-phase smart energy meter using GSM module not only benefits the electricity distribution board but also the consumers as it provides clear and precise energy consumption, accurate billing and accurate electricity outage information in an area, thus leading to fast recovery, much better and faster customer service, elimination of manual laborious work, which would help to reduce the cost and inadequacies of manual reading, smart automated process, accurate data from network load to optimise maintenance, detection of illegal tampering with energy meter, precise demand and distribution management and control of energy consumption and production. All these would be useful for planning and power allocation purposes. As of now, the smart meter penetration in India is barely around 1%. That is, roughly about 3 million smart meters are operational compared to the 270 million classic meters that are operational even now. This percentage is much less than the mature markets such as the United States where smart meters usage is 65–75%; smart meters are used in France to the extent of 60–70% and in China it is 40–55%. Previously in Bihar, 25,000 smart prepaid meters had been installed from the 28,000 smart meter deployment that provided average daily recharge revenue of INR 5000,000 (US$6,900) [2]. Although

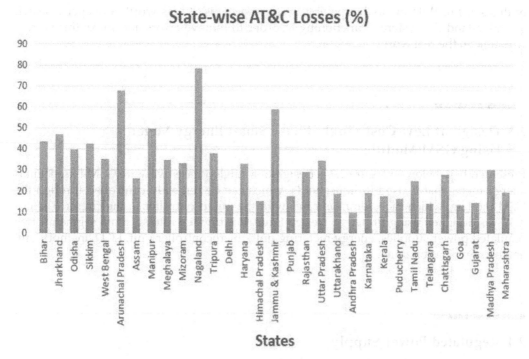

FIGURE 2.1
State-wise energy theft percentage in India [1].

smart meters have been considered a relatively mature technology, there are issues that should be solved in order to have a more widespread and efficient deployment of the smart meters.

Also, as mentioned in Figure 2.1 we can see that the amount of energy theft in India is so high that this solution will reduce the losses to electricity companies

- Currently, the smart meters communicate with the server through mobile networks, which is unreliable in certain areas (like rural areas). Thus to avoid the confusion over bills between consumers and the energy companies, a proper solution must be created.
- More functions and minimum functional requirements can be developed in the smart meters.

Currently, there is an increase in the solar-powered systems. Thus, the meters can be modified so that it could individually measure both the energy provided by the energy companies and the solar power consumed.

2.2 Gap Analysis

Earlier research has dwelt on the usage of these type of meters to stop electricity theft. However, some studies added that network issues can hamper in the smooth functioning of this system. With errors happening in these systems, it was worth a deeper research to understand the system's functioning in order to remove errors and make this system workable in the real world.

2.3 Design of Low-Cost Single-Phase Smart Energy Meter Using GSM Module

Presented here below in Figure 2.2 is design of a single-phase two-wire GSM-based smart energy meter that is used in households, which can be remotely controlled through the GSM modem, which then communicates with the microcontroller in the circuit. The circuit was designed using Proteus 8 Design Suite. It is divided into six main segments: two regulated power supplies, energy metering unit, microcontroller unit, LCD, memory unit and communication units.

2.4 Regulated Power Supply

The circuit has two regulated power supply units, each of which has a 5 V voltage regulator IC7805 in common.

2.4.1 Regulated Power Supply

As seen below in Figure 2.3, It consists of a current limiting capacitor, a rectifier and a Zener diode, filter chokes (bead core), a metal oxide varistor and a 5 V voltage regulator. Its main function is to power the energy metering IC ADE7757 with 5 V.

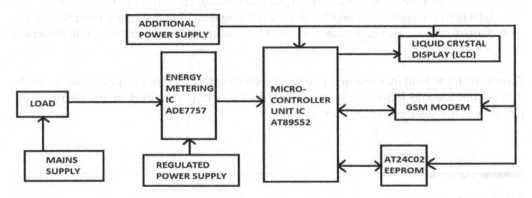

FIGURE 2.2
System block diagram hardware design and circuit analysis.

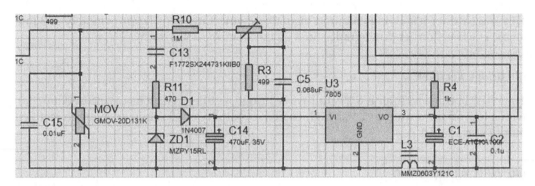

FIGURE 2.3
Regulated power supply.

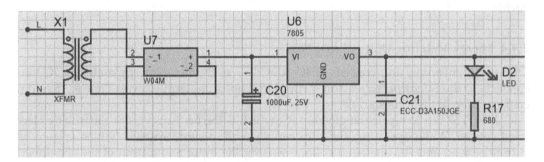

FIGURE 2.4
Additional regulated power supply [4].

2.4.2 Additional Regulated Power Supply

It contains a standard 5 V voltage regulator circuit including a bridge rectifier, which is connected directly to 230/9 V 500 mA secondary transformer, a smoothing capacitor and a LED. The main microcontroller takes the energy reading from the optocoupler and stores the readings in the EEPROM and simultaneously displays on the LCD and sends it to the GSM modem. This process requires an additional regulated 5 V supply. Refer below at Figure 2.4 for overall circuit diagram of Additional regulated power supply

2.4.3 IC L7805

It has a 5 V fixed output voltage because of three terminal positive regulators. It provides confined on-card synchronisation that eliminates the dispersal issues related to single-point regulation. Its utilities internal current limiting, thermal shutdown and safe area conservation, which makes it crucially sturdy.

(i) Secondary Transformer [3]

A 230/9 V 500m A centre-tapped step-down transformer is an all-around shell scaling the mains transformer. It has 230 V primary winding and centre-tapped secondary winding.

This transformer has flying coloured insulated connecting leads (approximately 100 mm long). The transformer downgrades the voltage from AC 230 V to AC 9 V.

(ii) Bridge Rectifier

The W04M bridge rectifier is a 1 A full-wave bridge rectifier, which has a diffused junction with a low forward drop of 1 V, a high current capability of 40 A and an average rectified output current of 1 A.

(iii) Filtering Capacitors

The filtering capacitors in this circuit are used to smooth the ripple of the rectified output. The capacitors are selected on the basis of important parameters such as capacitance, working voltage and percentage ripple. The capacitors are used provide safety for the circuit.

2.4.4 Energy Metering Unit (IC ADE7757)

The energy metering unit consists of IC ADE7757 as the main energy metering IC that connects to the microcontroller unit through the optocoupler. Below in Figure 2.5 is pin configuration of the IC is shown.

IC ADE7757 is a low-price single-chip IC, which is the best answer for measuring electrical energy. While operating, the chip couples with a shunt resistor (which is used as current sensor) and AC analogue voltage-sensing the input and output of the consumed energy. It has two analogue input channels that are designated as V1 and V2, respectively. Channel V1 (current channel) is utilised for current sensing and channel V2 (voltage channel) is utilised for voltage sensing. Between the input pins V1P and V1N, the differential output from the current-sensing resistor is connected while between the output pins, the differential output signal proportional to the AC line voltage is connected. IC ADE7757 has a reference circuit and a fixed DSP function for calculating the real power. A highly

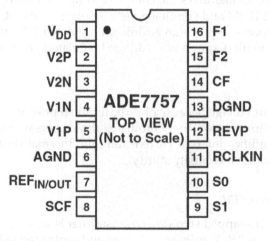

FIGURE 2.5
Pin configuration of IC ADE7757.

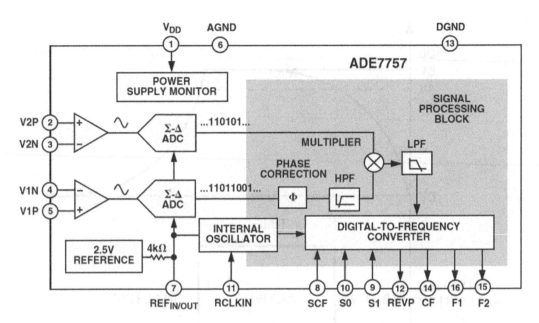

FIGURE 2.6
Block diagram of ADE7757.

stable oscillator is built into the chip that provides the necessary clock for the chip. The average real-power information is supplied on the F1 and F2 low-frequency outputs. The meter has been designed for 100 pulses/KWh and this can be measured by any counter for the energy consumption calculation. In this meter, microcontroller AT89S52 is used for measuring the pulses. ADE7757 gives a high-frequency output at the calibration frequency (CF) pin, that is, 3,200 pulses/KWh, that is picked up via pins S1 and S2. The high-frequency output gives the instantaneous real-power information, which is used to accelerate the calibration process. The block diagram of ADE7757 is shown in Figure 2.6.

The power supply required for IC ADE7757 is directly taken from the mains using the capacitor divider network comprising C13 and C14. Voltage is reduced across the capacitor C13 (0.47uF polyester capacitor rated for 630 V), while the resistor R11 (470-ohm, 1 W) is used as the current limiter. The output across C14 is locked at 15 V DC that is used as an input to the voltage regulator in the first regulated power supply unit. The regulated 5 V is then provided to IC ADE7757. The F1 output in IC ADE7757 is coupled to the port pin P3.2 of the IC AT89S52 via optocoupler IC MCT2E. LED1 specifies whether IC ADE7757 is active or not. Figure 2.7 shows the state of the chipset.

2.4.5 IC MCT2E

As seen in Figure 2.8 , this device contains a gallium arsenide infrared emitting diode optically coupled to a monolithic silicon phototransistor detector. Here in this circuit, it is used for interfacing and coupling of IC ADE7757 and IC AT89S52.

2.4.6 Microcontroller Unit

As cited in Figure 2.9 is the microcontroller unit IC AT89S52 chipset which is an energy-saving highly efficient CMOS 8-bit microcontroller having 8k bytes of in-system

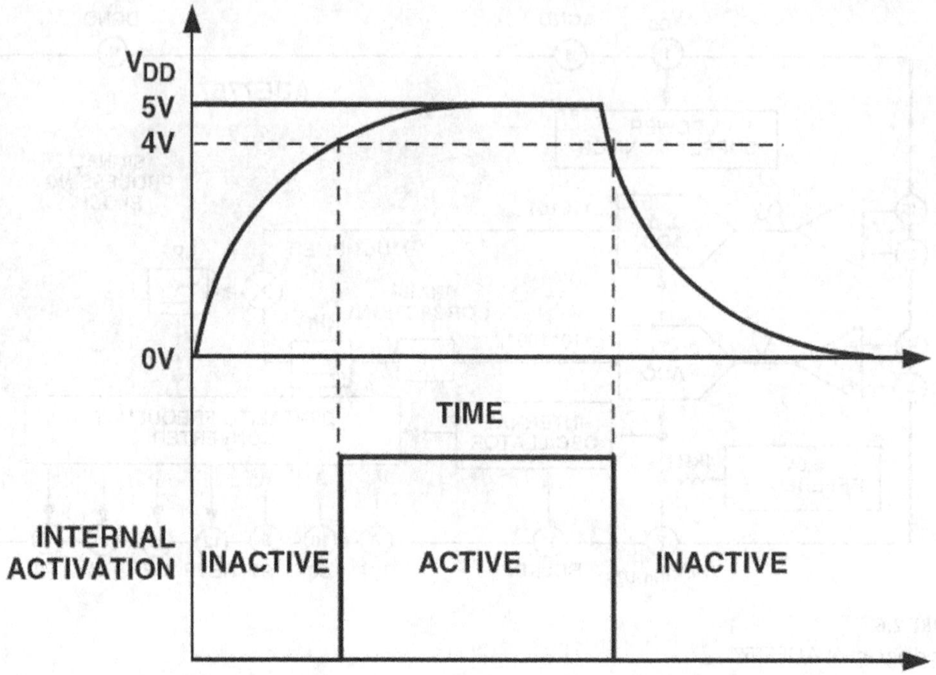
VDD
5V
4V
0V
TIME
INTERNAL ACTIVATION
INACTIVE
ACTIVE
INACTIVE

FIGURE 2.7
On-chip power supply monitor in ADE7757.

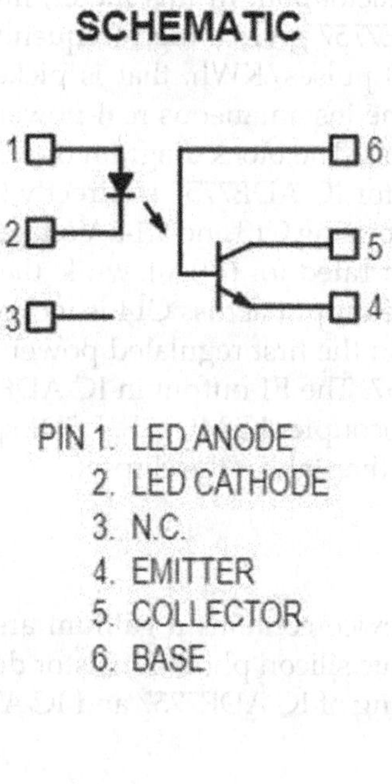
SCHEMATIC
1
2
3
6
5
4
PIN 1. LED ANODE
2. LED CATHODE
3. N.C.
4. EMITTER
5. COLLECTOR
6. BASE

FIGURE 2.8
Schematic of optocoupler ICMCT2E.

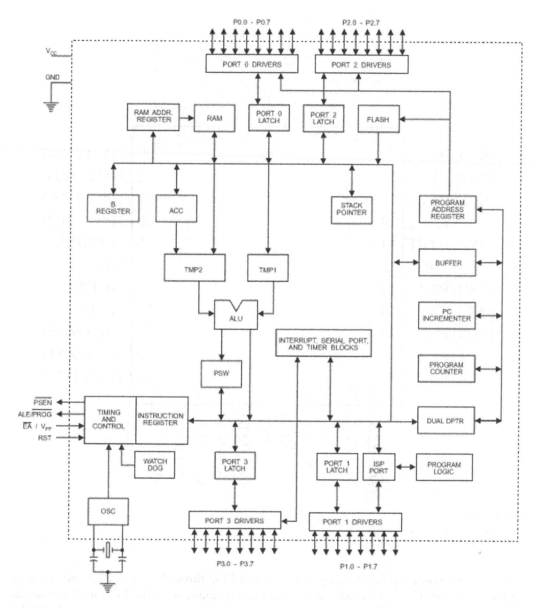

FIGURE 2.9
Block diagram of IC AT89S52.

flash-programmable memory, 256 bytes of RAM, 32 i/o lines, watchdog timer, two data pointers, three 16-bit timer/counters, a full duplex serial port, on-chip oscillator and a clock circuitry.

IC AT89S52 supports in-system programming in both page and byte modes for the flash memory and can also be reprogrammed easily and simply by using a normal computer. It has a quick programming time with 10,000 read/write cycles. Its operational frequency is 33 MHz max, which can be altered for saving energy. One of the reasons for selecting the microcontroller IC AT89S52 is that it directly interfaces with the GSM modem without the need of third-party ICs such as IC MAX323. Refer to Figure 2.10 for the pinout diagram.

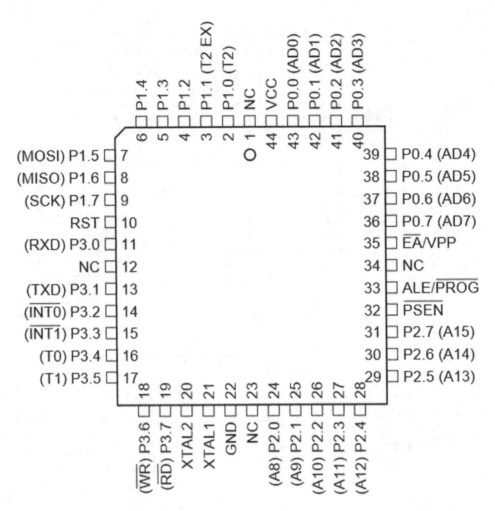

FIGURE 2.10
Pin configuration of IC AT89S52.

It takes the energy meter reading from IC ADE7757 through its pin P3.2 and stacks it in the EEPROM IC AT24C02 and simultaneously displays it on the LCD and also sends it to the GSM modem. This process requires an extra 5 V regulated and isolated supply. A standard 5 V regulator circuit, which has a BR1 bridge rectifier, C20 a smoothing capacitor and a regulator IC 7805, was utilised for this purpose. Figure 2.11 shows the additional power supply used in this system. Pins P2.0 to P2.7 of IC AT89S52 are connected to the LCD data pins D0 to D7, respectively, and P3.5, P3.6 and P3.7 of the IC AT89S52 are connected with the control pins RS, R/W and EN of the LCD, respectively. Power-on reset is provided by the combination of the capacitor C16 and resistor R14. Switch S1 is used for the manual reset. A 12 MHz crystal along with the two capacitors of 22pF each provides basic clock frequency to the microcontroller. Preset VR2 has been connected with the pin 3 of the LCD for contrast control.

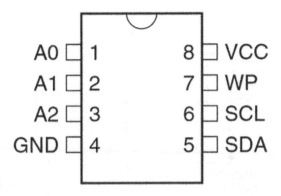

FIGURE 2.11
Pin configuration of EEPROM IC AT2402.

2.4.7 Memory Unit (IC AT2402)

We can see the temperatures can even touch up to 58°C. An all-liner test was done on an average summer day as there is less airflow in the environment. The radius of the range decreased as the temperature increased. This cannot be major issue for small homes but devices connected at edge of the map radius can face disconnection issues. So, we applied thermal paste followed by aluminium heat sink on top of both RAM and CPU chips.

IC AT2402, as shown in Figures 2.11 and 2.12, provides 2,048 serial electrically erasable and programmable read-only memory that is organised as 256 words, each of which is 8 bits. It is IC AT89S52-bus compatible 2KB EEPROM that has endurance of 1 million write cycles and can retain data for maximum 100 years. In case of power failure, it can obviate the loss of latest setting and the microcontroller can store all the data of the user in the EEPROM. Its memory ensures that when the power resumes, the microcontroller will read the last saved data from EEPROM. By using the lines SCL and SDA of EEPROM, the microcontroller can read/write the data from/to the IC AT2402 memory. The lines SCL and SDA of the IC AT2402 are interfaced to the pin P1.0 and P1.1 of the microcontroller IC AT89S52, respectively.

2.4.8 LCD Display

An LCD is an electronic device that is used to show the numbers or text. LCDs are easily programmable and have no limitations of displaying special characters (unlike in seven-segment LED display). Here we have used a 16×2 LCD, which displays 20 lines per line, having such two lines. It has two registers:

(i) *Command register*: This stores the command instructions given to the LCD display. The command that is given to the LCD is a predefined task such as initialising it, clearing its screen, setting the display, etc.
(ii) *Data register*: The data which is to be displayed on the LCD is stored. This data is the ASCII value of the character that is to be displayed on the LCD.

The LCD has 11 lines as seen in Figure 2.13 that can be directly connected to the microcontroller IC. The 10k preset connected to the pin 3 of the LCD is used to adjust the contrast of the display.

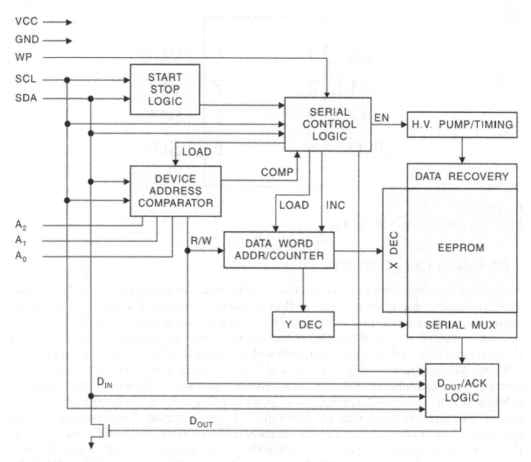

FIGURE 2.12
Block diagram of EEPROM IC AT240.

2.4.9 Communication Unit (GSM Module)

A GSM modem/module is a hardware that uses a GSM mobile telephone technology to provide a data link. This module needs a SIM to be identified on the network. The communication unit used in this model is the GSM module SIM900D (only available GSM module in Proteus 8 Design Suite). Currently, the latest GSM module available in market that can be used in our design is SIM7600EI and SIM900A.

As shown in Figure 2.14 we can see what GSM Kit looks like, It's very easy to interface the GSM module with the IC AT89S52 microcontroller. For that, we need to send the AT command from the microcontroller and receive the response from the GSM modem. To communicate with the GSM modem, we have to use the serial ports of the microcontroller that is using pin P3.0 and pin P3.1 (TXD). Before selecting the GSM module, we first have to check whether the selected GSM modem is capable of working at TTL logic; that is, basically if the GSM modem has RX and TX (with GND) pins on the board, then it can work on TTL logic. If not, then we need to use MAX323 IC when connecting to the microcontroller. Also the serial data has to be converted into TTL logic because the microcontroller can only work on TTL logic. Since in our case, we have both the RX and TX pins available in our GSM modem so we have directly connected them to the microcontroller pins TXD

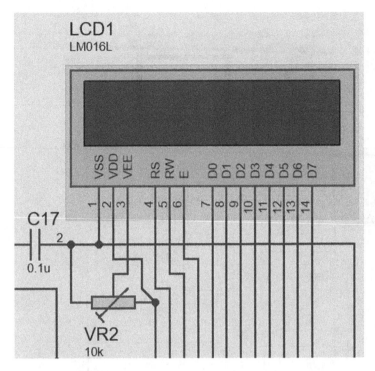

FIGURE 2.13
Pin configuration of liquid crystal display (LCD).

FIGURE 2.14
GSM module (SIM900A).

and RXD, respectively. When the connections are done, we just need to write program to send the AT commands to the GSM modem. Then the GSM modem connects with the web server (cloud) by the information that is provided in the code. Then the energy companies and the consumers can access their data through the web server [4]. And, as shown in Figure 2.15 we can see overall configuration or block diagram of the system

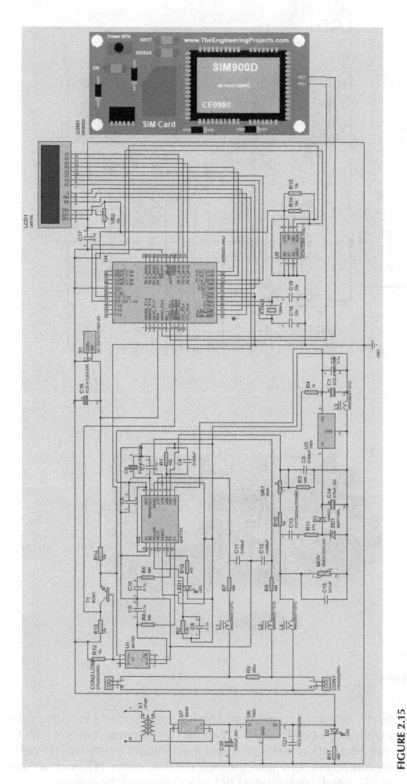

FIGURE 2.15

Circuit diagram of the smart energy meter.

2.5 Advantages

Updating the current system with smart meters will help us achieve security and economical use of resources for both the electricity producer and consumers. It also has a great positive impact on the environment.

- Smart meters send real-time data to the electricity supplier so it reduces disparity in data (related to consumption and billing) between both the parties.
- It provides transparency into the energy usage so that the households can track their real-time consumption and identify the waste points and control the energy spending based on the informed strategy on power consumption.
- These smart grids are great in reducing carbon emissions and are sustainable.
- It helps the energy suppliers to balance the load on the power grid to avoid failures.
- A positive impact on the environment is also a benefit of a smart energy meter.
- The combined data such as consumer demand, load and weather can help the energy companies to optimise and predict the production of the energy, which will help to promote clean energy.
- Another important benefit of smart meters is that it can prevent energy theft. Tampering with meter can easily be detected by the change in the real-time data provided by smart meters. By calculating the average consumption from the data of an area, the unusual energy consumption changes can be detected.
- Smart meters not only provide the homeowners with the energy usage data but also help to observe the load, which can detect any issues and errors in the operation of the electrical devices. It can also help to avoid the local outages and can improve fire safety.

2.6 Conclusion

The modern civilisation would be brought to its knees and the society would completely collapse if a crisis of electricity scarcity ever arises. Thus in the today's world, there is undeniably a need for uninterruptible electricity to ensure the development of any nation. From the design of the system in this chapter, it is clearly realised that the GSM-based smart energy meter meets the objectives of ensuring uninterrupted power supply as its design is capable of controlling the activities of the meter remotely, making it beneficial to both the energy companies and the consumers. Thus, it meets the requirements of providing a solution to the power theft, load control and proper documentation of individual consumer energy usage data over a period of time, which helps the energy company to make a proper plan and design of sufficient infrastructure equipment for power transmission.

References

1. Lehri D., Choudhary A. (2021) A Survey of Energy Theft Detection Approaches in Smart Meters. In: Shorif Uddin M., Sharma A., Agarwal K.L., Saraswat M. (eds) *Intelligent Energy Management Technologies. Algorithms for Intelligent Systems.* Springer, Singapore. https://doi.org/10.1007/978-981-15-8820-4_2
2. www.financialexpress.com/industry/smart-meters-time-to-make-that-smart-switch/2092936/
3. www.electronicsforu.com/electronics-projects/hardware-diy/energy-meter
4. https://circuitdigest.com/microcontroller-projects/gsm-module-interfacing-with-8051-at89s52

3

Yoga Posture Detection Using Machine Learning

Pradip Mukundrao Paithane

CONTENTS

3.1 Introduction

Yoga pose detection is an essential part of physical body structure [1]. In our work, we detect the user's pose from real-time webcam and verify it with real dataset data [2]. We have detected the poses by a set of a reference model of valid data. The first motive is the detection of the body skeleton coordinate joints [3]. By using the coordinates, we can see the poses. The system that can monitor the accuracy of different yoga poses can aid the user to practice yoga correctly [4]. A webcam is used to find other points of the body in real camera. All the collected joint points are stored in a file. It measures and shows the accuracy of a specific yoga pose for a user and also gives the name of that yoga pose [5]. Our system can prosperously identify various yoga poses in real-time. The practice of yoga leads to great physiological method improvements. Its effects are prominent in the vital signs of heart rate and body weight. Analysis suggests that the benefits of the yoga include an upgrade of wellness and improved and increased vital capacity. In the presence of a yoga trainer, yoga can be completed in a yoga center, which can give certain victims (of accidents, for example) a remedial helping hand. Our solution suggests a foreign yoga training approach without the trainer where the patient performs yoga poses correctly without the necessity of a trainer but by using a tool [6]. The human pose detection is done in real-time. An important area of specialization is the depth of images to find the human pose. The human posture by webcam becomes easy to understand.

DOI: 10.1201/9781003342755-4

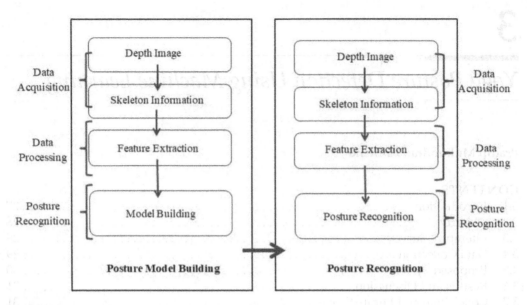

FIGURE 3.1
Step for the proposed system.

3.2 Objective

Basically, freedom of our body and meditative posture to keep balance of our body is important. Our proposed system can monitor a given human body pose and show accuracy of that yoga pose. The webcam capture pose is done in real-time and successfully identifies the pose. Steps of Proposed System are shown in Figure 3.1.

3.3 Literature Survey

Behere et al. [1] used profound CNN and Opencv using classifiers for grouping hand movements of five developments. Two classifiers were independently used with a F1 score of 0.93 and 0.95. Quality of live camera with a goal of 640 × 480 magnification was employed. Five volunteers performed six postures. By utilizing a foundation reduction method, they separated 21,000 casings from the live camera with a 74% precision. Maddala et al. [7] proposed yoga asana recognition using deep learning. A dataset contains six yoga asanas, which were created using 15 people using a RGB webcam. This webcam is easily available. There are a total 45 frames. It executes framewise prediction and polling approach on 45 frames for model and training method. Maybel Chan Thar et al. [8] differentiate a yoga pose with a live webcam. From five yoga poses, 300 recordings of 12 yoga instances were gathered. To acquire perfection, the near view part is divided from the cut and the star skeleton is used. An acquired perfection of 99.33% was achieved. Toshev amd Szegedy [9] describe the holistic view of human pose using deep neural networks (DNN) for estimation. The pose estimation is formulated as a joint regression problem and the authors successfully showed how poses can be fit into DNN settings. DNN is used for capturing each body joint by using seven-layer generic convolutional network. These cascades are used for increased precision for joint localization. For all processes, deep learning model was used for pose estimation. Wu et al. [10] proposed different posture discovery methodology that put live camera to use. Chen Tsung Huang [6] describes how to recognize posture by using star skeleton. The body map is captured first. After that, the body lines are extracted using which the star skeleton is computed. The posture performed by the practitioner is described by using the star skeleton. On the other side, we prebuild the module of yoga postures from experts of yoga. To evaluate the dissimilarity between two skeletons, the distance function is used. Finally, the pose is recognized by choosing most similar skeleton. A system achieves an accuracy of 99.33% in yoga pose recognition. Using the live camera, Maddala et al. [7] proposed a position admit methodology. In this study, RFC classifier was used to depict the exercises. Finally, an overall accuracy of 84.6% was achieved. The classifier helps to arrive at an efficient accuracy. Maybel Chan Thar [8] explains a method for self-learners of yoga pose assessment using their pose detection. At first, the method detects the pose using open pose and PC camera. It uses a method for calculating the "difference of the body angles between the instructor and user". By giving the different signals, the method suggests the correction if it is larger than the given threshold. Here pose estimation is used for recognition of moving joints with their points and rigid parts, using which feature extraction is done. Finally, these features are used for detecting the pose. The results shown in four levels depend on the understanding level of the user.

Guo and coworkers [10] describe the POAD method for yoga learning and self-instruction. This is the process which initiates the thinking process to solve different problems. The system gives self-instruction, and theory and skill learning to improve the yoga poses. The trainer provides a detailed explanation of the steps. Wu et. al [10] describes the two different methods for practice and feedback. The video self-evaluation (VSE) method is used for evaluating the yoga pose. The participants screen their pose on a video immediately after participating in the pose and the pose is evaluated using task analysis. The user can practice yoga subsequently. They can see the recorded practice video and finally self-evaluation is done by the users themselves. Another method is video feedback (VB). The researchers record the video the first time when the user practices yoga. They then provide the practice video to the participant.

3.4 Data Collection

We collected the dataset by taking real-time images through a webcam. By using MediaPipe, we created the human skeleton in a 3D view. We computed joint body points from that skeleton. The MediaPipe gives a live insight of the human pose, face landmarks and the hand tracking in real-time [11]. Separate models are integrated for face, pose, and hand landmarks using MediaPipe Holistic pipeline. We created two body structures: holistic and drawing. From the holistic structure, we take joint points and draw through a drawing method. The defined points on the drawing are visible on the holistic structure through query view. Then we store those points in the CSV format [12]. In each yoga pose, we take points through drawing and holistic class. Then we convert all those points into the 3D form. After starting the conversion, we have 42 joints at a time. Each collective point has four values like X, Y, Z and visibility. For hidden body parts, it shows visibility as 0; otherwise 1. Finally, we store those real-time points in an Excel sheet [13,14].

3.5 Proposed System

This approach aims to give accuracy of the yoga asana with its matching pose. The primary system works when the webcam of the system continuously checks the yoga pose. Once the yoga pose is performed by the user, the image is captured through the webcam. It will fetch the key points with the help of a skeleton image of the yoga pose and then shows the joint points. Then data is collected at end using MediaPipe Holistic.

The collected data is spilled into train and test dataset in the ratio of 70:30. The classification models used are logistic regression, ridge classifier, random forest classifier, and gradient boosting classifier with a different parameter for efficient accuracy. Among these classifiers, the ridge classifier gives more efficient accuracy than others. After the final evaluation, accuracy was found with the name of the yoga pose.

Algorithm

---

1) *Input Train data set T1 = {t1, t2, t3 ....tn}*
    Where T1 is the input of train data set t1,t2, t3 ....tn are the train image.
2) *Input Testing data set T2 = {s1, s2, s3 ....sn}*
    Where T2 is the input testing data set s1,s2, s3 ....sn are the test image.
3) *Identify yoga pose*
    Y = { y1, y2, y3 ....yn }
    Where "Y" is main set of Yoga
4) *Capture live image*
    I= { i1, i2, i3 ....in }
    Where, "I" is used for live image set capture by camera

Algorithm: *Classification of yoga pose*

If y1 ε Σ i1, i2, i3 ....in
I ← y1
If yn ε Σ i1, i2, i3 ....in
I← yn
Where,
        y1, y2, y3 ....yn = processed image (yoga pose) I = classification of live capture image
Calculating yoga pose polarity
Y = T / I
Where,
Y = polarity of Yoga pose
T = polarity for train data set I = total no of the captured image.

Algorithm: Process Model

Step 1 : Start
Step 2 : Yoga Pose

Step 3 : Webcam
Step 4 : Image Process
Step 5: Fetch Keypoints
Step 6: A Skeleton of Yoga Pose
Step 7 : Show Join Pose
Step 8: Detect Pose
Step 9 : Result
Step 10 : Stop

3.6 Results and Discussion

For calculating the results, we select the yoga asana, as shown in Figure 3.2 and calculate the accuracy of the yoga pose. And also, we find which asana it is. The accuracy is enhanced after comparing holistic and drawing structures.

3.7 Conclusion and Future Scope

The aim is to preserve the Indian yoga tradition by conducting workshops and seminars around the world. We also wish to bring a specific amount of self-discipline within the operations of the yoga institutions. Our tool would help in the certifications of yoga professionals and yoga schools. Different courses for imparting yoga education, training,

a) Dhanurasan

b) Gomukhasan

c) Shavasan

d) Bhadrasan

FIGURE 3.2
Yoga asana posture.

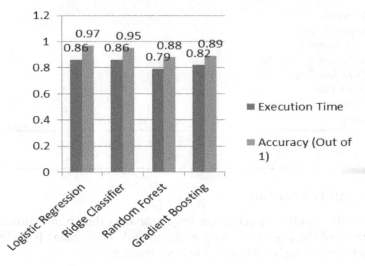

FIGURE 3.3
Comparison with classifiers.

TABLE 3.1
Highest Accuracy Score of Yoga Pose

S. No	Class	Accuracy
1	Dhanurasana	1.0
2	Vajrasan	1.0
3	Shavasan	0.99
4	Gomukhasan	1.0
5	Bhadrasan	1.0

TABLE 3.2
Comparison with Classifiers

Classifier Model	Execution Time	Accuracy
Logistic Regression	0.86	0.97
Ridge Classifier	0.86	0.95
Random Forest Classifier	0.79	0.88
Gradient Boosting Classifier	0.82	0.89

therapy, and research can be planned using the tool. The purpose of yoga is to achieve harmony within the physical, vital and mental attributes. It is important to improve self-awareness, self-control and self-worth about asanas. Our system helps to improve the posture and execution of yoga asanas. This model currently focuses on detecting the asana pose of a single person. However, Open Pose does come with the capabilities of detecting posture of multiple individuals in an image. Hence, we would like to improve our model to see multiple people in one frame. This would be beneficial for a group of people that are trying to learn or practice yoga at the same time. Our approach of input video would play a significant fundamental step in recognition of yoga pose efficiently with a large set of datasets. These results are presented in Figure 3.3, Table 3.1 and Table 3.2.

References

1. Behere, R. V., R. Arasappa, A. Jagannathan, S. Varambally, G. Venkatasubramanian, J. Thirthalli, D. K. Subbakrishna, H. R. Nagendra, and B.N. Gangadhar. "Effect of yogatherapy on facial emotion recognition deficits, symptoms and functioning in patients with schizophrenia." *Acta Psychiatrica Scandinavica* 123, no. 2 (2011): 147–153.
2. Yadav, Santosh Kumar, Amitojdeep Singh, Abhishek Gupta, and Jagdish Lal Raheja. "Real-time Yoga recognition using deep learning." *Neural Computing and Applications* 31, no. 12 (2019): 9349–9361.
3. Islam, Muhammad Usama, Hasan Mahmud, Faisal Bin Ashraf, Iqbal Hossain, and Md Kamrul Hasan. "Yoga posture recognition by detecting human joint points in real time using Microsoft Kinect." In *2017 IEEE Region 10 humanitarian technology conference (R10-HTC)*, pp. 668–673. IEEE, 2017.
4. H. E. Downs, R. Miltenberger, J. Biedronski, and L.Witherspoon, "The effects of video self-evaluation on skill acquisition with yoga postures," Journal of Applied Behavior Analysis, 484 (2015): 930–935.
5. Gochoo, Munkhjargal, Tan-Hsu Tan, Shih-Chia Huang, Tsedevdorj Batjargal, Jun-Wei Hsieh, Fady S. Alnajjar, and Yung-Fu Chen. "Novel IoT-based privacy-preserving yoga posture recognition system using low-resolution infrared sensors and deep learning." *IEEE Internet of Things Journal* 6, no. 4 (2019): 7192–7200.
6. Hua-Tsung, Chen, Yu-Zhen He, Chun-Chieh Hsu, Chien-Li Chou, Suh-Yin Lee, Bao-Shuh P. Lin, "Yoga posture recognition for selftraining." International Conference on Multimedia Modeling. Springer, pp. 496–505, 2014.
7. Maddala, Teja Kiran Kumar, P. V. V. Kishore, Kiran Kumar Eepuri, and Anil Kumar Dande. "YogaNet: 3-D yoga asana recognition using joint angular displacement maps with ConvNets." *IEEE Transactions on Multimedia* 21, no. 10 (2019): 2492–2503.
8. Maybel Chan Thar, Khine Zar Ne Winn, and Nobuo Funabiki. A Proposal of Yoga Pose Assessment Method Using Pose Detection for Self-Learning. University of Information Technology, Yangon, Myanmar Okayama University, Okayama, Japan. maybelchanthar@uit.edu.mm, khinezarnewinn@uit.edu.mm, funabiki@okayama-u.ac.jp
9. Toshev A., and C. Szegedy. DeepPose: human pose estimation via deep neural networks, 2013. https://doi.org/10.1109/cvpr.2014.214
10. Wu, W., W. Yin, and F. Guo. Learning and self-instruction expert system for Yoga. In: Proceedings of 2010 2nd International Work Intelligent System Application: ISA, pp. 2–5, 2010. https://doi.org/10.1109/iwisa.2010.5473592
11. Paithane P.M., S.N. Kakarwal, and D.V. Kurmude, "Automatic seeded region growing with level set technique used for segmentation of pancreas." Proceedings of the 12th International Conference on Soft Computing and Pattern Recognition (SoCPaR 2020). SoCPaR 2020. Advances in Intelligent Systems and Computing, vol 1383. Springer, Cham, 2021.
12. Paithane, P.M., S.N. Kakarwal, and D.V. Kurmude, "Top-down method used for pancreas segmentation." *International Journal Innovation Exploring Engineering* (IJITEE) 9(3) (2020): 1790–1793. ISSN 2278–3075.
13. Paithane, P.M. and S.A. Kinariwal. "Automatic determination number of cluster for NMKFC-means algorithm on image segmentation." *IOSR-JCE* 17(1) (2015): 12–19. Ver 2.
14. Paithane, P.M. and S.N. Kakarwal, "Automatic determination number of cluster for multi kernel NMKFCM algorithm on image segmentation." In: *Intelligent System Design and Applications*, pp. 80–89. Springer, Cham, 2018.

4

Smart Health Prediction System Using IoT

Kalpesh Joshi, Vipul Pisal, Rohan Awale, and Sanmit Patil

CONTENTS

4.1 Introduction

Human life has become more comfortable because of automation, and as a result, humans are jeopardizing their health. Patients who are elderly or bedridden will benefit more from the revolutionary health care predictions. In this paradigm, the Internet of Things (IoT) plays a critical role in data collection and processing of data from patients' wearable devices. Wireless communication is frequently used to transfer data to the server. Many existing systems monitor these data manually or through loosely coupled systems, resulting in less accurate prediction results. To enhance the process of smart health prediction, our proposed model uses IoT as the infrastructure to collect the data over the wireless paradigm and the whole process is weaved using K-means and artificial neural networks (ANN) techniques to provide accurate health predictions.

4.2 Literature Survey

Y. Jung [1] explores the ubiquity of smartphones and wireless technologies; as they have proliferated among the masses, it is highly unusual to meet a person without a phone nowadays. The authors propose a healthcare system that utilizes the wireless sensor

DOI: 10.1201/9781003342755-5

network for real-time monitoring of bio-signals. The researchers use expectation maximization for the processing of data acquired from electrocardiogram (EMG), electrocardiography (ECG), and electroencephalography (EEG) waveforms from a wearable device on the patient. N. Alshurafa [2] comments on the remote health monitoring (RHM) systems as they've become quite popular and widely accepted among doctors and patients alike. The authors reviewed Wanda-CVD, an RHM based on a smartphone that was utilized for assisting in the reduction of risks involving cardiovascular diseases. This was achieved through social support and feedback through wireless coaching. The authors noticed a pattern in the patients' success rates. Therefore, to understand the aspect, they developed a technique based on machine learning that can predict the risk factors for unsuccessful patients. S. Kesavan [3] expresses the advances in technology in the area of wireless sensor networks and other wearable devices. These devices can be used for processing health care with the help of sensors and trackers to monitor a patient's vital parameters. As it is cumbersome to connect various different devices wirelessly at the same time, the authors developed a gateway for the connection and utilization of various sensors together in a network. The network has proven to be highly efficient and also allows streaming data to the cloud at the same time. A. Massaro [4] proposes a method for automatic monitoring of patients staying at home alone. This provides better care for them in case of an emergency as the system is oriented to diagnose the heart rate and vitals of a person from the control room when the patient is in the comfortable confines of their home. The researchers defined a KNIME workflow that utilizes ANN (artificial neural network) and MLP (multilayer perceptron). The proposed technique can help patients a lot by providing an early discharge and helping them recuperate in the comfort of their homes. Arthi et al. [5] explore the health problems faced by individuals in the teaching profession. As most of the prediction systems for health care have a generalized view of the illnesses and most of them are specialized to a certain disease rather than a particular profession. Therefore, the authors propose a system that can predict diseases such as chronic laryngitis, asthma, and various other respiratory illnesses that occur due to the teaching profession. The researchers utilize the negEx algorithm to analyze the individual's medical records. The prediction is done by implementing DL (description logic), FOL (first order logic), and bio-ontology for prediction purposes. K. Navin [6] expresses concern over the detection of epidemics as the health care systems usually rely on the formal reports published by the center where the epidemic has been noticed. This leads to a delay and a possible increase in the spread of the disease even further. The authors, therefore, propose a method for health care surveillance based on smartphones as they are in widespread use by many individuals and help the epidemiologist in acquiring data on symptoms and diseases based on public opinion faster. The method has the potential to reduce and limit the spread of infectious disease. V. Jakkula states that the growth of technology has enabled convenience for everyone. This has also opened doors for advancements in the medical sector such as the health monitoring systems that can monitor the health of elderly patients in various situations and settings. The authors, therefore, present an exceptional method for the prediction of certain diseases and ailments integrated with an advanced smart home setting. This allows the system to observe the trends of ailments and diseases that occur over a period of time and provide accurate predictions for future events [7]. A. Yassine [8] explains that due to rapid urbanization, there is a large influx of people into the urban areas, which leads to heavy congestion that strains the in infrastructure. This also occurs in the health care sector where the small number of medical centers are strained with footfall and that would lead to a lapse in their practices. Therefore, the authors present a smart home system that utilizes various data generated by the homes to mine and analyze the energy consumption and monitor human activity to provide predictions based on it. These predictions can help identify serious flaws and assist the medical professionals in suggesting lifestyle choices and better diagnosing the patients. Y. Mehta [9] expresses concerns over rising air pollution in cities that is choking the inhabitants. Air pollution leads to a lot of respiratory illnesses; therefore, the authors present a system for tracking air quality throughout the city and relaying that information to the dwellers with the help of an app on their smartphones. This is enabled by deploying various IoT sensors throughout the city that measure the quality of air and relay that information to the cloud by using various wireless technologies. This information is then processed with the help of data from the city Road Transport Office and then transmitted to the app. G. Wang introduces a prevalent problem in epidemiological and community health studies, which is missing data. Missing data plagues the dataset and can reduce the quality of the system being tested with the data. If the missing data is purged, it results in a reduction in the size of the dataset. Even data imputation techniques aren't helpful as they inadvertently introduce unnecessary noise in the dataset. Therefore, the authors introduce an innovative technique for prediction involving missing data in datasets that utilizes an additive LS- SVM (least square support vector machine). This method is highly useful and increases the accuracy of the system [10]. M. Gillham [11] explores the concerns surrounding assistance to wheelchair-bound individuals. They require a high amount of assistance specifically in the area of collision avoidance. The authors design a weightless neural network architecture for the avoidance of obstacles based on sensor information from the wheelchair. It is essential not to usurp the control of the wheelchair from the user but the addition some kind of intelligence to the equipment to allow a more seamless experience that is safe and secure for the individual. The system efficiently utilizes pattern recognition and can provide non-intrusive assistance to the disabled individual. S. Rai [12] expresses concerns over the quality of life for people who are working as they tend to ignore general non-threatening ailments due to time and work constraints. This is a very bad habit that can cause a minor issue to have a domino effect and cause major issues to occur. To ameliorate this effect, the authors present a novel assistant based on ANN and artificial intelligence (AI) that can diagnose common symptoms and provide easy remedies and exercises to help busy people live a better lifestyle. Deep learning and AI help makes accurate predictions and enable an efficient diagnosis of the symptoms.

4.3 Implementation Details

The overview of the proposed system for health prediction using IoT is shown in Figure 4.1 and the steps involved in these methodologies are described below.

4.3.1 Deployment and Data Generation

The proposed model of health prediction is deployed in the distributed system where a patient panel is created to register the patient to get the service of the health prediction system. Once the patient is registered, he/she needs to complete the registration by feeding some facts related to their health like height, weight, smoking, alcohol, and

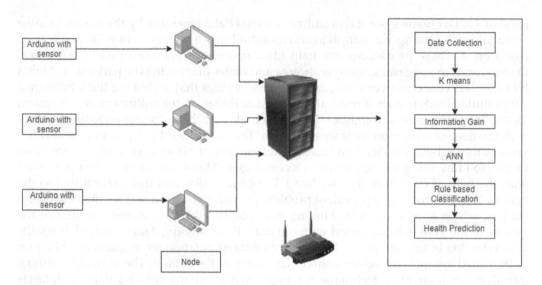

FIGURE 4.1
System diagram.

diabetes. Then the patient needs to wear the pulse sensor to get the pulse rate actively. All other parameters like the number of hours of sleep, systolic blood pressure, diastolic blood pressure, body temperature, and sugar level in mmol/L are generated based on some protocols as mentioned in www.webmd.com for given interval. This data is generated based on the random integer creation bounded by the protocols of the human body aesthetics. The generated data is sent to the prediction server, which is deployed in the local area network via a Wi-Fi connection.

4.3.2 Data Preprocessing

As the prediction server receives the data from the patient panel in the said interval, the particular patient is evaluated by extracting all his/her past data from the database. If the database of the particular patient is not enough to process, then the received data is stored in the database. As the data from the database is extracted, then it is subjected to preprocessing to collect only the columns which are actively changing for the given interval of time. The attributes like the number of hours of sleep, systolic bp, diastolic blood pressure, body temperature, blood sugar level, and pulse rate are selected in the preprocessed list.

4.3.3 K-Means Clustering

The preprocessed list is subjected to cluster formation based on the Euclidean distance. Euclidean distance is evaluated for each of the rows in the preprocessed list concerning all other rows to refer to them as row distance (RD). These individual row distances are summed up to get the average of all rows, which yields the Euclidean distance of the complete preprocessed list and is referred to as the Euclidean distance (ED). These rows are sorted based on RD. This ED is used to form the boundaries of the cluster along with the centroids. These centroids are randomly selected based on the values of K for the RD. Once these centroids are evaluated then, they are subjected to the form the boundaries of the clusters, which in the end yield the cluster of decided size. Euclidean distance formation can be shown in the equation below:

$$D = \sqrt{(x1 - x2)^2 + (y1 - y2)^2}$$ (4.1)

where D is the Euclidean distance, x1, x2, y1, and y2 are the attribute values.

4.3.3.1 Information Gain Estimation

Out of the created clusters, important clusters need to be selected based on the information gain theory. Here the highest factors which can cause ill health conditions are identified from the preprocessed list. And then each of the rows of a cluster is checked for the threshold of 75% of the highest ill-health parameters. Then the rows which are satisfying this rule are counted in a cluster to apply the gain theory. Then any cluster with non-zero gain values is selected for the further evaluation of ANN.

4.3.4 ANN

The neurons of ANN are formed for the selected clusters through information gain theory based on the mean and standard deviation of the row distances (RD). These neurons are formed with the protocols of the ranges inside the mean and standard deviation and ranges outside the mean and standard deviation. This can be shown with the below mentioned in Figure 4.2.

4.3.5 Rule-Based Classification

Once the neurons are formed, they tend to analyze the disease proneness based on the possible nearest threshold for the actively varying factors which are considered in the neurons. These optimized neurons are then evaluated for the second half of the received data of the respective patient. Once this second half data is evaluated, then it is binarized for the ill-health condition for the parameters like body mass index (BMI), smoking, alcohol, sleep hours, blood pressure, temperature, sugar level, and pulse rate. These binarized parameters are counted and checked for 50% of their ratio of total size to declare the patient with a specific ill-health proneness like obesity, anxiety, insomnia, diabetes, blood pressure, fever, or agoraphobia, If no ill health proneness is found, then the person is declared as healthy and same is intimating him/her via email.

4.4 Results and Discussion

The proposed methodology of the Smart Health Predicting System with IoT is deployed in the local area network using the D-Link double antenna Wi-Fi router. And the laptops are used for the deployment area of Core i5 with RAM of 6 GB configuration. And the patient panel laptops are equipped with a pulse sensor, which is connected to the laptops via Arduino UNO microcontroller board. To deploy the model, the proposed system uses

---

Algorithm 1: Neuron formation

// Input : Selected Clusters C_L
// Output : Neurons N_U
Function : neuronFormation(C_L)
Step 0: Start
Step 1: $N_U = \varnothing$
Step 2: *for* i=0 to size of C_L
Step 3: $S_G = C_{Li}$
Step 4: mean and Standard_deviation for S_G as (μ, α)
Step 5: *for* j=0 to size of S_G
Step 6: ROW=S_{Gj}
Step 7: R_D = ROW(ROW$_{SIZE}$ -1)
Step 8: **If**(RD> = (μ- α) AND R_D < =(μ+ α)
Step 9: $N_U = N_U + ROW$
Step 10: *ELSE*
Step 11: *If* R_D> μ+ α , **THEN**
Step 12: $N_U = N_U + ROW$
Step 13: *ELSE*
Step 14: *If* R_D < μ- α , **THEN**
Step 15: $N_U = N_U + ROW$
Step 16: **End** *for*
Step 17: **End** *for*
Step 18: return N_U
Step 19: Stop

FIGURE 4.2
Neuron formation algorithm.

the Java programming language and Netbeans as IDE along with MySQL as the database server. Further experiments are conducted to measure the effectiveness of the system using precision and recall. Precision and recall are considered the best parameters to evaluate any prediction system. Precision and recall can be described below:

A = The number of relevant predictions
B = The number of irrelevant predictions
C = The number of relevant predictions not predicted

Therefore,

Precision = (A / (A+ B)) *100
Recall = (A / (A+ C)) *100

On observing the reading and plot for the precision and recall from Table 4.1 and Figure 4.3, it can be seen that the proposed model achieves around 87% of precision and 94% recall. This is a good sign of a system in our first attempt to predict ill-health conditions.

TABLE 4.1
Precision and Recall Values

Testing Experiments with No. of Trials	Relevant Predictions Identified (A)	Irrelevant Predictions Identified (B)	Relevant Predictions Not Identified (C)	Precision %	Recall %
5	5	0	0	10	10
1	8	2	0	8	10
1	1	1	1	93.33333	93.33333
2	1	5	3	7	83.33333
2	2	3	1	8	95.6521739

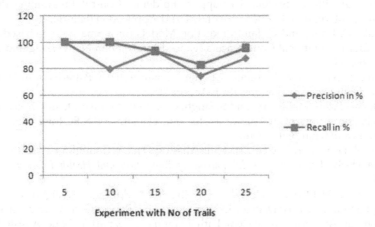

FIGURE 4.3
Precision and recall comparison.

4.5 Conclusion

The proposed model for ill-health condition prediction using IoT and machine learning is deployed using the combination of random health attribute generation. This is based on strict medical field protocols along with the real-time data capturing of the pulse rate using the pulse sensor. The model uses the ANN and K-means clustering along with the rule-based classification model, which yields better precision and recall; this, in turn, proves the effectiveness of the proposed model.

This model can be enhanced in the future for many other parameters like ECG and EEG signals using the real-time sensors using the IoT in the internet paradigm.

References

1. Y. Jung and Y. Yoon, Prediction Model for Mental and Physical Health Condition using Risk Ratio EM, International Conference on Information Networking (ICOIN), 2015.

2. N. Alshurafa, C. Sideris, M. Pourhomayun, H. Kalantarian, M. Sarrafzadeh, and J. Eastwood, Remote Health Monitoring Outcome Success Prediction Using Baseline and First Month Intervention Data, *IEEE Journal of Biomedical and Health Informatics*, 21(2), 507–514, 2016.

3. S. Kesavan and G. Kalambettu, IOT enabled comprehensive, plug and play gateway framework for smart health, Second International Conference on Advances in Electronics, Computer and Communications ICAECC, 2018.

4. A. Massaro, V. Maritati, A. Galiano, and N. Savino, Neural Networks for Automated Smart Health Platforms oriented on /heart Predictive Diagnostic Big Data Systems, AEIT International Annual Conference, 2018.

5. C. Arthi, R. Priya, and R. Rautela, Analysis and Prediction of Health Issues for Teaching Profession Using Semantic Techniques, International Conference on Smart City and Emerging Technology (ICSCET), 2018.

6. K. Navin, M. Krishnan, S. Lavanya, and A. Shanthini, A Mobile Health-Based Smart Hybrid Epidemic Surveillance System To Support Epidemic Control Programme Public Health Informatics, International Conference on IoT and Application (ICIOT), 2017.

7. V. Jakkula, D. Cook, and G. Jain, Prediction Models for a Smart Home-based Health Care System, 21st International Conference advanced Information Networking and Applications Workshops, 2007.

8. A. Yassine, S. Singh, and A. Alamri, Mining Human Activity Patterns from SmartHome Big Data for Healthcare Applications, IEEE Access, 2017.

9. Y. Mehta, M. Pai, S. Mallissery, and S. Singh, Cloud-enabled Air Quality Detection, Analysis and Prediction: A Smart CityApplication for Smart Health, 3rd MEC International Conference on Big Data and Smart City, 2016.

10. G. Wang, Z. Deng, and K. Choi, Tackling Missing Data in Community Health Studies Using Additive LS-SVM Classifier, *IEEE Journal of Biomedical and Health Informatics*, 22(2), 579–587, 2016.

11. M. Gillham, B. McElroy, G. Howells, S. Kelly, and S. Spurgeon, Weightless Neural System Employing Simple Sensor Data for Efficient Real-TimeRound Corner, Junction and Doorway Detection for Autonomous System Path Planning in Smart Robotic Assisted Healthcare Wheelchairs, Third International Conference on Emerging Security Technologies, 2012.

12. S. Rai, A. Raut, A. Savaliya, and R. Shankarmani, Darwin: Convolutional Neural Network based Intelligent Health Assistant, Proceedings of the 2nd International conference on Electronics, Communication and Aerospace Technology (ICECA), 2018.

5

Real-Time CNN-Based Face Mask Detection System

Suvarna Pawar, Mrudul Jain, Prathamesh Akole, Suyog Mahagaonkar, and Rupesh Kapse

CONTENTS

5.1 Introduction

COVID-19 has been creating ripples across the globe owing to its rapid spread. It has also been declared a global pandemic. There are various symptoms ranging from simple cold to infection of severe acute respiratory syndrome (SARS) virus. The basic precaution to stop the spread of COVID-19 is using face masks. It is necessary to wear face masks or else the disease will spread rapidly and again infect the masses. Research shows that wearing a mask reduces the possibility of contracting COVID-19 by more than 70% [1, 2]. It has also been observed during the various and multiple waves of COVID-19 that when the face masks usage reduced, the disease started spreading locally. Due to negligence of a few people, the community as a whole is placed at a high risk. Hence, face mask detection is of utmost importance to stop the cycle of community spread. Machine learning, deep learning, and computer vision can be used to detect the presence of people without masks. There are several other studies on COVID-19, and in this study, we will focus on the comparison of various machine learning techniques using computer vision for classifying maskless people using datasets [3].

DOI: 10.1201/9781003342755-6

5.2 Literature Survey

The American Journal of Infection Control [4] conducted numerous experiments to check the effectiveness of face masks in preventing COVID-19. The study was done on completely different populations, countries, and mask varieties. In all, over 5,178 eligible articles were searched in databases and references. The results showed that normally, carrying a mask was related to a considerably reduced risk of COVID-19 infection (OR = zero.38, 95% CI: 0.21–0.69, I2 = 54.1%). For the tending staff cluster, masks were shown to possess a reduced risk of infection by nearly 70%. Sensitivity analysis showed that the results were sturdy. A study by the School of Mathematical and Statistical Sciences, Arizona State University, and authored by Steffen E. Eikenberry et al. [5] further corroborated the findings of the previous study. The researchers sought out to model the potential that face masks had to curtail the spread of the COVID-19, and for the same, constructed a Kermack-McKendrick-type compartmentalized a mathematical model. They used the model to simulate COVID-19 dynamics using relevant data in the US states of New York and Washington. Multiple hypothetical mask adoption scenarios were simulated, and the results were as follows:

A. In the state of New York, it was established that 80% adoption of moderately effective masks (50% effectiveness) would be able to prevent the deaths caused by COVID-19 in the order ranging from 17% to 45% over a time span of two months while decreasing the peak daily death rate by 34–58%.
B. Even low-quality masks (20% effectiveness) were found to subdue the mortality rate by a factor of 2–9% and the peak daily mortality rate by factor of 9–18% in New York whereas, in the state of Washington, where the baseline transmission rate was quite lower, such masks could reduce the mortality rate by 24–65% and the peak daily mortality rate by 15–69%.
C. Using a time-series model compiled by John Hopkins University combined with least squares algorithm in MATLAB, it was observed that, in general, even having 50% coverage and 50% mask effectiveness diminished the virus transmission rate by half. [This study was performed for simulated epidemics with a true β_0 of 1.5, 1, or 0.5 day^{-1}.]

The authors also examined multiple types of masks varying from a simple home-made mask to surgical masks worn by medical professionals to estimate the inward and outward efficiency used for their own model. It was concluded by studying multiple dissertations (Davies et al. (2013) [6], Driessche et al. (2015) [7], Stockwell et al., (2018) [8], van der Sande et al. (2008) [9]) that the inward efficiencies could vary between 20% and 80% for home-made cloth masks, 70–90% for medical grade surgical masks and over 95% for properly work N95 masks. Similarly, outward efficiencies ranged between 0% and 80% for home-made cloth masks, 50–90% for surgical masks and 70–100% for N95 Masks. Masks were endorsed to be especially invaluable against coughing-based diseases for both control as well as prevention purposes (Patel et al. (2016) [10], Lai et al. (2012) [11]). In conclusion, the researchers doubled down on the importance of using masks in public spaces to diminish the effectiveness of the virus. Their models are quite constituent with previous research on this subject [10,11] and have showed us that there are quite strong benefits to general face mask use as compared to not masking at all. Hence, these results validate the necessity of face masks, especially for an even larger population in India and therefore support our reasons for building a real-time face mask detection model.

F.M. Javed Mehedi Shamrat et al. [12] projected the idea of comparing different types of pooling layers in their convolution neural networks (CNN) model. They created a model with three hidden layers and added pooling layers after each convolution. The authors compared three pooling layers: max pooling, average pooling and MobileNetV2 (which uses a global average pooling layer at the very end [13] instead of using it after every layer) on a dataset consisting of 1,845 images from the Web + 120 labeled images from the author's mobile and web cameras. The model with max pooling layers achieved 96.49% testing accuracy and 98.67% validation accuracy; on the other hand, the model with average pooling layers achieved 95.19% training accuracy and a validation accuracy of 96.23%. MobileNetV2 architecture achieved that highest accuracy of the lot at a staggering 99.72% for training and 99.82% for validation. The authors were therefore successful in proving that a global average pooling-based architecture is more effective that the fully connected layers of used in the CNN model. This can be explained by the fact that global average pooling is "more native to the convolution structure by enforcing correspondences between feature maps and categories" [14] and also overfitting is avoided at the last layer as there is no parameter left to optimize. Javed Mehedi and others' findings support our own conclusions in that MobileNet is the most preferred architecture for our use case while making a face detection model. Unlike their model however, we have used an even larger dataset with more variety of images. Similarly, a model developed by B. Varshini et al. [15] involved MobileNetV2 as their pre-trained model too. They also combined their model with a feature for the temperature measurement and counting the number of individuals in question at any time. The completely trained model had a good accuracy of 97%. The CNN model they developed with a 32-batch size and run for 20 epochs had an excellent validation accuracy of about 99% and the testing accuracy of the model on basis of the performance was 98.55%. B. Varshini and others, however, proposed a "smart door" solution, which had a specific use case of being fitted into homeowner's doors. Our model was primarily designed to be deployed in public spaces. Both these research papers did support our cause for developing a software-based application for the real-time detection of face masks using MobileNet. A study by students of electrical engineering politeknik Negeri Batam, Indonesia [16], proposed a yolo v4 deep learning algorithm for face mask detection. They have shown experimental results in images that were taken at the premises of politeknik college, Negeri Batam. Their model supports multiple moving persons at a time. The hardware they have used consists of a digital webcam camera to recognize the face mask, a PC and a speaker. All the face detection was done on a computer that is mounted for GPU to increase user interaction and it enhances the graphical calculation. Their machine model detects such people who don't wear masks and their model instructs that person to wear a mask. Their model firstly looks for a person by detecting the backbone and neck. After that, it detects a person with a mask or without a mask. They are using PANet for neck detection and backbone level detection. There is no mention of the accuracy of their model. Their hardware has to be installed in the public, which may lead to extra costs for installation and maintenance of the device. Their model cannot integrate with other low computational devices such as public security cameras, CCTV and due to these disadvantages, we have gone with our model, which has negligible setup cost and is suitable for low computational devices.

Bala Balamurugan et al.'s [17] model is completely based on the real-time face detection where it detects and produces the output depending on the person wearing a face mask or not and it also includes an alert system using deep learning and machine learning techniques by use of CNN. The model is trained using CNN, Tenser-Flow (Keras) and the VGG-16 transfer learning model. The model was able to achieve 96% result for performance and accuracy and it led the device to maintain the highest possible accuracy, throughput, and efficiency. The device is more feasible as it was developed with cheaper materials and made sure it is accessed by everyone in the world. In addition to it, the device has an alarm system to alert the people by making a sound along with red light if the person is not wearing the mask and with a green light if the person is wearing the mask. The disadvantages of the author's work are that VGG-16 CNN requires huge training time and resources due to the abundant number of parameters it supports (138 million). Just training the model on a NVIDIA Titan GPU takes 5–6 hours. The size of VGG-16 trained ImageNet is also relatively larger than other architectures (about 528 MB h5file). A lot of disk space and bandwidth get utilized in this model, which makes this model unfit to be deployed on low computational devices. The hardware built is not portable. It makes it difficult for the users to utilize it in different places according to their needs. The unnecessary use of the alarm system is increasing the cost of the product. Instead, one can give an alert using a software-based message alert too.

5.3 Module-wise Implementation

5.3.1 Dataset Collection

The dataset used in this work is open-source available on Kaggle and GitHub, which currently consists of a total of 3,833 images. These two types of images are stored in two different directories named: with_mask and without_mask, which contain 1,915 and 1,918 images, respectively, as shown in Figures 5.1 and 5.2. To avoid overfitting, we combined data from multiple sources and generated two unique datasets of our own which are: real-world masked face dataset (RMFD) [18] and simulated masked face dataset (SMFD) [3]. We then applied these datasets to train and test our model.

FIGURE 5.1
Dataset without face_mask: Sample Images from the dataset of people without masks.

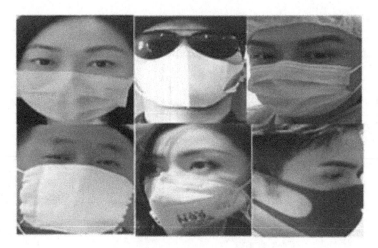

FIGURE 5.2
Dataset with face_mask: Sample Images from the dataset of people with masks.

5.3.2 Dataset Preprocessing

The images within the dataset are of different sizes, quality, and pixel density, so we needed to make all of them uniform before running CNN over it, hence we had to pre-process the images within our dataset. Our dataset was quite vast and preprocessing all the images manually wasn't possible. Therefore, we used Keras' image data generator method to resize all of the images to 224 × 224 pixels and normalized them. To process the images faster, we converted them into NumPy arrays. The amount of data gathered from the images was increased by zooming, horizontal flipping, rotating, and shearing the images.

5.3.3 Convolutional Neural Network

For image classification and processing, CNN (ConvNet) is used. CNN is a deep learning algorithm that takes an input image and assigns it importance (on the basis of weights, biases) with the aim to find important features that help differentiate one part of the image from another as shown in Figure 5.3.

Hence, we effectively work inside one part of the image rather than working with the full image. Our CNN is made up multiple layers including an input as well as output layer. In our model, we have applied CNN over 20 epochs (iterations) to get high training accuracy. We preferred CNN over other models as preprocessing required in CNN/ConvNet is much lower compared to other classification algorithms.

After passing through the first CNN layer, max pooling is used to obtain the most notable information. It helps us gather important information from an image and also decreases the size of the images, hence reducing complexity.

Max pooling is a pooling operation, shown in Figure 5.4 that selects the maximum element from the region of the feature map covered by the filter.. Therefore, the output after max pooling layer will be a feature map that contains the most prominent features of the previous feature map. It divides the data into 2 × 2 matrixes and selects the pieces of image with the highest values (which were generated using ConvNet). After that, the data is passed to the second convolution layer. The resultant image matrix obtained is then flattened and trained.

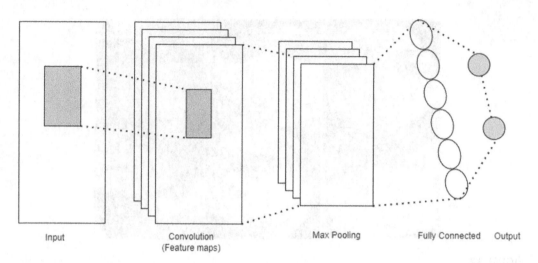

FIGURE 5.3
CNN Architecture: Flow of the convolutional neural network's architecture.

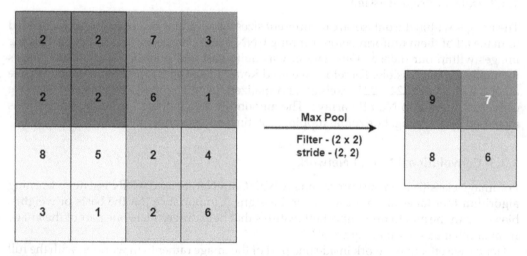

FIGURE 5.4
Max pooling example: Pictorial representation of a 4 × 4 image matrix max pooled into a 2 × 2 matrix.

Flattening is the process we use to convert data into a one-dimensional layer for inputting to into the next layer of the process. We flatten the output of the CNN algorithm and create a single extended feature vector, which is then used for output generation. About 20% of the dataset's images were used to judge the performance and accuracy of the model.

5.3.4 MobileNetV2 Architecture

MobileNetV2 is a CNN-based architecture, shown in Figure 5.5, provides a higher performance on mobile devices. MobileNets have an efficient design that uses severable convolutions to create lightweight deep neural network (DNN). As it is lightweight DNN,

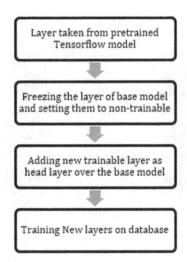

FIGURE 5.5
MobileNetV2 architecture: Flow diagram of MobileNetV2 architecture.

MobileNet has fewer parameters and high classification accuracy. Basically, it's a really effective in extracting features in object detection and segmentation. It decreases the complexity as well as model size of the network, which increases its effectiveness while being used on mobile devices, or any other device with low computational power [19].

MobileNetV2 Architecture is shown in Figure 5.5. In this architecture, firstly, the base layer of MobileNetV2 is removed and a new trainable layer is added. And now, the trainable layer uses the previous dataset to improve itself. The model analyzes the information and extracts the vital pieces of data from our image. For the mask detection from a picture or any live video, OpenCV is used. The mask detection classifier receives the output face detected image. It has very quick and high accuracy while detecting masks in live video. In the MobileNet architecture, it has few parameters, so it doesn't make an overfitted model and has a better accuracy than other comparable models. MobileNet has been applied to variety of various applications like the FaceNet model, which is a progressive face recognition model. Generally, up to 95% accuracy was obtained for training and 95% for validation.

5.3.5 ResNet50

In neural networks, a common problem while updating weights and biases is known as the vanishing gradient problem, which makes the model hard to validate and train. When we use the backpropagation algorithm for updating weights (which is based off of chain rules in calculus), multiple multiplications take place, which may make weights and biases extremely small (tending to 0). ResNet has a solution to this vanishing gradient problem.

Residual neural network uses the concept called skip connections [20] to resolve this problem, shown in Figure 5.6. In a traditional neural network, convolutions layers are stacked one after another and data travels layer by layer whereas, in ResNets, we have also added original input to the output of the convolutional block. So, we have input that will layer as input in a normal traditional way and by skipping one or more than one convolutional block. These are called skip connections.

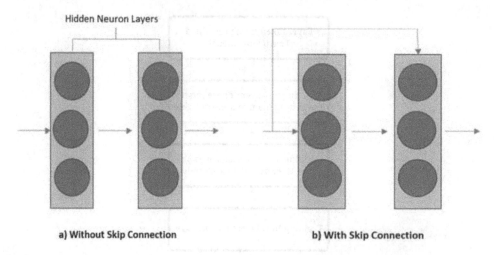

FIGURE 5.6
Skip connections in ResNets: (a) hidden layers in ResNet without skip connection. (b) Hidden layers in ResNet with skip connection.

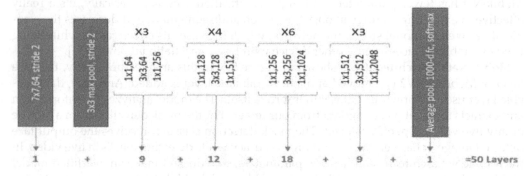

FIGURE 5.7
ResNet architecture: Representation of ResNet architecture consisting of 50 layers.

In skip connections, we are skipping some of the layers, and therefore, the updated values do not manage to reach a very small value. This technique helps relieve the difficulty in optimization due to non-linearity by propagating a linear component through the neural network layers [21]. Hence, this is technique used by ResNets to avoid the vanishing gradient problem.

ResNet50 is a ResNet layer structure that contains exactly 50 layers as shown below.

ResNet50 has the first default layer of filter size 7×7 and has 64 filters with stride = 2, shown in Figures 5.7 and 5.8, there is a max pool of size 3×3 with stride = 2. After that, there are 48 such layers of different filter sizes and several filters. The last layer has a SoftMax function with an average pooling layer. We worked on ResNet50 too with input shapes (150,150,3) with the same dataset. Along with that, the model has one flattened layer and two dense layers. This model has an accuracy of 97.60%.

(a) Stem Block; (b) Stage1 – Block 1; (c) Stage1 – Block 2; (d) FC block.

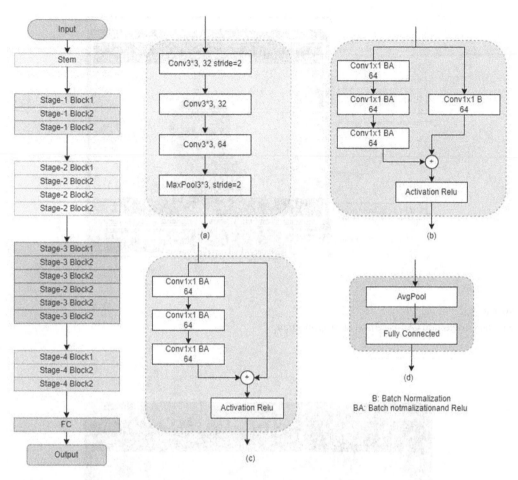

FIGURE 5.8
Detailed architecture of ResNet-50-vd.

5.4 Results and Analysis

While implementing the model to detect masks, we used images which contained both masked and unmasked faces shown in Figures 5.9–5.11. The training and validation accuracy after using deep CNN with max pooling as well as the MobileNetV2 is shown in Table 5.1. The highest training accuracy is 99.18% and the validation accuracy is 99.35% shown in Figures 5.12–5.16. The graph representing the accuracy against the epochs is also shown. It was observed that MobileNetV2 significantly increased the accuracy of the model.

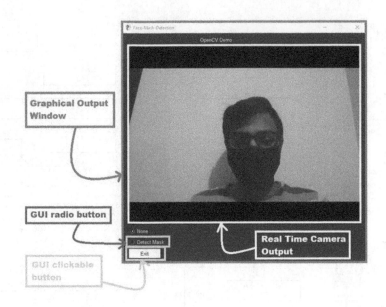

FIGURE 5.9
Face mask detection GUI-based desktop application.

FIGURE 5.10
App correctly detects masks for multiple people within the same frame.

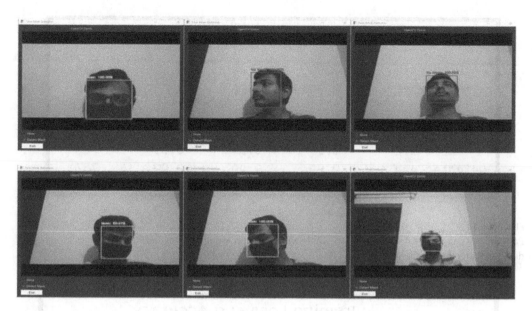

FIGURE 5.11
Working shown in multiple angles.

TABLE 5.1
Epoch versus Accuracy Table for MobileNetV2

Epoch	Training Loss	Training Accuracy	Validation Loss	Validation Accuracy
1	0.4169	0.8451	0.1508	0.9844
2	0.1538	0.9634	0.0756	0.9909
3	0.1005	0.9756	0.0549	0.9909
4	0.0803	0.9763	0.0451	0.9922
5	0.0638	0.9822	0.0395	0.9922
6	0.0604	0.9825	0.0382	0.9922
7	0.0525	0.9835	0.0351	0.9922
8	0.052	0.9819	0.034	0.9922
9	0.0436	0.9881	0.0319	0.9922
10	0.0377	0.9901	0.0317	0.9909
11	0.0394	0.9885	0.0305	0.9896
12	0.0412	0.9891	0.0304	0.9922
13	0.037	0.9865	0.0306	0.9922
14	0.0353	0.9901	0.0287	0.9922
15	0.029	0.9908	0.0278	0.9909
16	0.0302	0.9908	0.0306	0.9896
17	0.0286	0.9904	0.0379	0.9922
18	0.0297	0.9914	0.027	0.9922
19	0.0301	0.9914	0.0289	0.9935
20	0.0263	0.9918	0.0265	0.9922

	precision	recall	f1-score	support
with_mask	0.99	0.99	0.99	383
without_mask	0.99	0.99	0.99	384
accuracy			0.99	767
macro avg	0.99	0.99	0.99	767
weighted avg	0.99	0.99	0.99	767

FIGURE 5.12
Performance parameters for MobileNetV2: Table with precision, recall, f1score and support values for images detected with mask, without mask.

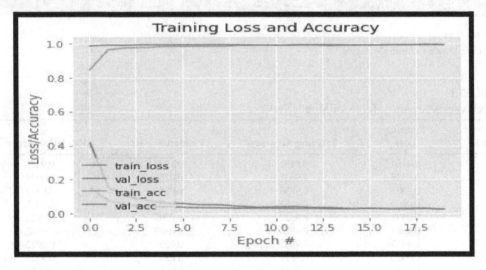

FIGURE 5.13
Loss v/s epoch graph: MobileNetV2.

5.5 Conclusion and Future Scope

We implemented the model using the deep learning based CNN architecture with max pooling as well as MobileNetV2. Our main motive behind this study was to present a highly accurate compatible model so that the identification of people without masks in public spaces will become easier henceforth. To scale the performance of the model when applied to a larger dataset, we may add different models and then compare their accuracy with Mobilenetv2. We can also integrate it with IoT devices such as CCTV cameras and other small computation devices and automate the model so that there is no need of human interference.

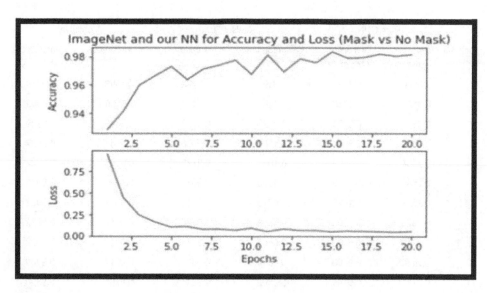

FIGURE 5.14
Loss and accuracy graph for ImageNet.

Layer (type)	Output Shape	Param #
inception_resnet_v2 (Functio	(None, 3, 3, 1536)	54336736
flatten_1 (Flatten)	(None, 13824)	0
dense_2 (Dense)	(None, 256)	3539200
dense_3 (Dense)	(None, 2)	514

Total params: 57,876,450
Trainable params: 3,539,714
Non-trainable params: 54,336,736

FIGURE 5.15
Inception ResNet model summary.

Acknowledgment

We would like to extend our sincere gratitude and thanks to our head of the department, Dr. Pravin Futane, for his invaluable guidance and for giving us useful inputs and encouragement time and again. The project wouldn't have gone so well without his care and support.

Epoch	Pure CNN		ResNet 50		MobileNet	
	Validation Loss	Validation Accuracy	Validation Loss	Validation Accuracy	Validation Loss	Validation Accuracy
1	3.3246	0.7839	0.9497	0.9289	0.1508	0.9844
2	0.3122	0.8756	0.4487	0.9417	0.0756	0.9909
3	0.3169	0.8699	0.2423	0.9600	0.0549	0.9909
4	0.2659	0.8985	0.1069	0.9666	0.0451	0.9922
5	0.2654	0.8965	0.1034	0.9730	0.0395	0.9922
6	0.2560	0.9019	0.1085	0.9639	0.0382	0.9922
7	0.2533	0.8978	0.0778	0.9713	0.0351	0.9922
8	0.2376	0.9069	0.0808	0.9740	0.0340	0.9922
9	0.2342	0.9053	0.0661	0.9774	0.0319	0.9922
10	0.2416	0.9100	0.0898	0.9676	0.0317	0.9909
11	0.2184	0.9160	0.0505	0.9811	0.0305	0.9896
12	0.2249	0.9113	0.0816	0.9693	0.0304	0.9922
13	0.2215	0.9096	0.0633	0.9784	0.0306	0.9922
14	0.2214	0.9137	0.0637	0.9757	0.0287	0.9922
15	0.2170	0.9130	0.0489	**0.9835**	0.0278	0.9909
16	0.2129	0.9184	0.0592	0.9791	0.0306	0.9896
17	0.1998	0.9184	0.0543	0.9794	0.0379	0.9922
18	0.1908	**0.9272**	0.0493	0.9818	0.0270	0.9922
19	0.1967	0.9272	0.0436	0.9804	0.0289	**0.9935**
20	0.1880	0.9241	0.0528	0.9815	0.0265	0.9922

FIGURE 5.16
Comparative study of transfer learning architectures.

References

1. Yanni Li et al. "Face Masks to Prevent Transmission of COVID-19: A Systematic Review and Meta-Analysis." *American Journal of Infection Control*, Mosby, 19 December 2020, www.scienc edirect.com/science/article/pii/S0196655320310439
2. *The New Indian Express*. "Only 44 per cent of India Is Wearing a Face Mask." 4 May 2021, www.newindianexpress.com/nation/2021/may/04/only-44-per-cent-of-india-is-wearing-a-face-mask-2298187.html
3. Gurav Omkar. "Face Mask Detection Dataset." Kaggle, 31 July 2020, www.kaggle.com/omk argurav/face-mask-dataset.
4. Yanni Li, Mingming Liang, Liang Gao, Mubashir Ayaz Ahmed, John Patrick Uy, Ce Cheng, Qin Zhou, and Chenyu Sun. "Face Masks to Prevent Transmission of COVID-19: A Systematic Review and Meta-analysis," *American Journal of Infection Control*, 49(7), 2021, 900–906, ISSN 0196 6553, www.sciencedirect.com/science/article/pii/S0196655320310439

5. Steffen E. Eikenberry et al. "To Mask or Not to Mask: Modelling the Potential for Face Mask Use by the General Public to Curtail the COVID-19 Pandemic." Infectious Disease Modelling, Elsevier, 21 April 2020, www.sciencedirect.com/science/article/pii/S2468042720300117

6. A. Davies, K.A. Thompson, K. Giri, G. Kafatos, J. Walker, and A. Bennett. "Testing the Efficacy of Homemade Masks: Would They Protect in an Influenza Pandemic?" *Disaster Medicine and Public Health Preparedness*, 7 (4) (2013), 413–418.

7. K.V. Driessche, N. Hens, P. Tilley, B.S. Quon, M.A. Chilvers, R. de Groot, et al. "Surgical Masks Reduce Airborne Spread of *Pseudomonas aeruginosa* in Colonized Patients with Cystic Fibrosis". *American Journal of Respiratory and Critical Care Medicine*, 192 (7) (2015), 897–899.

8. R.E. Stockwell, M.E. Wood, C. He, L.J. Sherrard, E.L. Ballard, T.J. Kidd, et al. "Face Masks Reduce the Release of *Pseudomonas aeruginosa* Cough Aerosols When Worn for Clinically Relevant Periods". *American Journal of Respiratory and Critical Care Medicine*, 198 (10) (2018), 1339–1342.

9. M. van der Sande, P. Teunis, and R. Sabel. "Professional and Home-made Face Masks Reduce Exposure to Respiratory Infections among the General Population". *PloS One*, 3(7), (2008), 1–6.

10. R.B. Patel, S.D. Skaria, M.M. Mansour, and G.C. Smaldone. "Respiratory Source Control Using a Surgical Mask: An in Vitro Study". *Journal of Occupational and Environmental Hygiene*, 13 (7) (2016), 569–576.

11. A.C.K. Lai, C.K.M. Poon, and A.C.T. Cheung. "Effectiveness of Facemasks to Reduce Exposure Hazards for Airborne Infections among General Populations". *Journal of The Royal Society Interface*, 9 (70) (2012), 938–948.

12. F. M. J. Mehedi Shamrat, S. Chakraborty, M. M. Billah, M. A. Jubair, M. S. Islam, and R. Ranjan, "Face Mask Detection using Convolutional Neural Network (CNN) to reduce the spread of Covid-19," 2021 5th International Conference on Trends in Electronics and Informatics (ICOEI), 2021, pp. 1231–1237, https://ieeexplore.ieee.org/abstract/document/9452836

13. Matthijs Hollemans. "MobileNet Version 2." https://machinethink.net/blog/mobilenet-v2/

14. EkaEka 2, et al. "What Is Global Max Pooling Layer and What Is Its Advantage over Maxpooling Layer?" Cross Validated, 1 September 1964, https://stats.stackexchange.com/questions/257321/what-is-global-max-pooling-layer-and-what-is-its-advantage-over-max pooling-layer

15. B. Varshini, H.R. Yogesh, Syed Danish Pasha, Maaz Suhail, V. Madhumitha, and Arachana Sasi. IoT-Enabled Smart Doors for Monitoring Body Temperate and Face Mask Detection, *Global Transitions Proceedings*, 2(2) (2021) 246–254, ISSN 2666-285X, https://doi.org/10.1016/j.gltp.2021.08.071, (www.sciencedirect.com/science/article/pii/S2666285X21000996)

16. S. Susanto, F. A. Putra, R. Analia, and I. K. L. N. Suciningtyas, "The Face Mask Detection for Preventing the Spread of COVID-19 at Politeknik Negeri Batam," 2020 3rd International Conference on Applied Engineering (ICAE), 2020, pp. 1–5, https://ieeexplore.ieee.org/document/9350556

17. B. Bala Balamurugan, T. Ananth Kumar, R. Rajmohan, and P. Praveen Kumar, A Brief Survey on AI Based Face Mask Detection System for Public Places (28 March 2021). *Irish Interdisciplinary Journal of Science and Research* (IIJSR) 2021, Available at SSRN: https://ssrn.com/abstract=3814341

18. X-zhangyang. "X-Zhangyang/Real-World-Masked-Face-Dataset: Real-World Masked Face Dataset, 口罩人脸数据集." GitHub, https://github.com/X-zhangyang/Real-World-Mas ked-Face-Dataset

19. Andrew G. Howard et al. "MobileNets: Efficient Convolutional Neural Networks for Mobile Vision Applications." ArXiv.org, 17 April 2017, https://arxiv.org/abs/1704.04861.

20. Priya Dwivedi. "Understanding and Coding a ResNet in Keras." Medium, Towards Data Science, 27 March 2019, https://towardsdatascience.com/understanding-and-coding-a-res net-in-keras-446d7ff84d33?gi=7f410de18cfc

21. Fenglin Liu et al. "Rethinking Skip Connection with Layer Normalization in Transformers and Resnets." ArXiv.org, 15 May 2021, https://arxiv.org/abs/2105.07205.

6

AI-Powered COVID Detection App Using Chest X-Ray

Jay Shimpi, Ajinkya Hapase, Ajinkya Sawadkar,
Pranav Wagh, Rutuja Patil, and Pravin Futane

CONTENTS

6.1 Introduction

Coronaviruses are a broad cluster of viruses that may cause sicknesses starting from the respiratory illness to a lot of serious conditions like the Middle East respiratory syndrome (MERS) and severe acute respiratory syndrome (SARS). Within the Chinese town of Wuhan, a brand-new coronavirus (COVID-19) was discovered. This is perhaps the first time a coronavirus has been found in humans. Early automated diagnosis would be extremely beneficial in limiting the spread of this disease. Since December 2019, the COVID-19 pandemic has become a serious public health issue [1,2]. In about 74% of the cases, the COVID-19 infections were mild (18%) or moderate (56%) [3]. On the other hand, the opposite effects range from minorly severe (20%) to severe (6%) [3]. When only a small image dataset is available, deep learning is among the most successful intelligent retrieval methods for diagnosing infections caused by medical image data like chest radiographs. COVID-19 has previously been identified using augmented reality through chest radiographs in previous investigations. Blended with artificial intelligence, chest X-ray data can do exceptional work by giving out the results for the person's positivity or negativity. A total of 300 COVID-affected and normal images have been considered for training, testing, and validation.

The following are the research's primary benefits and contributions:

1. A COVID-19 prediction app has been developed, which would inordinately decrease the testing time.
2. The use of the app would increase the number of tests enormously without any healthcare equipment involved.
3. The use of technology (here, deep learning algorithm) is effective in the form of an Android app.
4. Radiographic imaging techniques are utilized to emphasize the presentation of chest X-beams with various types of cases, namely positive coronavirus, non-coronavirus, and pneumonitis cases.
5. Physically disabled persons can get their COVID result within a few seconds.
6. This app can be integrated into very popular health apps of the Central government so that people will get to know about their COVID-19 status without any healthcare equipment.

Unexpectedly, the limit of the proposed technique is that it centers just around chest radiograph dataset, whereas there are further clinical data sets that can be used to identify the novel coronavirus that causes COVID-19. Also, a model once trained cannot be updated in real-time based on the data it receives. The accuracy of the model depends on chest X-ray images. So, any discrepancy in the image would lead to model giving wrong predictions.

6.2 Related Work

There hasn't been a clinical trial for the proposed approach. As a result, it cannot be used to substitute a medical diagnosis because a larger dataset might allow for a more complete study. Our effort adds to the cause in these cases. Our method offers a precise, automated, quick, and inexpensive methodology as a way for aiding the designation of COVID-19 images of a chest X-ray [1]. To train the object detector, combining the virtual dataset with numerous real datasets improves performance. We also look into the possibility of employing purposefully designed virtual datasets to test the trained models on a certain element [4]. Novel Coronavirus Pneumonia (NCP) seen on CT imaging as patchy ground glass opacities in the pleura's periphery, with partial consolidation that will be absorbed with the creation of fibrotic stripes if the condition improves. CT scanning can help in early NCP diagnosis and treatment [3]. The most common method for diagnosing COVID-19 is real-time reverse transcription-polymerase chain reaction (RT-PCR). Early detection and treatment of the condition need radiographic images of the chest, such as CT scans and X-rays. Because RT-PCR has a low sensitivity (60–70%), symptoms can be detected by looking at a patient's radiographic images, even if the findings are negative. CT could be a sensitive procedure for COVID-19 respiratory illness diagnosis and should be used as an Associate in Nursing RT-PCR screening procedure. Patients often get a CT scan within the first 0–2 days of presenting with symptoms, and the findings are sometimes not known for many days. That's why these lengthy procedures are not considered in our implementation. The ones which facilitate and quicken the process in getting results faster are built into the implementation.

6.3 Proposed Methodology

A X-beam is a quick, convenient examination that creates images of the patterns inside your frame, particularly your bones. X-rays pass through your frame and might be worth a lot of money depending on the thickness of the material they pass through. On X-rays, thick materials like bone and metal appear white. The air in your lungs appears to be as black. Fat and muscle seem like dark sunshades. For positive forms of X-ray tests, a distinction medium – like iodine or barium – is familiar into your frame, which supply extra enormous subtlety at the images. X-rays had been used to look at the lungs for many years and are a beneficial method for diagnosing COVID-19 infections and for determining if they are especially rapid. They have the capacity to create images that depict areas within the lungs. Because X-rays are rapid and inexpensive, they may be used to triage sufferers in regions in which healthcare structures have failed or in which sufferers are some distance from massive centers in which extra superior strategies are available as shown in Figures 6.1a and b, respectively. There is also a portable X-ray gadget that may be easily brought anywhere you want it. There also are compact X-ray gadgets which can be moved without problems to the spot in which they may be required. CT scans are a kind of X-ray that analyses the tender tissues of the frame the use of superior X-ray principles. It's additionally applied to enhance the readability of organ and tender tissue imaging. X-rays, on the other hand, require much less radiation, hence they may be faster, much less hazardous, and much less high priced than CT scans. Using convolution neural networks (CNNs), we provide an AI-powered utility to categorize chest X-ray images from COVID-19 sufferers or healthful sufferers in this research. The COVID-19 class in dataset is made from 300 chest X-ray images taken from human beings identified with COVID-19 [5,6].

We construct a sub-dataset for every CNN configuration made from units of capabilities gathered from every image inside the real datasets [7]. Upon successful implementation of the model, we discovered that there was room for improvement as the accuracy without any modification was around 91%. Upon hyper parameter tuning, the accuracy jumped to 96.8. However, the difference is quite small yet very impactful in such health-related

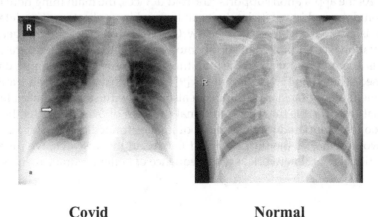

Covid   **Normal**

FIGURE 6.1
Chest x-ray images [COVID]. (b) Chest x-ray images [normal].

application. The approach for categorizing an X-ray acquired through a wholesome affected person or a affected person with COVID-19 is defined below. We'd begin by going over how to obtain the image datasets for this research and then we'll look at the feature extraction technique. Finally, we specify the measures that will be used to assess the results and compare them to those of alternative methodologies.

6.4 Experimental Design

Using crossover balanced COVID-19 class images, we advise enhancing the existing X-ray dataset. Our goal is to show how the raw dataset's uneven distributions have a negative impact on performance. The more the imbalance data the more we get discrepancy in our result. So, the task is to maintain the balance of positive and negative samples perfectly in 1:1 ratio. The data we got from dataset had unbalanced positive and negative samples. So, we aimed to fix it via various techniques by sampling and duplicating data. Outcomes were the classification of positive and negative samples and thereby generating a trained model file. Multiple classes (normal and COVID) and indices 0 and 1 were associated with the data. For the training, testing and validation, a dataset was broken down into chunks of 70%, 15%, and 15%, respectively.

Cross validation is a simple holdout technique that involves using some data for trying out and the rest for training. More data may be utilized in training than testing using recurrent arbitrator while still assuring a valid test. Using unbiased samples from the coronavirus dataset, the distinct go-validations are utilized to gain a few ranges in findings and to cast off any outliers for averaging. For the detection and classification of COVID-19 in X-rays, variety of conditions were used. The model's outcome is calculating the usage of a 10-fold go validation method for binary category issues. The training records employ 70% of the X-ray pictures for the training stage and 15% for the testing stage. The approach is iterated 20 times using the final dataset selected during the pre-processing step. As a result, upon training the model, we save it in Android-suitable format, that is, .tflite file (by converting .h5 to .tflite). As the application supports Android devices, the main thing here is the how is the conversion done and how efficiently it can be used in application. The detailed section for the same is covered in the section below CNN. To construct a more generic model, data augmentation was employed to supply more input data. In the literature, augmenting training sets is a common strategy in the literature [8]. To provide extra input, data augmentation was used. The related transformations [9] are the most widely used transformations for data augmentation. Transfer learning can also work with such kind of dataset, and the only thing that restricts it is the very traditional problem of overfitting. As the chest X-ray images are too less compared to the number of images trained on transfer learning model so, using it wouldn't serve the purpose. That is why, in this research, we preferred going with convolutional neural network as a consequence of better accuracy metrics.

6.5 Convolutional Neural Network

Layers of CNN: CNN is intended to reduce the image size so it can be processed more quickly without loss of features that can lead to accurate prediction. The convolutional layer, the pooling layer, and the fully connected layer are the three layers that make up this system.

- Pixel features are recognized using a convolutional layer.
- A pooling layer abstracts these features.
- A fully connected layer uses the acquired features in prediction.

Convolution layer: CNNs are built on convolution layers, which allow them to recognize pictures on their own. It might be challenging to train a neural network due to the massive quantity of data created by the convolution process. To compress the data, we must pool it.

Pooling layer: The convolutional layer's result is condensed by the pooling layer. In most cases, the pooling layer reduces a 2 × 2 square (patches) as the input. When using a 2 × 2 filter, each feature map would have a quarter the pixels. If feature map is 10*10, the resultant would be 5*5. Multiple functions can be used for pooling. The most common include the maximum value for each patch on the feature map is obtained using maximum pooling and the average value for each patch on the feature map is derived using average pooling. The pooling layer produces pooled feature maps, which are summed-up representations of the characteristics in the input. CNNs are more stable due to the pooling layer. In the past, even little alterations in pixels would lead the model to misclassify; today, the convolutional layer will identify changes in feature placement, resulting in a pooled feature map with the same feature. The input must now be flattened (converted into a column vector) before being sent to a standard neural network for classification. Back propagation is done to each training cycle after feeding the flattened output to a feed-forward neural network. Finally, this layer is capable of understanding images: each input pixel communicates with each output class. Convolution is a mathematical operation which makes it possible to merge two sets of information. Convolution is used to the input data in CNN to filter the data and create a feature map. This filter is known to be a kernel, or function sensor, and its dimensions can be, for instance, 3 × 3. The kernel goes across the input frame to perform the convolution, making the matrix multiplication element after the element. On the features map, the outcome of each receptive field (the region where convolution occurs) is noted. The filter is dragged until the feature map is complete.

6.6 Model Summary

Model summary enhances the knowledge about the model architecture. The number of parameters the model trained on and the information about type of layers used is very vividly mentioned in the summary. A precise idea of model architecture is grasped via model summary, shown in Figure 6.2.

The model's accuracy refers to how often it correctly classifies data. The harmonic mean of sensitivity and precision is defined as the F1 score; this measure may provide a value that indicates the method's overall quality. The FPR is the percentage of correctly identified healthy patients. The number of times the model correctly classified the images as COVID-19 is known as true positives (TP).

There are several techniques to evaluate the success of your classification model, but none has lasted as long as the confusion matrix. It enables us to assess how well our model performed, identify where it went wrong, and provide suggestions on how to adjust our approach. An $N \times N$ matrix is used to guage the performance of a classification model,

```
Model: "sequential_1"
_____
Layer (type)                 Output Shape              Param #
=================================================================
conv2d_4 (Conv2D)            (None, 222, 222, 32)      896

conv2d_5 (Conv2D)            (None, 220, 220, 64)      18496

max_pooling2d_3 (MaxPooling  (None, 110, 110, 64)      0
2D)

dropout_4 (Dropout)          (None, 110, 110, 64)      0

conv2d_6 (Conv2D)            (None, 108, 108, 64)      36928

max_pooling2d_4 (MaxPooling  (None, 54, 54, 64)        0
2D)

dropout_5 (Dropout)          (None, 54, 54, 64)        0

conv2d_7 (Conv2D)            (None, 52, 52, 128)       73856

max_pooling2d_5 (MaxPooling  (None, 26, 26, 128)       0
2D)

dropout_6 (Dropout)          (None, 26, 26, 128)       0

conv2d_8 (Conv2D)            (None, 24, 24, 256)       295168

max_pooling2d_6 (MaxPooling  (None, 12, 12, 256)       0
2D)

dropout_7 (Dropout)          (None, 12, 12, 256)       0

flatten_1 (Flatten)          (None, 36864)             0

dense_2 (Dense)              (None, 64)                2359360

dropout_8 (Dropout)          (None, 64)                0

dense_3 (Dense)              (None, 1)                 65

=================================================================
Total params: 2,784,769
Trainable params: 2,784,769
Non-trainable params: 0
_____
```

FIGURE 6.2
Model summary.

wherever N is that the range of target classes. The matrix compares the particular goal values to the machine learning model' predictions. This provides us with a comprehensive image of however well our classification model is functioning and therefore the varieties of errors it makes.

The number of false negatives (FN) pertains to the number of times COVID-19 pictures were incorrectly labeled as coming from a healthy patient. The number of times the model mistakenly categorized a healthy patient is known as false positives (FP). The number of correctly categorized healthy patient photos is determined by true negatives (TN). An FN happens when a person who is intended to be a member of a certain group is instead

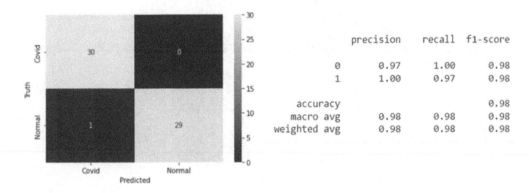

FIGURE 6.3
Confusion matrix and classification report.

excluded from it. The accuracy (Acc), score, exactness (PPV), specificity (Spc), sensitivity (Sen), and Matthew parametric statistic (MCC) were used to value the functioning of the varied networks on the validation/test dataset [8].

Explaining the terms in Figure 6.3:

- Precision = tp / (tp + fp)
- Accuracy = (tp+tn)/(tp+tn+fp+fn)
- F1 score = 2*(precision*recall)/(precision+recall)

where, tp, tn, fp, and fn stands for true positive, true negative, false positive and false negative, respectively.

Figure 6.4 describes loss and accuracy relationship. As the epochs increase, accuracy increases and loss decreases.

6.7 Android Implementation and Results

With extensive accessibility of smartphones, dedication of COVID-19 utilizing X-ray images have gotten to be simpler. But the association of the organized knowledge display straightforwardly in a mobile telephone can be a project as it misuses the computing resources. To neutralize this issue, the organized TensorFlow display has been modified over to TensorFlow Lite display utilizing the TensorFlow Lite converter that is an open-supply apparatus. The transformed version has been at that factor coordinates with the Android software. The display is rehashed for every display and measurements of the X-ray pix entered have to be altered that allows the display to be accomplished on this code. Trials utilizing the telephone were completed with the images in the take-a-look-at dataset, which accommodates of many types of everyday images and coronavirus classes individually. As it is able to be a preparatory take into account and because of the difficulty in obtaining the important X-ray photos for coronavirus category, the computerize pictures on the automaton phone are used. The basic pillar of an app is the trained model. Whenever the user chooses a picture (chest radiograph) to discover COVID-19 within

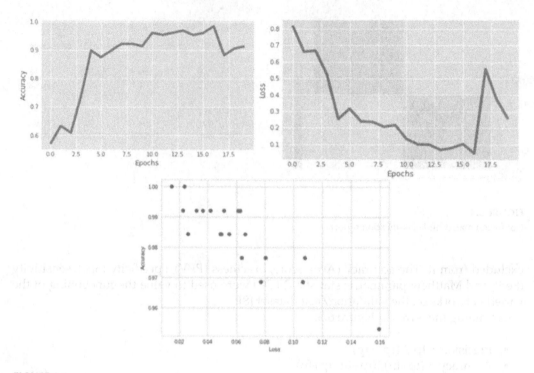

FIGURE 6.4
Accuracy vs. loss.

the backend, the saved model fetches the necessary results and upon toggling the predict button, the result gets displayed with a message as shown in Figure 6.5.

6.8 Gap Analysis

As mentioned in abstract, the peak accuracy of 96.88% was achieved on test dataset. More the images, more the data as a consequence, the initial record of 91% accuracy was surpassed, thereby taking model to a peak accuracy of 96.88%. Also, not only the size of dataset but also various hyperparameter tuning techniques contributed to this accuracy like the increase in the number of dense layers, max pooling layers, and dropout layers. We also performed certain performance metrics to evaluate the model and to maximize its potential.

6.9 Conclusion and Future Work

By its relatively contagious nature, the COVID-19 contamination threatens the lives of billions of people. According to world health organization (WHO), the quantity of inflamed

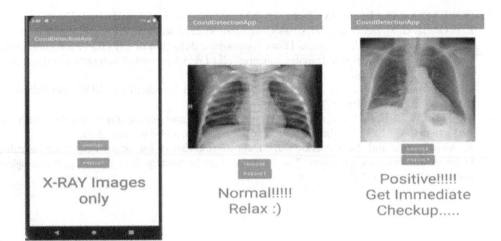

FIGURE 6.5
Interface of the application.

sufferers and deaths is speedily increasing. Infected people's lungs get infected because of this viral illness. As a result, a chest x-ray is one of the possible strategies for figuring out such infections. With the use of an AI-powered Android application, we segregated COVID-19 instances from pneumonia and healthy instances using chest x-ray images. We examined numerous deep switch getting to know models, and the effects have been evaluated by the use of numerous overall performance measures, with convolution neural network imparting a fine accuracy. First and foremost, we use an imbalanced dataset to test the proposed approach. We also suggested that our technology can be integrated into a free online picture classification system like LINDA. without needing to create their own classification system. Healing centers and helpful clinics all round the world would be ready to distinguish diseases in chest X-ray pictures. Apart from that, we want to compare the recommended method to fine-tuning procedures.

References

1. K. Roosa, Y. Lee, R. Luo, A. Kirpich, R. Rothenberg, J. M. Hyman, P. Yan, and G. Chowell, "Real-time forecasts of the COVID-19 epidemic in China from February 5th to February 24th, 2020," *Infect. Dis. Model.*, vol. 5, pp. 256–263, Feb. 2020.
2. L. Yan, H. T. Zhang, Y. Xiao, M. L. Wang, C. Sun, J. Liang, S. S. Li, M. Y. Zhang, Y. Q. Guo, Y. Xiao, X. C. Tang, H. S. Cao, X. Tan, N. N. Huang, B. Jiao, A. L. Luo, Z. G. Cao, H. Xu, and Y. Yuan, "Prediction of criticality in patients with severe COVID-19 infection using three clinical features: A machine learning-based prognostic model with clinical data in Wuhan," *medRxiv*, 2020.
3. Y. H. Xu, J. H. Dong, W. M. An, X. Y. Lv, X. P. Yin, J. Z. Zhang, L. Dong, X. Ma, H. J. Zhang, and B. L. Gao, "Clinical and computed tomographic imaging features of novel coronavirus pneumonia caused by SARS-CoV-2," *J. Infect.*, vol. 80, no. 4, pp. 394–400, Apr. 2020.
4. J. P. Cohen, P. Morrison, and L. Dao, "Covid-19 image data collection," arXiv preprint arXiv: 2003.11597, 2020.

5. COVID-19 X rays. Online. Available: www.kaggle.com/andre- wmvd/convid19-x-rays.

6. E. F. Ohata, G. M. Bezerra, J. V. S. das Chagas, A. V. L. Neto, A. B. Albuquerque, V. H. C. de Albuquerque, and P. P. Reboucas Filho. "Automatic detection of COVID-19 infection using chest X-Ray images through transfer learning", *IEEE/CAA Journal of Automatica Sinica*, vol. 8, no. 1, pp. 239–248, 2021.

7. D. M. Powers, "Evaluation: from precision, recall and F-measure to ROC, informedness, markedness and correlation," 2020.

8. Y. L. Tian, X. Li, K. F. Wang, and F. Y. Wang, "Training and testing object detectors with virtual images," *IEEE/CAA J. Autom. Sinica*, vol. 5, no. 2, pp. 539–546, Mar. 2018.

9. A. Mikołajczyk and M. Grochowski, "Data augmentation for improving deep learning in image classification problem, " in *Proc. Int. Interdisciplinary PhD Workshop*, Swinoujście, Poland, 2018, pp. 117122.

Section II

Advances in Sensor and Chip Design, Controls, Communication, and Signal Processing

7

Software-Defined Networking: Research Challenges

Kumbhar A. Kalpana and Prachi Mukherji

CONTENTS

7.1 Introduction

In the current network system, multiple users are connected to the network, enjoying network services. Multiple routes for communication are available and used. Open shortest path first protocol is used for switching or routing [1]. Routing tables are used to send the data packets. The switch gets down when it is attacked. Centralized control is not possible here. These switches are running at three different layers of network. No centralized solution is available to solve this. As shown in Figure 7.1, three different layers of network are hardware, operating system and application. The global view of this network is not known by the switches. Switches do not have dynamic configuration according to the network requirement. According to the operating system, switches can be configured [2]. In the current network system, centralized control system is not possible. Traditional networks have three layers: data plane, control plane and application layer. They are vendor-specific. Hardware and software are bundled together. Devices are function-specific [2].

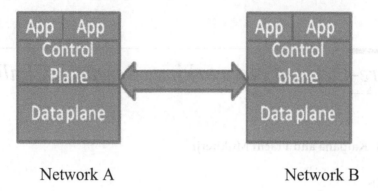

Network A   Network B

FIGURE 7.1
Basic network system [2].

Software-defined networking is one of the solutions for abovementioned issues [2]. Centralized control system is used to manage a network. Through the centralized network, security, routing, monitoring and load balancing can be done. The complex interactions with each other when managing the above applications becomes difficult to execute. The problem increases because of network events such as failure of devices, cyber attacks and traffic shifts. With each application, network has to be reconfigured. Combining and configuring different applications is very challenging task with all advantages of the network. SDN is used for distributing changes across network devices in different layers. In SDN network, control unit and hardware (switches) are separated from each other. Control unit is designed in a centralized way and controls entire network including switches. In SDN, the control logic is defined in a centralized manner. Application program interface is used for controlling data plane, control logic and application plane.

1. *Traffic flow control*: To control the traffic flow from other devices, alternate or duplicate flows are created. These get inserted in the data plane or control plane.
2. *Unguarded switches*: Switches with an error create other security issues. Switches with security issues lead to other weakness in the network or exploit the network.
3. *Communications in the control plane*: If an attack persists in between the communication channel of control plane and data plane, it can stop communication or disturb the communication. There are no more effects of other attacks on the communication channel between control plane and data plane.
4. *Sensitivity of the controller*: These attacks are similar to attacks by the communication channel, but are more severe. Trading off with the controller, complete control over the network can be taken by the attacker.
5. *Certainty between controller and applications*: There is no certainty between the controller and applications. Any alternative also do exist by controller. There should be certainty for applications which are running on controller as applications have the same view like the controller.
6. *Accountability in administration stations*: Different administration stations should be protected from attacks by the controller programming. If this is not protected, then the attack can reprogram the controller and control the whole network.
7. *Juristic issues*: Many of the resources have not been provided by OpenFlow to solve the difficulties that may occur in the network and also authentication mechanism is not provided to cross check sources of statistics by calculations or analysis.

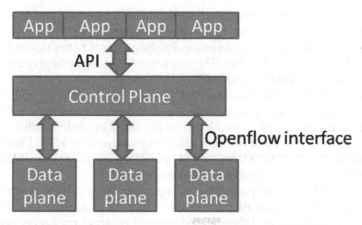

FIGURE 7.2
SDN architecture diagram [11].

7.2 Architecture of SDN

SDN architecture is shown in Figure 7.2.

SDN controller: Controller is placed at the control plane, which controls south-bound application program interface and north-bound application program interface. The switches and routers are left in data plane only. All these are controlled through software. Few SDN controllers are NOX/POX, Ryu, Trema, Pyretic and Frenetic [2]. SDN controller is used as the control element in a feedback loop, responding to events of the network to recover from network failure and resource allocation by reoptimization.

South-bound application program interfaces (APIs): South-bound APIs (OpenFlow APIs) is used to manage switching in data plane and communicates with the switches in data forwarding plane.

North-bound APIs: North-bound APIs is an interface between controller and applications. These are managed by controller from control plane.

OpenFlow: OpenFlow interface generates messages for interaction between data plane and controller.

7.3 Benefits of SDN

SDN provides benefits over the conventional network.

Virtualization: The physical location of switches is not known, but then also network resources can be used. Multiple virtual networks can be possible with network virtualization on same physical hardware. Existing virtual networks and new networks can be isolated from each other. The implementation of networks can be done with isolation tool using routing protocol.

Orchestration: With the SDN, thousands of devices can be managed and controlled with one command. The routing algorithms topology of data center, control functions configuration and scheduling network can be provided by orchestration.

Programmable: The behavior of the network can be changed by SDN. Configuration time can be reduced with SDN. Management operations are programmable and controller based. SDN is recommended in cloud data centers.

Dynamic scaling: With the help of SDN, change in size of the network and scalable data centers networks are possible. Static network devices are used in data center network, which are based on Ethernet and internet protocol packet connections.

Automation: With the use of operational expenditures (OpEx), manual involvement can be minimized. It provides network automation and virtualization for WAN and LAN resource allocation and connectivity [3]. It can be used for following troubleshooting, reduce downtime, policy enforcement, provisioning, reprovisioning/segmentation of resources add new workloads, sites, devices and resources.

Visibility: Minimum visibility of network is provided due to SDN.

Performance: The performance of SDN can measured based on two metrics: The number of flows per second that the controller can handle and flow setup time. Optimization and utilization of devices in SDN as in the traffic engineering/bandwidth management, capacity optimization, load balancing, high utilization, and fast failure handling [4].

Multi-tenancy: Tenants are used for control over addresses, security, topology and routing. Cloud-pushed network function virtualization (NFV) needs multi-tenancy to support use of a software-based network. SDN is a solution for this. This software consists a set of virtual switches and tunnels that oppose sudden changes in virtual network functions.

Service integration: In service integration of SDN intrusion detection systems (IDS), load balancers and firewalls are used and at the end, they are placed in the path of traffic [5].

7.4 SDN Applications

7.4.1 Software-Defined Mobile Network

It is used to design mobile networks. In terms of software all protocol-specific software features are designed with increasing use of hardware and maximizing the use of common software for core network and access network. An extension of SDN system gives mobile network specific functionality.

7.4.2 Software-Defined Wide Area Network

SDN can manage wide area network (WAN). The driver of SD-WAN is the solution for use of commercially available leased lines and also on more expensive lines, which give lower

WAN costs [6]. Hardware with central controllers are used for easier administration and configuration. Management and control is administered separately in SDWAN.

7.4.3 Software-Defined Local Area Network

SDN can be used for local area networking (LAN). In integration of these two things, topologies, security signals and data planes are designed in such a way that architecture enables both wired and wireless LANs [7]. Without use of physical controller, cloud management system and connectivity of wireless LAN are characterized.

7.4.4 Security Using the SDN Paradigm

In SDN, data plane is reprogrammable and controller's central view is also reprogrammable [5]. Due to this, security-related issues get enabled and enhanced. SDN is used for security applications. Mitigation and detection of distributed denial of service (DDOS) is one the important applications. Different types of propagation are used for collecting statistics of the network from the forwarding plane using standard method such as overflow and then detecting anomalies with the classification based on statistics calculated previously. In order to mitigate, application instructs controller to make changes in data plane.

7.4.5 Research Challenges

- Selection of the controller.
- Need of the number of controllers based on the complexity of problem statement.
- Controller selection should be such that it should take backup and do not get shut down.
- Controller selection depends on load balancing.
- Based on complexity of the problem, memory backup handling capacity of controller has to be present.
- Number of flows handling capacity of controller.
- Selection of hardware switches at the physical layer.
- Placement of controller is necessary; if not placed at a proper place, it causes delay.
- Communication between SDN and non-SDN parts run.

7.5 Quality Parameters of Software-Defined Networking

SDN is used for enhancing the quality of service, traffic engineering, network segmentation, security, network provisioning and configuration.

7.5.1 Quality of Service and Traffic Engineering

Pradip Kumar Sharma et al. [1] proposed a model based on block chain technology for a distributed cloud architecture, which provides on-demand access with high security and low cost. Performance is improved by reducing the response time and reducing the induced delay, with low performance overheads, increasing the ability to detect real-time attacks and throughput in the IoT network. Xiaoming Li et al. [2] proposed an SDN architecture to detect and control congestion in traffic. SDN-based traffic engineering improves quality of service (QoS) and increases network utilization, efficiency and flexibility of the traffic flow management. Yu-Jia Chen et al. [8] demonstrate delay analysis with use of SDN. The measurement of network parameters can provide deterministic quality of service (QoS).With this, particular delay can be derived by recursive method. The amount of delay is generated by the calculation of parameters and it is provided to the network with future delay. Hilmi E. Egilmez et al. [9] proposes (i) a general optimization substructure for getting QoS, flow-based solution over multi-scope networks, (ii) topology and aggregation link summative methods for getting control over and access the network topologies and (iii) communication between two controllers for sending messages with its address for securing routine for getting quality of service and design of separate control plane. Payman Samadi et al. [10] designed self-working control plane for getting required bandwidth allocation, which provides inter/intra network architecture for data centers. This architecture can support both multi- and single-rate data planes and it uses physical layer connections (dynamic and background). This provides connectivity with fixed and lagging time. Gergely Biczók et al. [11] showed that SDN and NFV facilitate 5G exchange (5GEx). 5GEx is to be used with 5G multioperating services. It also provides coordination of virtually interconnected management factors and memory resources. They present possible 5GEx use cases and value proposition. Pitchai Mohana Priya et al. [12] use the Wi-Fi networks data to secure and for getting best interconnectivity between different nodes. This is achieved in application layer to divide bandwidth from the long-term evolution (LTE). Wei Huang et al. [13] use the north-bound API. This API learns the condition in the multi-path transmission. Thus it solves the network conditions of malicious routes. Ying Duan et al. [13] propose that use of big data in mobile communication engineering (MCE) with the best network method for accessing such as data storage, emerging trends and network bandwidth. Real-time traffic change, issues and challenges in network users can be studied. Klaus-Tycho Foerster et al. [14] characterize the delay performance and design an analytical method. They propose a network design for time-sensitive network and also use solution with the optimal traversal path.

7.5.2 Wireless Sensor Networking

Schulz-Zander et al. improved software-defined wireless sensor network (improved SD-WSN). It manages the network and coverage of the network is solved with this wireless network. The reliability of the network is also can be improved. Node failure is addressed by the framework [15].

7.6 Proposed Methodology

It is concluded that SDN can be used for various applications such as improving quality of service of traffic engineering, Internet of Things (IoT), networking and internetworking design for current and future networks. With the SDN for IoT, different parameters can be improved like bandwidth utilization and packet loss rate in the network. SDN controllers can be used for integrating and managing all the parameters. In this work, quality of service is improved. The network of the existing SDN architecture using Mininet, Miniedit,

Floodlight and similar platforms is simulated for further processing to improve bandwidth utilization and packet loss rate as it improves the quality of service.

7.6.1 Mininet

Mininet is one of the platforms for designing a virtual network. In Mininet, virtual design of the network can be done by selecting the host, controllers, links and switches virtually.

7.6.1.1 '3' Hosts and a Switch Network Design

This considers the following steps when the virtual box get created with login and password as Mininet operates with the virtual box. Run the virtual box and find the IP address of the available Ethernet. Enter this IP address on the command prompt to enter in Putty. By putting command sudo, Mininet creates the default Mininet with default settings, as shown in Figure 7.3.

In Putty, we can be seen the available nodes, create nodes and hosts, as shown in Figure 7.4

Check for available nodes and create nodes. It is possible to change node settings, as in Figure 7.5.

With Ping h2 from h1, transmission of packets between h1 and h2 can be seen in Figure 7.6. Ping commands also can be used with IP address, shown in Figure 7.7

7.6.2 Miniedit

Miniedit is GUI editor for Mininet. Miniedit is an experimental tool. Miniedit is created to demonstrate how Mininet can be extended. Using Miniedit, it is possible to add

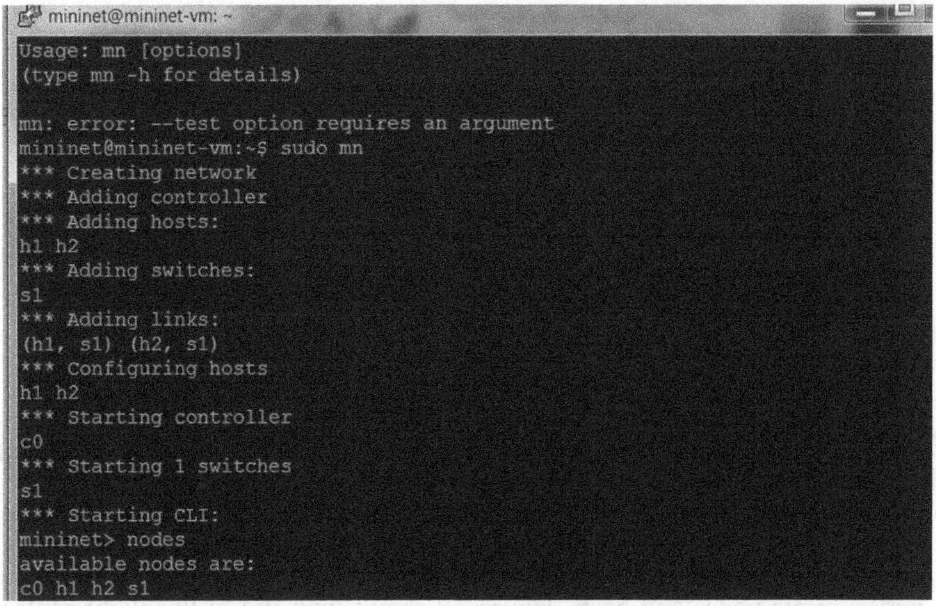

FIGURE 7.3
Sudo Mininet generation.

```
Microsoft Windows [Version 6.1.7600]
Copyright (c) 2009 Microsoft Corporation.  All rights reserved.

C:\Users\admin>putty.exe -X mininet@10.0.2.255

C:\Users\admin>putty.exe -X mininet@10.0.2.15

C:\Users\admin>putty.exe -X mininet@10.0.2.15

C:\Users\admin>putty.exe -X mininet@10.0.2.15

C:\Users\admin>putty.exe -X mininet@10.0.2.255

C:\Users\admin>putty.exe -X mininet@10.0.2.15

C:\Users\admin>putty.exe -X mininet@192.168.56.101
```

FIGURE 7.4
IP address on command prompt to enter in Putty.

```
c0
*** Starting 1 switches
s1
*** Starting CLI:
mininet> nodes
available nodes are:
c0 h1 h2 s1
mininet>
```

FIGURE 7.5
Creation of nodes.

```
login.gpcc.itd.umich.edu - PuTTY
login as: uniqname
uniqname@login.itd.umich.edu's password: █
```

FIGURE 7.6
Nodes on network.

host, switches and controllers virtually. It is useful to save the network topology, particularly when its complexity increases. Miniedit enables to save the topology to a file. Configurations of the controllers can be changed in Miniedit. Once the network is created, it can be run on terminal. Figure 7.8 shows topology in Miniedit.

These networks can be run to study different parameters. In Putty, we can see the available nodes, create nodes and hosts. Figure 7.9 shows with use of floodlight controller, which is working like a firewall to get the traffic filtered as per rules specified.

```
*** Unknown command: Xterm h1
mininet> xterm h1
mininet> Ping test
*** Unknown command: Ping test
mininet> dpct
*** Unknown command: dpct
mininet> dpct
*** Unknown command: dpct
mininet> Xterm h2
*** Unknown command: Xterm h2
mininet> h1 ping -c3 h2


PING 10.0.0.2 (10.0.0.2) 56(84) bytes of data.
From 10.0.0.1 icmp_seq=1 Destination Host Unreachable
From 10.0.0.1 icmp_seq=2 Destination Host Unreachable
From 10.0.0.1 icmp_seq=3 Destination Host Unreachable

--- 10.0.0.2 ping statistics ---
3 packets transmitted, 0 received, +3 errors, 100% packet loss, time 6964ms
pipe 2
mininet>
```

FIGURE 7.7
Ping test from h1 to h2.

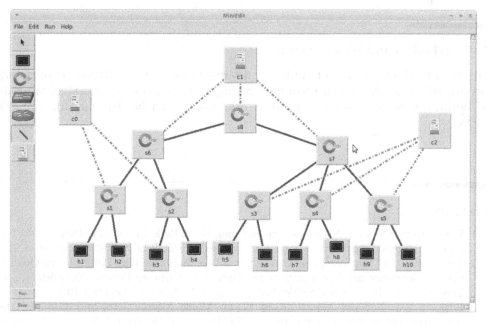

FIGURE 7.8
Topology in Miniedit.

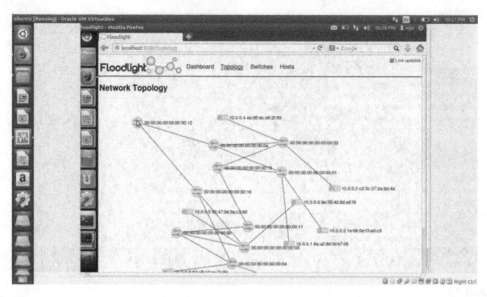

FIGURE 7.9
GUI representation of fat tree topology creation.

7.7 Conclusion and Future Work

With above method, with use of Mininet and Miniedit for SDN simulation, it is concluded that network parameters can be identified and improved with use of some SDN controllers and optimization techniques. In future work, attacks can be detected and mitigated in SDN.

References

1. Pradip Kumar Sharma, Mu-yen Chen, and Jong Hyuk Park. 'A Software Defined Fog Node Based Distributed Block chain Cloud Architecture for IoT', *IEEE Access*, Vol. 16, No. 4, 2018.
2. Yu-Jia Chen, Li-Chun Wang, Feng-Yi Lin, and Bao-Shuh Paul Lin. 'Deterministic Quality of Service Guarantee for Dynamic Service Chaining in Software Defined Networking'. *IEEE Transactions On Network And Service Management*, Vol. 14, No. 4, December 2017.
3. Bilal Ahmed, Nadeem Ahmed, Asad Waqar Malik, Mohsin Jafri, and Taimur Hafeez. 'Fingerprinting SDN Policy Parameters', *IEEE Access*, Vol. 16, No. 4, 2020.
4. Xiaoyue Zou, Qun Huang, Jing Zheng, and Patrick P.C. Lee, 'Dynamic Packet Forwarding Verification in SDN', *IEEE*, 2018.
5. Matheus P. Novaes, Luiz F. Carvalho, Jaime Lloret Mario, and Lemes Proença. 'Long Short-Term Memory and Fuzzy Logic for Anomaly Detection and Mitigation in Software-Defined Network Environment', *IEEE Transactions On Network And Service Management*, Vol. 4, 2020.
6. Marcos V. O. de Assis, Matheus P. Novaes, Cinara B. Zerbini, Luiz F. Carvalho, Taufik Abrão, and Mario Proença. 'Fast Defense System Against Attacks In Software Defined Networks', *IEEE Access*, 2018.

7. Maninderpal Singh, Gagangeet Singh Aujla, Amritpal Singh, Neeraj Kumar, and Sahil Garg. 'Deep Learning Based Blockchain Framework For Secure Software Defined Industrial Networks', *IEEE Transactions On Network And Service Management*, Vol. 4, 2020.
8. Hilmi E. Egilmez and A. Murat Tekalp, 'Distributed QoS Architectures for Multimedia Streaming Over Software Defined Networks' *IEEE Transactions On Multimedia*, Vol. 16, No. 6, October 2014.
9. Payman Samadi, Varun Gupta, Junjie Xu, Howard Wang, Gil Zussman, Keren Bergman, 'Optical multicast system for data center networks,',Optics Express, Vol. 13, Issue 17, December 2015.
10. Tong Xu, Deyun Gao, Ping Dong, Chuan Heng Foh, Hongke Zhang. 'Mitigating the Table-Overflow Attack in Software-Defined Networking', *IEEE Transactions on Network and Service Management*, Vol .14, No. 4, October 2017.
11. Sahrish Khan Tayyaba, Hasan Ali Khattak, Mahmad Almogren, Munam Ali Shah, Ikram Ud Din, Ibrahim Alkhalifa, and Mohsen Guizani.'5G Vehicular Network Resource Management for Improving Radio Access Through Machine Learning', *IEEE Access*, IF3.367, January 2020.
12. Catherine Nayer Tadros and Mohamed R. M. Rizk. 'Software Defined Network-Based Management for Enhanced 5G Network Services', *IEEE Access*, 2020.
13. Nan Hu, Fangjun Luan, Xiaoxi Tian, and Chengdong Wu. 'A Novel SDN-Based Application-Awareness Mechanism by Using Deep Learning', *IEEE Access*, Vol. 16, No. 4, 2017.
14. Erdal Akin And Turgay Korkmaz, 'Comparison of Routing Algorithms with Static And Dynamic Link Cost In Software Defined Networking (SDN)', *IEEE Access*, Vol. 14, No. 4, September 2019.
15. Jacob H. Cox and Russel Clark, 'Leveraging SDN And Webrtc for Rogue Access Point Security', *IEEE Transactions on Network and Service Management*, Vol. 14, 2017.

8

Channel Allocation Techniques for Deadline-Driven Edge Computing Framework

Radhika Purandare, Archana Ratnaparkhi, Pallavi Deshpande,
Arti Bang, Gauri Ghule, Shraddha Habbu, and Rohini Chavan

CONTENTS

8.1 Introduction

In today's world, IoT is playing a huge role and has been used in diverse applications. In projects such as intelligent houses [1] and intelligent sensor-based buildings [2], to get the sensor data a low-power wireless network has been used on sensor data like gyroscope, pressure, temperature and smart cameras [3,4]. Cloud computing started around 2005 and drastically changed the way of data computing [5]. Google services, Twitter, Facebook, and Instagram, all these platforms have become a part of our day-to-day life [6]. To achieve a given deadline, sensor data need to reach the sink node for further processing. It helps to monitor real-time targets [7]. The intelligent infrastructures, machines, and engines are deployed to support cloud services that will help businesses to run smoothly, for instance, Google File System [8], MapReduce [9], Apache Hadoop [10], and Apache Spark [11] as mentioned in literature. In 1999 IoT, that is, networks controlled by embedded systems were introduced to the world [12], As soon as this technology was introduced to the world, it was adopted by the health sector in public and private segments [13,14]. Now vast use of IoT in different sectors where a huge quantity of data will be gathered from devices, frequently used in day-to-day life, will be used by business applications for research and development purposes. By 2023, more than 500 zettabytes of data will be gathered from human beings, machinery, and others, as per the report provided by standard agencies such as Cisco. IP traffic in the global data center is also set to increase by 10.4 zettabytes [15]. According to [15], IoT-created data has been stored, analyzed, processed, and acted upon on massive scale and , as per the report, 45% of the data was being used commercially [16]. The Cisco Internet Business Solutions Group proposed long back that in 2020 billions of IoT devices shall be deployed [17]. For assisting the deadline in IoT networks, it takes into consideration of the restraint in allocating channels [18–23]. Dao et al. [24] showed , with a guarantee that those packets could be delivered prior to the deadline but with a certain probability and augment the consumption of energy coherently. Alinia et al. [25] keenly gave a focus on the construction of an optimal tree with the constraints of deadline in WSNs, which had the aggression of data. For collision avoidance, time division multiple access (TDMA) permits us to schedule the transmission of each node. For the already existing works, primarily we observe three major limitations. First, it is preconceived that every time the transmission can be successful within the single slot, which is not the real-world scenario. However, the enlarged slot will definitely add up to the delay for all links that are composed with decent qualities because the slots must be the same for all nodes to be synchronized [26]. We need to anticipate the quality of the link, which is a basic parameter for adaptation. Albeit for low-power wireless nodes, the task of predicting link quality can use enormous energy as well as time, because of the hardware's energy constraint [27–29].Lastly, the impact of allotting sequences for various paths is overlooked when allotting channels in the flow path's network. Computing and data communication are two major parts of IoT infrastructure. Both issues need to be managed efficiently for optimum overall performance. To overcome such limitations and to improve the dependability prior to the deadline, researchers have proposed novel channel allocation algorithms for multiple channels in the wireless scenario. With edge computing architecture, determination of the packet delivery ratio (PDR) of the nodes of IoT can be offloaded to edge servers. Edge computing-based techniques significantly help in reducing delay in the applications of IoT in the recent age [30–34]. Edge computing gives services with edge servers that are quite close to the user compared to cloud services. With the help of these edge servers, bandwidth can be saved taking into consideration of lower delay response. Researchers have proposed the use of Recurrent Neural Network (RNN) based modality for edge servers as speculation on link quality to be carried out in low-energy framework. Some researchers have detailed the study of computation on edge devices reducing the burden of data communication, concentrating on a single metric such as energy savings, application deadline, retransmissions, efficiency, or overload due to transmission of a large volume of data.

8.2 Motivation

8.2.1 Effect of Unreliable Wireless Communication Links: Unreliable Case

An example, as discussed in the literature [35], illustrates the effect of link quality in TDMA-based channel allocation. In the given Figure 8.1, we can see two links: Node A transmits a packet via Node C to Node B.

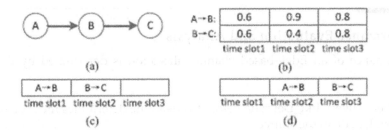

FIGURE 8.1
Packet transmission between nodes [35].

Assume a situation where the links as shown in the diagram. Due to the inherent lossy nature of wireless links, the nodes will respectively experience different link qualities at different time slots. There is only one channel and the quality for which is being given in decimals in the table. If we consider the scheme in which it assigns links with a minimum time slot, links will be assigned to the initial two-time slots, which guarantees the transmission deadline. However, if packet delivery ratios are low, it results in poor throughput and an added delay if failed transmission links are retransmitted in the following slot frames. The solution is to assign high-quality links with a minimum number of slots to maintain the application deadline.

8.2.2 Effects of Path Assignment Order

External interference to IEEE 802.15.4 channels is due to a smaller number of channels available out of which the maximum number of channels overlaps with the three commonly used Wi-Fi channels. The thumb rule is, that noninterfering links can be assigned the same channel. But while maintaining this channel allocation, application deadline must not be overlooked. In general, only four channels avoid overlapping with Wi-Fi and only a few partially overlap. Inefficient channel assignment priority could be another valid reason for the limitation. Ineffective channel assignment could lead to less than optimum use of resources.

8.2.3 Impact of Retransmissions

Ideally, the packet delivery should be over in one or least transmission attempts, but practically it is not true. Increasing the slot length can reduce retransmission in one slot. But this increase causes the delay to increase for a lower packet loss scenario.

An optimization opportunity is identified, from the above-illustrated examples, which is as follows:

1. In the channel assignment, it is assumed that wireless links would be lossy in nature. If retransmission happens, packet delivery will be delayed because of packet losses and increased security risks.
2. The channel assignment sequence should be carefully designed. If links utilize the same channel, conflict might arise for links in their corresponding area.

8.3 Performance Evaluation and Analysis

The performance of an Edge-based channel allocation is determined by the following metrics:

a. Packet delivery Pkt_Del ratio before the deadline determines the ratio of packets at the sink node to the source.
b. Resource utilization: A number of slots/channels are allocated during the channel allocation scheme.
c. Insufficient paths: Lack of slots for path assignment.
d. The number of retransmissions: A certain amount of retransmission helps improve the transmission liability.

8.3.1 Simulation Evaluation

To evaluate the simulation wave [21], a low-power channel allocation scheme for wireless networks was plotted against the Edge-based channel allocation (ECA) Using Tossim, the Pkt_Del ratio, is evaluated for 50 nodes: one sink node and 49 source nodes. Time slot size was set at 100 ms and in a duty cycle, there were up to 200 time slots. On the basis of least hop count, packets traverse from source to the sink node. Here alpha determines urgency and path length is 0.5.

Different packet loss and path lengths generate different PDR-BD as seen in Figure 8.2(a). Pkt_Del ratio in the second case with no retransmission is smaller than the ECA, as it selects channels with better link quality. The use of extra channels improves data collection significantly, which improves the performance of ECA with retransmission. In Figure 8.2(b), resource utilization is compared between ECA and wave. Assigned channels over the total channels give the utilization. For a limited number of channels, ECA does not assign channels with low quality, and as a result, conflicts occur. The performance of ECA is enhanced as the number of channels increase and retransmission is allowed. Using deadline postpone and fixed deadline, the insufficient paths are compared for ECA and wave. Wave will always have more insufficient paths as compared to ECA. Figure 8.2(c) highlights results for deadline postponed, using a fixed number of channels, insufficient paths are decreased.

In Figure 8.2(d), by fixing the deadline and accounting for the inadequate paths, the number of channels increases. No matter if the number of channels or deadline increases, ECA will schedule colliding paths when slots are available, gaining an advantage.

Transmission statistics are compared in Figure 8.3(a): 29% of links do not need retransmission and about 39% need one retransmission. Around 22% and 8% of the links required two and three retransmissions, respectively. Only 2% of the links require four retransmissions. Links with retransmission greatly improve the PDR-BD.

8.3.2 Performance Evaluation with Testbed

In the experiments 20 TelosB motes were used and the performance of centralized ECA was evaluated. One mote acts as a server that is connected to the PC. TelosB is a low-power wireless device, mainly used for experimentation. For practical purposes, nodes are connected to the ceiling. Three channels, channels – 11, 18, and 26 – are used for data transmission, as shown in Figure 8.3(b). Using the shortest path, data is transmitted to

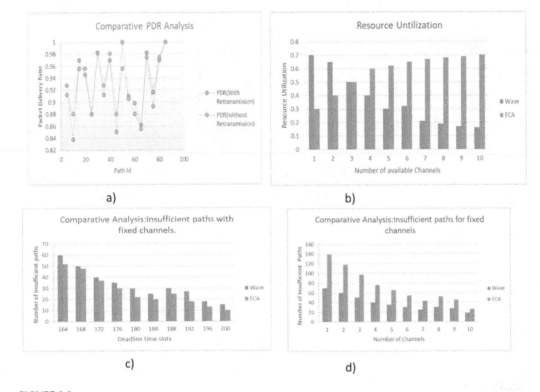

FIGURE 8.2

(a) Packet Delivery Ratio (Before Deadline(BD)). Figure 8.2(b) Comparison of resource utilization. Figure 8.2(c) Inadequate paths (channel numbers fixed). Figure 8.2(d) Inadequate paths (fixed deadline).

node 20. In Figure 8.3(c) and Figure 8.3(d), 80% of links are better in link quality and have a value greater than 0.6. All links above 0.6 demonstrate that the Pkt_Del ratio of ECA is greater than that of the wave. ECA considers higher quality links and takes advantage of retransmission links, and as a result, the average PDR-BD has improved by around 22%. ECA delays a few links with lesser priority, which sometimes increase the PDR-BD of the wave than that of ECA, but in the process increases the overall performance.

8.4 Methodology

8.4.1 Overview

As lower power wireless nodes have limited ability for processing, it is hard to implement link prediction. Edge computing servers are used to perform these tasks and return the results to low-power nodes. The framework that depends on edge computing is proposed for channel allocation. Edge servers can execute all computing tasks such as low-power nodes and incur additional overhead and real-time channel allocation.

For the sake of dealing with channels of time variation, we can run allocation as a result. Approaching ECA has two parts: path-based assigning is suggested as a first stage where

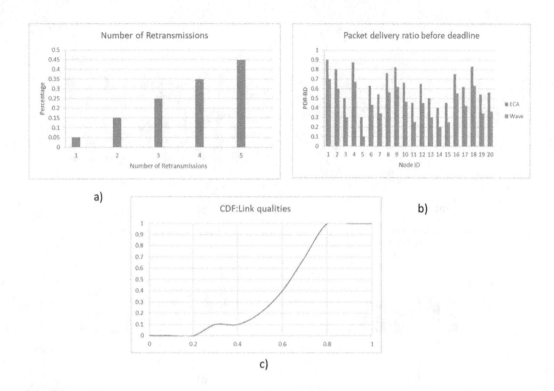

FIGURE 8.3
(a) Inadequate paths (fixed deadline). Figure 8.3(b) Retransmission rates. Figure 8.3(c) Link qualities. Figure 8.3(d) PDR BD.

links are scheduled successively. In the second stage after the assignment, a scheme of novel retransmission is adopted for the sake of PDR improvisation to reuse time slots and channels that are not yet used.

8.4.2 Measurement of Data on Edge Servers

The slots and links can get composed from networks since IoT networks are getting targeted by having specific deployment. Obtaining quality links of time variation for provided slots and channels is the main difficulty. As we are using edge servers, we can also use a method of prediction for links where the link quality depends on a famous method of 4 bits. An RNN got trained using a Kalman filter with POS for channel condition prediction. This method, depending on RNN, is absolutely capable of predicting link qualities with accuracy. This method can even reach to 0.0001 mean square error of prediction.

8.4.3 Assignment of Channels on the Basis of Paths

1. *Extension of link schedule to the path schedule*: Total traffic traveling has ordered the links for assignment of data collection through them and also assigned time slots in sequence from early time slots to reduce collection delay. According to its quality, every link has its own preferences of time slots and channels. The best quality slot

assigned to a link can cause two unacceptable issues: first is that the transmission order gets conflicted due to the preference of time slots of various links. And another one is that the slots might not be sufficient for the packets arriving before the deadline if slots and channels are chosen by link.

2. *Path prioritization*: For maximizing the received packet ratio before the data collection deadline, ECA is intended for the assignment of channels and time slots of good quality to links. Until all paths get assigned, only one path is processed by the algorithm, and among paths in the network channels and time slots got assigned by ECA.

As more slots get used by long paths compared to short ones, the performance of channel allocation gets influenced by its assigning sequence.

On one side, due to its urgent deadline, the slots and channels are less residual as early as they get allocated. On the other side, channels and residual time should be considered jointly. Before the deadline, all the data of every IoT node should be sent to its sink node.

The path urgency can be given by:

$$u_i = d_i - l_i, u_i = d_i - l_i$$

where d_i suggests the path deadline
l_i suggests the path length.

In case non-urgent paths occupy the time slots, the urgent paths should be allocated early. The conflict relation among links has a significant impact on the order of assignment with immediate deadline constraints. If time slots or channels conflict with assigned links while a link is not permitted with its usage, there is an availability of multiple channels on time slots, hence channels and time slots have limited availability. As unavailability of time slots may happen due to the extension of channels of conflict, the urgency and conflict impacts are intertwined.

The set of links on conflict is used for demonstrating the path's relationship to conflict. A number of conflict links with the worst case in path ^{i} are $c_i = \mathbf{maxC}$
where C is the set of conflict link numbers.

The paths having larger indicate a high probability of conflicting with other links.

The metric of path prioritization is proposed for the conclusion as follows:

$$m_i = \alpha u_i + (1-\alpha)c_i$$

where α suggests weight factor which determines the priority of data urgency priority and conditions of conflict

3. *Link quality-aware channel allocation*: The time slots and channels are assigned to links as per the priority of the path where link quality varies according to channels and time. This allocation depends on the quality of the average link in the time slot.

Channels and time slots are assigned to various paths with path priority. Link quality differs between channels and slots and is allocated on the basis of average link quality. The links dependency might be broken by the preferable link time slots or channels, which will lead to channel allocation complexity. The problem of allocation along with the constraint of path assignment sequence as well as links conflicts is as follows:

$$max \prod_{b_{t,ch}=1} P_{t,ch}^l max \prod_{b_{t,ch}=1} P_{t,ch}^l, (l, P_i, t \in T, ch \in C) P_i, t \in T, ch \in C)$$

$$s.t. \forall l. \in .P_i, t_l < t_{l+1} P_i, t_l < t_{l+1}$$

$$\forall l. \in .P_i, 0 < t_l < d P_i, 0 < t_l < d$$

$$\forall l. \in .P_i, \forall m \in As, b_{t,ch} \neq 1, if\ hear(recv(m), l)$$

$$\forall l. \in .P_i, \forall m \in$$

$$As, b_t^l \neq 1, if\ adjacent(m, l)$$

where $P_{t,ch}^l$ denotes the link quality
P_i is the path I,
t_l is the time slot,
d suggests the data deadline,
$b_{t,ch}^l$ suggests if a link transmits data.

The initial two limitations suggest that data should be transmitted by link before its preceding link while the other two mean the adjacent links and interference effect, where two links can't be transmitted concurrently in the time slot or channel.

ALGORITHM 1: Scheduling of link in a path

Input: The set of links in the path, L
          The number of links, ll The number
          of available time slots, n The link
          quality of link s in time slot t and
          channel ch, $q_{t,ch}^s q_{t,ch}^s$

Output: Link scheduling, $b_{t,ch} b_{t,ch}$
for each s $\in$ L **do**
    Judge(s)
end
for each s $\in$ L **do**
Judge(s)
End
Function Judge(s)

If $t = arc\max\left(q_{t,ch}^s\right) \in \left(t_{min}, t_{min} + \frac{n}{l}\right) t = arc\max\left(q_{t,ch}^s\right) \in \left(t_{min}, t_{min} + \frac{n}{l}\right)$ **then**
$N = n - \left(t - t_{min} t_{min}\right)$
$l = l - 1$
End
Else
Remove$\left(q_{t,ch}^s q_{t,ch}^s\right)$
Judge(s)
End

8.4.4 Allocation of Scheme for Retransmission

The unused channels and time slot for retransmitting are used for improving the ratio of PDR-BD as the packets can't reach the sink node because of varying link quality. Here researchers have proposed a retransmission scheme for considering link quality improvement and channel and time slots availability of retransmission link.

The two-level sorting process includes quality profit and chances of retransmission, that is, number of available retransmission slots. The quality profit for retransmission on a particular time slot and channel for the available link is

$$pr_i = 1 - (1 - q_b)(1 - q_n) - q_b$$

where the q_b is succeeding probability without retransmission,
q_n is the succeeding probability with retransmission on this channel/slot,
q_b is the probability of successful transmission.

Once retransmission is assigned to the link, the q_b will turn to q_n and the profit of the next retransmission will decrease such that the link already retransmitted has a lower chance on other time slots for retransmission. If time slots or channels do not interfere with each other, we can concurrently assign its pairs to multiple retransmission to extend the quality profit. The quality profit of a link set can be expressed as:

$$pr_g = \sum_{i=1}^{G} pr_i$$

where G represents the set of links which can be assigned retransmissions concurrently with the same channel.. To prioritize the waiting links for retransmission, a specific metric is proposed as:

$$mr_g = \beta pr_g + (1 - \beta) \sum_{i=1}^{g} r_i$$

where r_i represents available time slots for the retransmit link i.

8.4.5 Discussion on the Additional Overhead of Retransmission

Here, to guarantee the constraint of the deadline for the same duty cycle the lost packets are retransmitted. The retransmission slots allocated might be idle if packet losses, the extra latency and overhead of energy are occurring, and the energy overhead is related to link PDR. Low PDR links got slots of high quality for retransmission from ECA to reduce retransmission overhead.

Algorithm complexity analysis
The time slot and channel allocation algorithm for the wireless networks have time complexity of **O(L ∗ (C ∗ T)log(C ∗ T))**
    where **L** represents the number of links in the given network.
    C and **T** is channel number and time slot respectively

Algorithm overhead is dependent on network scaleAlgorithm overhead is dependent on network scale.

ALGORITHM 2: Distributed Allocation

```
while ready(i) do
        Sort(ch, p);                    //Finding the best channel
        pri=Prioritize(ch);             //Calculating its priority
        Notice(Ready, ch [0], pri);     //Notifying its neighbors
        Receive();
        Decide();
End
Function Decide()
//Comparing with priorities of neighbors
for each j ∈ Ni do
        if chj == chi then
                C.append(j);
        End
End
if pri > max(prj ∈ C) then
        Send();
        if Fail then
                Update(pr i); //If failed, updating its priority
        End
End
Else
        Del(c,c[0]); //Validating the second best channel
        Decide();
End
```

8.4.6 Distributed ECA

The global information of the network is required for ECA operations. For the adaptation of application scenario dynamics, and dealing with difficulty in global information collection, the central scheme in practice might not be apt. Nodes will consume estimation energy not as accurate as the RNN method as distributed ECA needs nodes to locally estimate link quality. The powerful method for the prediction of link quality can increase the advantage of distributed ECA.

8.5 Conclusion

In recent times, it is observed that many services are shifting from cloud services to edge services as it offers better time response and reliability compared to cloud services. Also, it can save significant amounts of bandwidth if the larger portion of the data would be handled at the edge rather than uploading it to the cloud. The advancements in IoT and ubiquitous mobile applications changed the work and role of edge computing in the data field. This chapter shows the motive of using edge computing in the propinquity of the data. The chapter also discusses the performance evaluation and analysis of edge-based channel allocation by different metrics. A low-power channel allocation scheme for the wireless network was plotted against the edge-based allocation and showed desired outputs. And in performance evaluation with a testbed using 20 TelosB motes, the performance of centralized ECA was discussed. It also showed the modus operandi for assigning the time slots and also the channels for making links to process data using the edge servers and the details about data gauging and types of channel allocations in different conditions. Edge computing carries a lot of potential for future applications and we hope this chapter will help you in understanding this new-age technology.

References

1. S. Feng, P. Setoodeh, and S. Haykin, "Smart home: Cognitive interactive people-centric internet of things," *IEEE Communications Magazine*, vol. 55, no. 2, pp. 34–39, 2017.
2. O. Guerra-Santin, S. Silvester, and N. R. Herrera, "Building monitoring to determine occupancy patterns in renovation projects," in Proceedings Conference Sustainable Built Environment: Transition Zero, 2016.
3. Y. Gao, W. Dong, K. Guo, X. Liu, Y. Chen, X. Liu, J. Bu, and C. Chen, "Mosaic: A low-cost mobile sensing system for urban air quality monitoring," in Proceedings of IEEE INFOCOM, 2016, pp. 1–9.
4. A. Fabre, K. Martinez, G. M. Bragg, P. J. Basford, J. Hart, S. Bader, and O. M. Bragg, "Deploying a 6lowpan, coap, low power, wireless sensor network: Poster abstract," in Proceedings of ACM Sensys, 2016.
5. Weifeng Gao, Zhiwei Zhao, Zhang Xin yu§, Geyong Min, Minhang Yang and Wenjie Huang. Edge Computing based Channel Allocation for Deadline-driven IoT Networks, *IEEE Transactions on Industrial Informatics*, vol. 16, no. 10, pp. 6693–6702, 2020.
6. Shi, W., Cao, J., Zhang, Q., Li, Y., & Xu, L. (2016). Edge computing: Vision and challenges. *IEEE Internet of Things Journal*, 3(5), 637–646.
7. E. Fadel, V. C. Gungor, L. Nassef, N. Akkari, M. A. Malik, S. Almasri and I. F. Akyildiz, "A survey on wireless sensor networks for smart grid," *Computer Communications*, vol. 71, pp. 22–33, 2015.
8. S. Ghemawat, H. Gobioff, and S.-T. Leung, "The google file system," in *ACM SIGOPS Operating Systems Review*, vol. 37, no. 5, pp. 29–43, ACM 2003.
9. J. Dean and S. Ghemawat, "Mapreduce: simplified data processing on large clusters," *Communications of the ACM*, vol. 51, no. 1, pp. 107–113, 2008.
10. K. Shvachko, H. Kuang, S. Radia, and R. Chansler, "The hadoop distributed file system," in Mass Storage Systems and Technologies (MSST), 2010 IEEE 26th Symposium on. IEEE, 2010, pp. 1–10.
11. M. Zaharia, M. Chowdhury, M. J. Franklin, S. Shenker, and I. Stoica, "Spark: cluster computing with working sets," in Proceedings of the 2nd USENIX conference on Hot topics in cloud computing, vol. 10, 2010, p. 10.
12. K. Ashton, "That internet of things thing," *RFiD Journal*, vol. 22, no. 7, pp. 97–114, 2009.
13. H. Sundmaeker, P. Guillemin, P. Friess, and S. Woelffle, "Vision and ' challenges for realising the internet of things," 2010.
14. J. Gubbi, R. Buyya, S. Marusic, and M. Palaniswami, "Internet of things (iot): A vision, architectural elements, and future directions," *Future Generation Computer Systems*, vol. 29, no. 7, pp. 1645–1660, 2013.
15. "Cisco global cloud index: Forecast and methodology, 2014–2019 white paper," 2014.
16. "IDC futurescape: Worldwide internet of things 2016 predictions," 2015.

17. D. Evans, "The internet of things: How the next evolution of the internet is changing every-thing," CISCO white paper, vol. 1, p. 14, 2011.

18. M. Bagaa, M. Younis, D. Djenouri, A. Derhab, and N. Badache, "Distributed low-latency data aggregation scheduling in wireless sensor networks," *ACM Transactions on Sensor Networks*, vol. 11, p. 49, 2015.

19. M. Bagaa, M. Younis, and I. Balasingham, "Optimal strategies for data aggregation sched-uling in wireless sensor networks," in Proceedings of IEEE GLOBECOM, 2015, pp. 1–6.

20. M. Dong, K. Ota, A. Liu, and M. Guo, "Joint optimization of lifetime and transport delay under reliability constraint wireless sensor networks," *IEEE Transactions on Parallel and Distributed Systems*, vol. 27, no. 1, pp. 225–236, 2015.

21. R. Soua, P. Minet, and E. Livolant, "Disca: A distributed scheduling for convergecast in multichannel wireless sensor networks," IFIP/IEEE International Symposium on Integrated Network Management, 2015.

22. D. De Guglielmo, G. Anastasi, and A. Seghetti, "From ieee 802.15. 4 to ieee 802.15. 4e: A step towards the internet of things," *Advances onto the Internet of Things*, pp. 135–152, 2014.

23. Y.-D. Lee and W.-Y. Chung, "Wireless sensor network based wearable smart shirt for ubi-quitous health and activity monitoring," *Sensors and Actuators B: Chemical*, vol. 140, no. 2, pp. 390–395, 2009.

24. T.-N. Dao, S. Yoon, and J. Kim, "A deadline-aware scheduling and forwarding scheme in wireless sensor networks," *Sensors*, vol. 16, no. 1, p. 59, 2016.

25. B. Alinia, M. H. Hajiesmaili, and A. Khonsari, "On the construction of maximum-quality aggregation trees in deadline-constrained WSNS," in Proceedings of IEEE INFOCOM, 2015, pp. 226–234.

26. A. Mihnea and M. Cardei, "Multi-channel wireless sensor networks," Recent Development in Wireless Sensor and Ad-hoc Networks, 2015.

27. Z. Zhao, W. Dong, J. Bu, T. Gu, and G. Min, "Accurate and generic sender selection for bulk data dissemination in low-power wireless networks," *IEEE/ACM Transactions on Networking*, vol. 25, no. 2, pp. 948–959, 2016.

28. B. Silva, R. M. Fisher, A. Kumar, and G. P. Hancke, "Experimental link quality characteriza-tion of wireless sensor networks for underground monitoring," *IEEE Transactions on Industrial Informatics*, vol. 11, no. 5, pp. 1099–1110, 2015.

29. T. Liu and A. E. Cerpa, "Data-driven link quality prediction using link features," *ACM Transactions on Sensor Networks*, vol. 10, p. 37, 2014.

30. W. Shi, J. Cao, Q. Zhang, Y. Li, and L. Xu, "Edge computing: Vision and challenges," *IEEE Internet of Things Journal*, vol. 3, no. 5, pp. 637–646, 2016.

31. N. Abbas, Y. Zhang, A. Taherkordi, and T. Skeie, "Mobile edge computing: A survey," *IEEE Internet of Things Journal*, vol. 5, no. 1, pp. 450–465, 2017.

32. Z. Wang, Z. Zhao, G. Min, X. Huang, Q. Ni, and R. Wang, "User mobility aware task assignment for mobile edge computing," *Future Generation Computer Systems*, vol. 85, pp. 1–8, 2018.

33. Z. Zhao, G. Min, W. Gao, Y. Wu, H. Duan, and Q. Ni, "Deploying edge computing nodes for large-scale iot: A diversity aware approach," *IEEE Internet of Things Journal*, vol. 5, no. 5, pp. 3606–3614, 2018.

34. C. Shu, Z. Zhao, Y. Han, G. Min, and H. Duan, "Multi-user offloading for edge computing networks: A dependency-aware and latency-optimal approach," *IEEE Internet of Things Journal*, vol. 7, no. 3, pp. 1678–1689, 2019.

35. Gao, W., Zhao, Z., Yu, Z., Min, G., Yang, M., & Huang, W. Edge-computing-based channel allocation for deadline-driven IoT networks. *IEEE Transactions on Industrial Informatics*, vol. 16, no. 10, pp. 6693–6702, 2020.

9

Optimal Cluster Head Selection in Wireless Sensor Network via Improved Moth Search Algorithm

Kale Navnath Dattatraya, S. Ananthakumaran, and K.V.D. Kiran

CONTENTS

9.1 Introduction

Wireless Sensor Network(WSN) seems to be a massive network of wirelessly interconnected nodes that collects a wide range of environmental data such as temperature, pressure, and motion capture [1–5]. Furthermore, WSNs may be used to gather data from their environments, which can be analyzed or studied by scientists and researchers. The use of such small devices is rapidly expanding in various fields, including monitored agriculture, animal tracking, and environmental monitoring. The intense nature of these networks is split down into clusters to facilitate communication. Clusters are the structured units of WSNs [6–10]. Compared to the traditional routing protocols, the clustering routing protocols hold many advantages based on robustness, scalability, and energy consumption. In each of the clusters, the CH is responsible for routing the information [11–14]. Initially, the data from the sink node is transmitted to the cluster head and then, from the cluster head, the data is sent to the base station after undergoing particular "fusion and aggregation" operations [15–18].

Generally, two types of nodes are used: (i) Lower Energy Sensor Node(LESN) and (ii) Higher Energy Sensor Node(HESN). Some Base Station(BS) knows about every other node's location and residual energy in the sensor network. Moreover, the node with the best residual energy is generally elected as the CH. However, CHS is challenging owing to the reduction in energy during each round of data transfer [19] [20]. The unique properties mentioned above make it difficult to set up a WSN and operate it with escalated lifetime and curtailed energy consumption. Optimum energy use is necessary as it becomes difficult to replace the batteries in sensor networks deployed in an unattended environment. Any clustering algorithm's most important task is to select the best cluster head (CH) under various restrictions such as energy consumption and delay. Yet, in the last few years, research has been carried out in WSN to limit the energy requirement by transferring the data via the CH. The meta-heuristic techniques are suggested as a promising approach for optimal CH selection with minimized energy requirement.

The major contribution of the presented work is:

> The moth's proclivity to fly toward light sources is determined by the moth search algorithm (MSA). In most cases, the moth travels in a straight line with the celestial light. The MSA provides larger convergence and does not get trapped into local optima. However, it suffered from slower convergence in certain complicated cases. To overcome this issue and optimally select the CH, a new modified algorithm is being proposed named modified moth search algorithm based on QoS parameter, distance, delay, and energy.

The rest of this work is ordered as follows: Section 9.2 portrays the review based on optimal CHS in WSN. Section 9.3 determines the adopted CHS model with MMSA-based defined multi-objectives, and Section 9.4 explains the defined multi-objective-based CH selection.

9.2 Literature Review

9.2.1 Related Works

In 2021, Alazab et al. introduced a novel approach for selecting the optimal CHs in the network using a modified Rider Optimization Algorithm(ROA). The proposed model had optimal CHS due to the numerous objectives, including energy sustainability, minimized delay, and inter-distance between the nodes and CH. The suggested approach divides the solutions into two groups based on the best fitness value. To accomplish the desired CH selection, optimization variables like as distance, delay, and energy utilized in IoT devices are examined. Finally, a comparative evaluation was made regarding normalized energy and alive node count [22].

In 2020, Malisetti et al. determined an efficient technique for optimally selecting the CHs based on energy conservation. The quasi-oppositional butterfly optimization algorithm (QOBOA) protocol was used to identify the best CH. In terms of network longevity and energy efficiency, the suggested method is compared to original butterfly optimization and particular current algorithms. Simulation results show that the QOBOA-based CH selection scheme outperforms the existing ones [4]. In 2019, Rambabu et al. have predominantly selected the cluster heads in WSN using the HABC-MBOA. This suggested HABC-MBOA also eliminates the potential of cluster heads being overloaded with a maximum number of sensor nodes, leading to sensor node mortality during the futile cluster head selection process. The simulation results showed that the network's number of living nodes is 18.92% higher than the benchmarked cluster head selection methodologies [15]. In 2019, Verma et al. [26] selected the optimal CH in terms of residual energy, node density, and sink distance using the Genetic Algorithm-based Optimized Clustering protocol(GAOC). In addition, the authors have introduced MS-GAOC for overcoming the issues regarding communication distance. The proposed work was validated to be more efficient than the traditional schemes based on the count of dead nodes, network throughput, stability, and network lifetime. MS-GAOC empirical investigations are conducted using protocols designed to operate with various data sinks in order to conduct a fair comparative study.

In 2018, Janakiraman et al. [27] effectively selected the CHs using the HACO-ABC-CHS technique. A comparative evaluation was made between the adopted and the traditional methods based on alive nodes count, residual energy, dead nodes count, and throughput.

Because wireless sensor networks (WSNs) use small batteries that can't be recharged or replaced, energy efficiency is seen as the most pressing concern. Energy consumption is a significant challenge in WSN research. Clustering is a useful strategy for reducing WSN energy consumption. No perfect approach is available to enable maximum stringent power expenditure requirements to be reliable and run unattended for a long time, which can be in years. We need to build a technique to enable strong cluster head selection for a better network lifetime.

9.3 Proposed CH Selection Model with MMSA-Based Defined Multi-Objectives

9.3.1 Simulation Environment

A wireless communication network is constructed with dimensions 100 m × 100 m with base station $Base_s$ at the center. The network is constructed with 100 counts of normal nodes. The node that satisfies the QoS parameter is chosen as the CH among these normal nodes. Since the cluster head communicates with base station, it needs to be selected optimally. To have almost advantageous data transmission, an optimal CH is selected in this research work using the MMSA model, which is based on the multi-objectives like QoS parameter, distance, delay, and energy. In this research work, ten counts of optimal cluster heads are formed, and so there are ten counts of clusters n^c. The nodes within the cluster are denoted as D_{ij} where $i = 1, 2, ...L$ and $j = 1, 2, ...M$. Once an optimal CH is chosen, the transmission data takes place significantly, and as outcomes of this, the network life span increases. Figure 9.1 shows architecture of the proposed work.

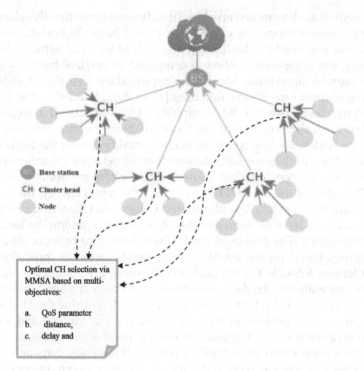

FIGURE 9.1
Proposed optimal CH selection model.

9.4 Defined Multi-Objectives-Based CH Selection

9.4.1 Overall Objective Function

Moreover, the optimal CH is chosen with a new MMSA model based on the multi-objectives like QoS parameter, distance, delay, and energy. The QoS parameter is the most essential constraint for well-organized network performance. The network's performance for data transmission enhances if the higher QoS, lower energy, lower delay, and lower distance are recorded. Mathematically, the objective function *(obj)* is given as per the following equation:

$$obj = \beta \times fit^2 + (1 - \beta) fit^1; 0 < \beta > 1 \tag{9.1}$$

in which

$$fit^1 = \gamma^1 * fit_i^{dist} + \gamma^2 * fit_i^{energy} + \gamma^3 * fit_i^{delay} \tag{9.2}$$

$$fit^2 = \frac{1}{n^c} \sum_{r=1}^{n^c} \| D_i - Base_s \| \tag{9.3}$$

In Equation (9.1), the constant $\beta = 0.3$. In addition, Equation (9.2) denotes the distance, energy, and delay parameters, respectively. Further, in Equation (9.3), the term $\| D_i - B_s \|$ refers to the distance among D_i (standard node) and base station $Base_s$. The notation fit_i^{dist} denotes the fitness function of ith normal node corresponding to the distance metric. The notation fit_i^{energy} represents the normal node's fitness functions corresponding to energy and delay metrics. A detailed explanation of fit_i^{dist} fit_i^{energy} fit_i^{delay} is explained in the forthcoming section.

9.4.2 Fitness Function in Terms of Energy

The required energy for a node to be a CH is computed using Equation (9.4). Further, the energy is the major criterion that chooses the network lifespan. In WSN, the node with greatest energy is selected as the optimal CH, and this selection will be made using the MMSA model.

$$fit^{energy} = \frac{fit^{energy}(q)}{fit^{energy}(p)} \tag{9.4}$$

in which

$$fit^{energy}(q) = \sum_{j=1}^{M} uEN(j) \tag{9.5}$$

$$uEN(j) = \sum_{i=1}^{i} \left(1 - EN(D_i) * EN(CH_j)\right); 1 \le j \le M \tag{9.6}$$

$$fit^{energy}(u) = M * \underset{i=1}{\overset{L}{Max}}(EN(D_i)) * \underset{j=1}{\overset{M}{Max}}(EN(CH_j)) \tag{9.7}$$

Here, the notation $EN(D_i)$ denotes the energy of the i-th normal node and the CH's energy $EN(CH_j)$.

9.4.3 Fitness Function in Terms of Distance

To have a reliable data transmission, the nodes close to CH join the cluster. The node close to the base station has a higher chance of acting as a CH. In this research work, the f^{dist} is fixed to be within the range of [0,1]. The node that lies within this range is optimally selected via the MMSA model. Mathematically, the fitness function in terms of distance is shown in Equation (9.8).

$$fit^{dist} = \frac{fit^{dist}(q)}{fit^{dist}(p)} \tag{9.8}$$

in which

$$fit^{dist}(q) = \sum_{i=1}^{L} \sum_{j=1}^{M} \| D_i - CH_j \| + \| CH_j - Base_s \| \tag{9.9}$$

$$fit^{dist}(p) = \sum_{i=1}^{L}\sum_{j=1}^{M}\| D_i - D_j \|$$ (9.10)

In Equation (9.9), the $f^{dist}(q)$ computes the difference in distance between D_i and $Base_s$ and the difference in distance between the jth cluster head CH_j and $Base_s$. Further, $fit^{dis\,tan\,ce}(q)$ in Equation (9.10) denotes the distance between two normal nodes.

9.4.4 Fitness Function in Terms of Delay

The delay is a key parameter that portrays the consistency of the data transmission. It is crucial to select the optimal CH to route the fresh data packets to the destination with negligible delays, as it is the mediator for data transmission. This research work will select the node with lower delay in data transmission as the optimal CH via the MMSA model. Here, fit^{delay} is set as within the range [0, 1]. The nodes within this range are selected optimally by the MMSA model. Mathematically, the data transmission delay is shown in Eq. (9.11).

$$fit^{delay} = \frac{Max(\sum_{j=1}^{M} CH_j)}{L}$$ (9.11)

The solution for minimizing the delay is to lower the cluster's nodes count. In Equation (9.11), $Max(\sum_{j=1}^{M} CH_j)$ denotes the available CH in the network, and L denotes the overall nodes count.

9.4.5 Fitness Function in Terms of QoS

The QoS can be achieved if the aforementioned criteria like the minimal delay, minimal distance, and maximal energy are satisfied.

9.5 MMSA Model and Its Solution

9.5.1 Solution Encoding

Though most of the nodes in the network might lie within the specified limits of distance, distance, and energy, it is critical to select the most optimal one, and this research work makes it possible with the introduced MMSA model. The solution encoding for MMSA is illustrated in Figure 9.2.

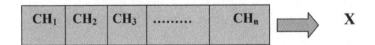

FIGURE 9.2
Solution encoding for proposed algorithm.

9.5.2 MMSA Model

The MSA [1] was developed based on the moths' tendency to fly toward the light sources. Because this behavior is still unknown, many theories have been proposed to explain it. One suggestion is that the heavenly is used in "transverse orientation" while the moths are flying. In general, the moth flies at a steady angle to the celestial light, without turning. The MSA has higher convergence and do not get trapped into local optima. But it suffers from lower convergence in case certain complicated cases. Therefore, a novel MMSA scheme is proposed in this work. Moreover, the steps involved in the adopted approach are depicted below:

> **Step 1:** First, set up the search agent's population Po with NP moths in a random manner. In addition, the current iteration is set as $iter$ and Max^{iter} is the maximal generation count.
> **Step 2:** Calculate the search agent's fitness in Equation (9.1).
> **Step 3:** While $iter<Max^{iter}$ do.
> **Step 4:** Arrange the solutions owing to the fitness function.
> **Step 5:** Among the sorted solutions, the first 30% of the solutions (i.e., the best solutions) are updated using the Levy flights update mechanism. These best solutions are symbolized as J_{best}^{iter+1}. Mathematically, it is shown in Equation (9.12).

$$J_{best}^{iter+1} = J_i^{iter} + \beta L(r) \tag{9.12}$$

in which, r denotes the step length, which is computed as per Equation (9.13).

$$r = \frac{u}{|x|^{1/\alpha - 1}} \tag{9.13}$$

in which α denotes the index and u and x are obtained from the normal distribution. In addition, the notation J_i^{iter} represents the current position of ith moth. In Equation (9.12), the step obtained from Levy distribution is denoted as $L(r)$ and β specifies the scaling factor. The mathematical formula for β is given in Equation (9.14):

$$\beta = \frac{R_{max}}{it^2} \tag{9.14}$$

Here, R_{max} represents the utmost walk step of the moths.
The mathematical formula for $L(r)$ is shown in Equation (9.15):

$$L(r) = \frac{(\alpha-1)\Gamma(\alpha-1)\sin\left(\frac{\pi(\alpha-1)}{2}\right)}{\pi r^\alpha} \tag{9.15}$$

In Equation (9.15), r refers to the random number and Γ stand for gamma function.

> **Step 6:** The next 30% of the solutions are updated using the straight line flight mechanism of MSA. These solutions are denoted as J_{med}^{iter+1}. Mathematically, J_{med}^{iter+1} is updated as per Equation (9.16).

$$J_{med}^{iter+1} = \eta \times \left(J_i^{iter} + \Phi \times \left(J_{best}^{iter} - J_i^{iter} \right) \right) \tag{9.16}$$

The moths that fly in the direction of the last position, which is away from the light source is modeled as per Equation (9.17).

$$J_{med}^{it+1} = \eta \times \left(J_i^{it} + \frac{1}{\Phi} \times \left(J_{best}^{it} - J_i^{it} \right) \right) \tag{9.17}$$

Step 7: The rest of the search agents are the worst fitness solutions and they are updated using the arithmetic crossover operation. Mathematically, it is shown in Equation (9.18):

$$J_{wor}^{iter+1} = A * J_{worst}^{iter+1} + (1-A).J_{best}^{iter} \tag{9.18}$$

Here, A denotes the random number among 0 to 1.

Step 8: Calculate the populations using the most recent positions.
Step 9: Increment the current iteration by 1.
Step 10: Attain the optimal solution.
Step 11: Terminate.

9.6 Results and Discussion

9.6.1 Simulation Procedure

The proposed CH selection model using MMSA was implemented in MATLAB. This evaluation is made by fixing the parametric values as: initial energy $EN^{In} = 0.5$, energy of free space model $EN^{fr} = 10$ pJ/bit/m2, energy of power amplifier $E^{power} = 0.0013$ pJ/ bit / m^2, transmitter energy $E^{tr} = 50$ nJ/bit/m^2, data aggregation energy $E^{Da} = 5$ nJ/bit/m^2. The proposed work was evaluated for 2,000 rounds. The evaluation of the projected method is evaluated to the existing schemes based on count of alive nodes (AN), convergence, network lifetime, and normalized network energy. This assessment was done among the adopted scheme (MMSA) and traditional works including MSA [1], CSA, GA, and GSO.

9.6.2 Analysis on Count of Alive Nodes

For a ceaseless information passage with negligible delay, the lifetime of the network need to higher. The network life span is based on the count of AN. In this section, the count of available ANs after each of the rounds (R) is recorded. This evaluation is performed by altering the number of R like 500, 1,000, 1,500, and 2,000 and the corresponding outcomes obtained are analyzed. From Figure 9.3, when compared to previous works, the proposed work appears to have a higher number of ANs. Initially, the count of ANs of MMSA model is 100 till $R =$1,200. Then, the count of ANs tends to decrease, and finally at the $R=$ 2,000, there is 38 counts of ANs, while the existing works has ANs below 32 numbers. Therefore, it is shown that the MMSA model has the maximum count of ANs from the overall assessment.

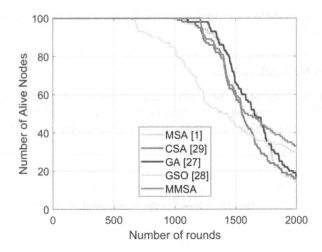

FIGURE 9.3
Analysis on count for MMSA and existing techniques.

TABLE 9.1
Overall Analysis on the Count of Alive Nodes for Every Round: Proposed versus Existing Techniques

Rounds	MSA [21]	CSA [25]	GA [23]	GSO [24]	MMSA
1	100	100	100	100	100
100	100	100	100	100	100
225	100	100	100	100	100
500	100	100	100	100	100
725	100	100	100	93	100
1000	100	100	100	85	100
1225	95	92	98	62	94
1500	66	59	66	44	61
1725	43	29	43	36	44
2000	14	16	17	30	33

An analysis on count of alive nodes using MMSA and existing techniques over number of rounds was done and result shows that MMSA contains more number of alive nodes compared with other existing techniques (Figure 9.3).

In addition, the results corresponding to the overall count of ANs recorded by MMSA model and the existing techniques are tabulated in Table 9.1. At the 2,000th round, the count of ANs in MMSA=33, which the highest count while comported to MSA=14, CSA= 16, GA=17, and GSO=30. Therefore, it is vivid that the MMSA model has the highest count of ANs even under higher count of nodes.

9.6.3 Analysis on Convergence

The convergence analysis dwells on the achievement of the defined objectives by the MMSA model as well as existing model. The defined multi-objective in Equation (9.1) is a minimization-based fitness function, and so the technique with the least cost function is said to be the appropriate technique for CH selection. This assessment is performed through altering count of iterations from 2, 4, 6, 8, and 10, respectively. From the recorded results in Figure 9.4, the MMSA model achieves the least cost function for every variation in the count of iterations.

9.6.4 Analysis on Network Lifetime

The expansion in life span of the network is a crucial challenge faced by the researchers in recent days. This research work overcomes this issue by optimally selecting the CH based on multi-objectives. The outcomes attained are shown in Figure 9.5, from which

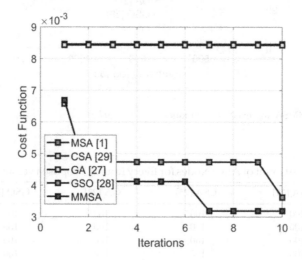

FIGURE 9.4
Convergence analysis of MMSA and existing techniques.

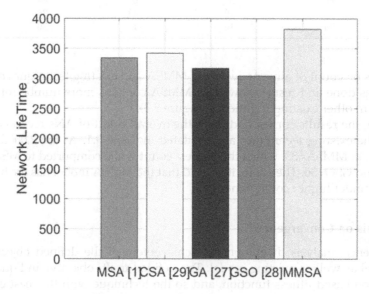

FIGURE 9.5
Analysis on network lifetime for MMSA and existing techniques.

an obvious ending is derived that the adopted scheme is much sufficient for optimal CH selection, since it has the capability of expanding the life span of the network.

9.6.5 Analysis on Normalized Network Energy

In order to enhance the network lifetime, the normalized energy of the network needs to be maintained as high as possible. In this section, the normalized energy recorded by both existing and proposed work is discussed by varying the count of rounds from 500, 1,000, 1,500, and 2,000, respectively. The corresponding outcomes obtained are given in Figure 9.6. For lower count of rounds, the normalized network energy seems to be higher. Initially, at the 0th round, the normalized network energy of both the existing as well as proposed technique is higher, and the corresponding value is between 0.5 and 0.6 pJ. Further, as the count of rounds tends to increase, the normalized network energy seems to lessen down gradually. Finally, at the 2,000th round, the normalized network energy of MSSA model is 0.9 pJ, while the normalized network energy of the existing techniques is below it. Therefore, the proposed work is suggested to be an apt technique for optimal CH selection.

In addition, the overall normalized network energy recorded by the adopted and extant technique for changing the count of rounds is depicted in Table 9.2. At the 2,000th round (i.e., highest round), the recorded normalized network energy by MMSA is 0.077099, which is the highest value than MSA=0.034355, CSA=0.040929, GA=0.035618, and GSO=0.04889. As a whole, the proposed work is indeed good in enhancing the network life span, and so it is suggested as a significant technique for optimal CH selection.

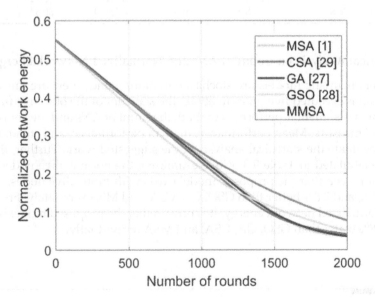

FIGURE 9.6
Analysis on normalized network energy of MMSA and existing techniques.

TABLE 9.2

Overall Analysis on the Normalized Network Energy for Every Round: Proposed versus Existing Techniques

Rounds	MSA [21]	CSA [25]	GA [23]	GSO [24]	MMSA
1	0.54969	0.54968	0.54969	0.54964	0.54966
100	0.51954	0.51808	0.51889	0.51454	0.51755
225	0.48135	0.47795	0.48006	0.47082	0.47756
500	0.39753	0.38997	0.39449	0.37494	0.39224
725	0.32884	0.31791	0.32438	0.29712	0.32747
1000	0.24499	0.23009	0.23895	0.21276	0.25534
1225	0.17633	0.15908	0.16988	0.15686	0.204
1500	0.097083	0.089983	0.095691	0.10973	0.15076
1725	0.05307	0.059369	0.05758	0.080016	0.11368
2000	0.034355	0.040929	0.035618	0.04889	0.077099

TABLE 9.3

Statistical Analysis on the Count of ANs and Normalized Network Energy for Every Round: Proposed versus Existing Techniques

	Mean		Median		Standard Deviation	
Approaches	Count of ANs	Normalized network energy	Count of ANs	Normalized network energy	Count of ANs	Normalized network energy
MSA[1]	76	0.25870	100	0.24499	37.656	0.20246
CSA[29]	75	0.25381	100	0.23009	37.457	0.20068
GA[27]	76.6	0.25673	100	0.23895	36.425	0.20177
GSO[28]	71.8	0.25217	85	0.21276	32.729	0.19175
MMSA	78.8	0.27860	100	0.25534	30.671	0.17854

9.6.6 Statistical Analysis on Count of ANs and Normalized Network Energy

Since the meta-heuristic models are stochastic in nature, and to ensure fair comparison, each algorithm is executed five times to obtain the statistics of the objective function minimization. This assessment is performed for both the count of ANs and the "normalized network energy" measure. Mean performance, median performance, and standard deviation are used to evaluate the statistical analysis of the suggested work. Further, the outcomes acquired are tabulated in Table 9.3. While examining the normal alive nodes of different techniques, it is seen that the proposed model exists with more alive nodes, which is 7%, 2.2%, 3%, 3.1%, and 2.8% better than GSO, GA, CSA, and MSA separately. From the investigation of normalized network energy, it is proven that the proposed model is 9.2%, 9.6%, 9.3%, and 9.8% better than GSO, GA, CSA, and MSA individually.

9.7 Conclusion

In this chapter, the selection of optimal CH was accomplished using the MMSA model based on the defined multi-objectives like QoS, delay, distance, and energy. The evaluation of the projected method was determined over the existing approaches based on count of alive nodes (AN), convergence, network lifetime, and normalized network energy. This assessment was performed among the adopted work (MMSA) as well as traditional works such as MSA, CSA, GA, and GSO. When compared to the previous works, the proposed work appears to have a higher number of ANs. Initially, the count of ANs of MMSA model is 100 till R =1,200. Then, the count of ANs tends to decrease, and finally at the R = 2,000, there are 38 counts of ANs, while the existing works have ANs below 32 numbers. Therefore, it is clear that the MMSA model has the maximum count of ANs from the overall assessment.

References

1. A. A.-H. Hassan, W. M. Shah, A.-H. H. Habeb, M. F. I. Othman and M. N. Al-Mhiqani, "An Improved Energy-Efficient Clustering Protocol to Prolong the Lifetime of the WSN-Based IoT," *IEEE Access*, vol. 8, pp. 200500–200517, 2020. doi: 10.1109/ACCESS.2020.3035624

2. S. Lata, S. Mehfuz, S. Urooj and F. Alrowais, "Fuzzy Clustering Algorithm for Enhancing Reliability and Network Lifetime of Wireless Sensor Networks," *IEEE Access*, vol. 8, pp. 66013–66024, 2020. doi: 10.1109/ACCESS.2020.2985495

3. J. Qiao and X. Zhang, "Compressive Data Gathering Based on Even Clustering for Wireless Sensor Networks," *IEEE Access*, vol. 6, pp. 24391-24410, 2018. doi: 10.1109/ACCESS.2018.2832626

4. Nageswara Rao Malisetti and Vinay Kumar Pamula,"Performance of Quasi Oppositional Butterfly Optimization Algorithm for Cluster Head Selection in WSNs", *Procedia Computer Science*, 2020.

5. N. Hemavathi, M. Meenalochani, and S. Sudha, "Influence of Received Signal Strength on Prediction of Cluster Head and Number of Rounds," *IEEE Transactions on Instrumentation and Measurement*, vol. 69, no. 6, pp. 3739–3749, June 2020. doi: 10.1109/TIM.2019.2932652.

6. Y. Han, G. Li, R. Xu, J. Su, J. Li, and G. Wen, "Clustering the Wireless Sensor Networks: A Meta-Heuristic Approach," *IEEE Access*, vol. 8, pp. 214551–214564, 2020. doi: 10.1109/ACCESS.2020.3041118.

7. J. Zhang, J. Tang, and F. Wang, "Cooperative Relay Selection for Load Balancing With Mobility in Hierarchical WSNs: A Multi-Armed Bandit Approach," *IEEE Access*, vol. 8, pp. 18110–18122, 2020. Doi: 10.1109/ACCESS.2020.2968562.

8. H. El Alami and A. Najid, "ECH: An Enhanced Clustering Hierarchy Approach to Maximize Lifetime of Wireless Sensor Networks," *IEEE Access*, vol. 7, pp. 107142–107153, 2019. doi: 10.1109/ACCESS.2019.2933052

9. A. Verma, S. Kumar, P. R. Gautam, T. Rashid, and A. Kumar, "Fuzzy Logic Based Effective Clustering of Homogeneous Wireless Sensor Networks for Mobile Sink," *IEEE Sensors Journal*, vol. 20, no. 10, pp. 5615–5623, 2020 doi: 10.1109/JSEN.2020.2969697

10. S. Vinusha and J.S. Abinaya, "Performance Analysis of the Adaptive Cuckoo Search Rate Optimization Scheme for the Congestion Control in the WSN", *Journal of Networking and Communication Systems*, vol. 1, no.1, pp.19–27, 2018.

11. Amit Kelotra and Prateek Pandey, "Energy-aware Cluster Head Selection in WSN using HPSOCS Algorithm", *Journal of Networking and Communication Systems*, vol.2, no. 1, pp. 24–33, 2019.

12. Fatema Murshid AlBalushi, "Chaotic based Hybrid Artificial Sheep Algorithm - Particle Swarm Optimization for Energy and Secure Aware in WSN", *Journal of Networking and Communication Systems*, vol.2, no. 2, pp. 37–48, 2019.

13. Jacob John and Paul Rodrigues, "Multi-objective HSDE Algorithm for Energy-Aware Cluster Head Selection in WSN", *Journal of Networking and Communication Systems*, vol.2, no.3, pp. 20–29, 2019.

14. Amit Sarkar and T. Senthil Murugan, "Adaptive Cuckoo Search and Squirrel Search Algorithm for Optimal Cluster Head Selection in WSN", *Journal of Networking and Communication Systems*, vol. 2, no. 3, pp. 30–39, 2019.

15. A. Bandi Rambabu, Venugopal Reddy, and Sengathir Janakiraman,"Hybrid Artificial Bee Colony and Monarchy Butterfly Optimization Algorithm (HABC-MBOA)-based Cluster Head Selection for WSNs", *Journal of King Saud University – Computer and Information Sciences*, vol. 34, no. 5, pp. 1–10, 2019.

16. Suresh Babu Chandanapalli, E. Sreenivasa Reddy, and D. Rajya Lakshmi, "Convolutional Neural Network for Water Quality Prediction in WSN", *Journal of Networking and Communication Systems*, vol. 2, no. 3, pp. 40–47, 2019.

17. Reeta Bhardwaj and Dinesh Kumar, "Hybrid GSDE: Hybrid Grasshopper Self Adaptive Differential Evolution Algorithm for Energy-Aware Routing in WSN", *Journal of Networking and Communication Systems*, vol. 2, no. 4, pp. 1–11, 2019.

18. Kale Navnath Dattatraya and K. Raghava Rao, "Hybrid FruitFly Optimization Algorithm and Wavelet Neural Network for Energy Efficiency in WSN", *Journal of Networking and Communication Systems*, vol. 3, no.1, pp. 41–49, 2020.

19. M Anandkumar, "Multicast Routing in WSN using Bat Algorithm with Genetic Operators for IoT Applications", *Journal of Networking and Communication Systems*, vol 3, no. 2, 2020.

20. Badriya Al Maqbali, "Sensor Activation in WSN using Improved Cuckoo Search and Squirrel Search Algorithm", *Journal of Networking and Communication Systems*, vol. 3, no. 2, pp. 1–5, 2020.

21. Gai-Ge Wang, "Moth Search Algorithm: a Bio-inspired Metaheuristic Algorithm for Global Optimization Problems", *Memetic Computing*, vol.10, no.1, pp. 151–154, June 2018.

22. Mamoun Alazab, Kuruva Lakshmanna, and Praveen Kumar Reddy Maddikunta,"Multi-objective Cluster Head Selection Using Fitness Averaged Rider Optimization Algorithm for IoT Networks in Smart Cities", *Sustainable Energy Technologies and Assessments*, vol. 43, pp. 10–29, 2021. doi:10.1016/j.seta.2020.100973

23. John McCall, " Genetic Algorithms for Modelling and Optimisation", *Journal of Computational and Applied Mathematics*, vol. 184, no. 1, pp. 205–222, 2005.

24. S. He, Q. H. Wu, and J. R. Saunders, "Group Search Optimizer: An Optimization Algorithm Inspired by Animal Searching Behavior," *IEEE Transactions on Evolutionary Computation*, vol. 13, no. 5, pp. 973–990, Oct. 2009.

25. Alireza Askarzadeh, "A Novel Metaheuristic Method for Solving Constrained Engineering Optimization Problems: Crow Search Algorithm", *Computers and Structures*, vol. 169, pp. 1–12, 2016 .

26. Sandeep Verma, Neetu Sood, and Ajay Kumar Sharma, "Genetic Algorithm-based Optimized Cluster Head Selection for Single and Multiple Data Sinks in Heterogeneous Wireless Sensor Network," *Applied Soft Computing Journal*, vol. 85, pp. 1–21, 2019. doi.org/10.1016/j.asoc.2019.105788.

27. Sengathir Janakiraman, "A Hybrid Ant Colony and Artificial Bee Colony Optimization Algorithm-based Cluster Head Selection for IoT," *ScienceDirect*, pp. 360–366, 2018.

28. T. M. Behera, S. K. Mohapatra, U. C. Samal, M. S. Khan, M. Daneshmand, and A. H. Gandomi, "Residual Energy-Based Cluster-Head Selection in WSNs for IoT Application," IEEE *Internet of Things Journal*, vol. 6, no. 3, pp. 5132–5139, June 2019. doi: 10.1109/JIOT.2019.2897119

29. T. M. Behera, S. K. Mohapatra, U. C. Samal, M. S. Khan, M. Daneshmand, and A. H. Gandomi, "I-SEP: An Improved Routing Protocol for Heterogeneous WSN for IoT-Based Environmental Monitoring," *IEEE Internet of Things Journal*, vol. 7, no. 1, pp. 710–717, January 2020. doi: 10.1109/JIOT.2019.2940988

10

Camera Calibration Using Robust Intrinsic and Extrinsic Parameters

Ketki P. Kshirsagar, Ashish Tathod, Rushikesh Dudhate,
Ajay Yadav, and Rudra Tarte

CONTENTS

10.1 Introduction

A plane of an image plus a lens makes a camera. The plane of the picture is where light hits the film or sensor, while the lens gives a transformation between the object and image space. Because of the distortions between the objects and points of image location, the transformation cannot be described with the perfect perspective. Distortions in lenses can be modeled. However, the model may only approximate the real relationship. The model will conform better to reality if the parameters might be approximated more precisely. The process of calibrating a lens is not easy. Numerous parameters must be considered, and the selection of these parameters is necessary but not sufficient to ensure that the calibration will be successful. Camera calibration may not be a hot research topic because of an apparent maturity of analytical self-calibration. In the mid-1980s, self-calibration was a hot topic in the early days of digital cameras. The photogrammetric industry has many different projects that it works on, including accident reconstruction and heritage recording. This has led to an increased interest in photogrammetry. Photogrammetrics are now interested in fully automatic calibration. Photogrammetry is the science of making measurements from photographs. Traditionally, this has been used for mapping and architectural purposes, but in recent years, it has become a popular technique in computer vision. In the context of photogrammetry and computer vision, one subject that is still being investigated is camera calibration. The use of calibration parameters for cameras is a popular topic.

DOI: 10.1201/9781003342755-12

Camera calibration is a process-driven method in which properties, including intrinsic and extrinsic, of the camera are calculated. After calibration, camera images can be utilized for the required purposes. Camera calibration is drastically needed in order to get fine-tuned parameters of the object plane. For the development of machine vision applications, camera calibration is a must to get camera-efficient object parameters. A camera is a visual sensor and is very important part for various technical branches, including image processing, automation, and surveillance as well as the entertainment sector. Camera calibration is a parameter-tuning process. This involves adjusting parameters of the camera to find an exact relationship between 3D coordinates and their corresponding 2D image object pixels captured by the calibrated camera. Specifically, these methods or techniques are used for finding the parameters. Intrinsic parameters of the camera lens are radial distortion, focal length, optical center and the lens coefficients. Orientation of the camera with respect to coordinates is included in extrinsic parameters. The most commonly used camera calibration techniques are pattern calibration, geometric clues and deep learning.

Geometric clues: Geometric clues involve straight lines, equally distributed or vanishing points in order to calibrate.

Pattern calibration: If taking a whole set of images; the appropriate method of calibration is to capture multiple object images of known dimensions from various coordinate points. In checkerboard pattern, circular patterns are also used for checkerboard-based method of known dimensions.

Deep learning based: If taking few imaging object information, deep learning method is better to use for the calibration of the camera (Figure 10.1).

The camera calibration determines the require parameters of the object image. It's very important process in many computer vision related applications and instruments. Applications and instruments, including the camera, are modeled with camera internal parameters including focal length, principal lines and skew of axis, and the orientation of the camera is explored in terms of extrinsic parameters, which include rotational and translational features. In linear or nonlinear processes, while finding internal and external camera parameters, orientation of the image plane as well as pixels in the image are required.

Those pixels and edges are presented as a pattern calibration with known geometrical structures, generally a flat chessboard. Various studies have focused on calibrating

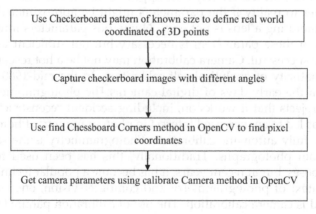

FIGURE 10.1
Generalize camera calibration flow chart.

methods. Majority of them emphasize on estimating parameters step and calibrating location factors. This calibrating problem is not always quantified during automatic calibration pattern detection.

Camera calibration is a common important and unavoidable topic, but because of the lack of powerful feature detection methods, automated calibration is a major issue. Calibration pattern recognition is a versatile task, where blur/drowsy light issues and high-end conviction are the important ultimatums. For reducing these problems, camera calibration application majorly needs user interaction for the right detection of the calibration points. The fine sharpening of points is monotone and a skillful task. These are various constraints and problems. However, the accuracy of these parameters may not be sufficient for an accurate reconstruction of a scene in order to increase the precision of this data; it may be useful to explore using a nonlinear model of light that considers the non-Euclidean nature of light. In other systems, parameters that are not of much interest are known as nuisance parameters. In the past, industrial cameras were used for a variety of tasks. Recently, consumer-grade digital cameras have been adopted for a number of measurements. In the 1950s and 1960s, lens calibration attracted a lot of attention. However, in the past few years, it has received less attention than it did before. The maturity of understanding aerial lenses has provided much of the impetus for lens calibration models and methods in the past. The future of technology will see demand for high-speed continuous measurements.

10.2 Related Work

J. Kannal et al. proposed a general camera model along with a calibrating method for figuring out the parameters of the given models. This is most appropriate for fish-eye lens cameras and cameras with wide-angle lenses [1]. In a study put forward by Azra Fetić et.al., the process of camera calibration of a charge couple device(CCD) [2] digital camera is described using the Calibrating Cameras Toolbox for MATLAB. It's based upon a perspective projection method to find accurate three-dimensional values from the images for various applications in the field of computer vision [3,4]. Some of the cameras today have multiple acquisition modes of images and videos. These have different values of aspect ratio, image resolution and field of view. Andrey Bushnev Skiy Lorenzo Sorgi et al. suggest in their work that each of these modes should be considered and calibrated separately. This task can be tedious and time-consuming, although this paper provides us with a better solution that is not only easier but also less prone to errors [5].

The study by Weidong Song et al. proposed an automatic camera calibration method [6]. This method suggests the use of new points of calibration and not the usual chessboard corners. This new way of calibration is said to give higher accuracy than the previous traditional methods [7]. Jia Sun et al., in their work on camera calibration review, analyze and compare the different methods of camera calibration for various future applications, both research and practical, since different methods have different levels of accuracy that affects the camera vision directly [8,9]. Qiuyu Zhu et al. propose a novel method for determining the parameters that are extrinsic of the camera matrix and also one of the intrinsic characteristics, the focal length of the camera, using just one image. To calculate the final extrinsic coordinate factors, a backward camera model and three of the indirect extrinsic coordinate factors are used. In comparison to previous approaches, this procedure is believed to be more accurate and have less computing complexity [10,11]. Calibrating camera with using not only MATLAB calibration toolbox but also genetic algorithm was proposed by Yuanyuan Dong Xuanzuo Ye et al. [12]. They have proposed a solution that involves finding the intrinsic parameters using the MATLAB calibration toolbox and then optimizing it using a genetic algorithm. Their method is not only simple and effective but also ensures accuracy [13,14]. I-Sak Choi etal. [8] proposed a calibrating camera method for the omni-stereo camera system. The vision system has eight horizontal cameras and two vertical cameras. The approach entails surrounding the omni-stereo system with a cubic-type calibration framework. All of the cameras may be calibrated in a single shot [15,16]. Wang Qi et al. [17] reviews camera calibration with different applications like robot navigation, biomedical, machine vision and 3D reconstruction applications. And also different methods like self, traditional and active vision calibration are reviewed. In mobile robot navigation application, camera calibration implies a crucial role in finding positioning accuracy. In machine vision application, camera calibration is done by a simple method with a high precision-automation process. In biomedical applications, camera calibration important when surgical operations are performed through a computer or a robot. This camera calibration improves surgical precision.

Wang, Li, and Zheng [18] proposed camera calibration by OpenCV with nonlinear tangential and radial distortion. OpenCV platform provides good support to the user as well as Windows and Linux computer platform and improve developing and execution accuracy with speed. Jen-Hui Chuang et al. proposed a new technique of camera calibration, which is based on a geometric approach [19]. The authors focused on two issues: to avoid computational outliner and fixation of camera focal length. This proposed new technique provides closed-form solution with internal and external parameters for calibration. The proposed technique provides better results on synthetic and real data with different focal length situations. Qian Zheng et al. [20] proposed optimization-based noisy camera calibration with internal and external parameters for a single image with glass. A single-image reflection separation is a major problem in camera calibration. Calibration cue is mapping reflective amplitude coefficient using internal and external parameters of the camera. The proposed camera calibration methodology solves high-level vision problems. Kai Guo, Hu Ye, Junhao Gu and Honglin Chen [21] proposed three-point prospective problem for the known position of camera calibration with intrinsic and extrinsic parameters. The proposed methodology provides unique numerical stability solution, accuracy for synthetic data and real images.

Jie Zhao et al. proposed intrinsic and extrinsic parameters used for multi-camera calibration. Intrinsic parameters are used to determine radial distortion coefficient with invisible fixed point. Extrinsic parameters are used for word coordinate system involving three collinear points. The authors claim that the calibration system observes the object perfectly in different orientations [22]. Kun Yan et al. [23] proposed a novel and high accuracy method for camera calibration. For optimal results, they compute the center with radial distortion and intrinsic parameters are solved linearly and independently. These decoupled processes calibrate the camera with high accuracy. The proposed technique can be powerfully applied on small images as well as large images and shows higher accuracy than classical methods. Sunil Kopparapu and Peter Corke [24] proposed a calibration problem for inaccurate and noisy digital images. The proposed system finds the relationship between intrinsic and extrinsic parameters and the calibration matrix. The calibration matrix is derived on the basis of Gaussian distribution. The above relationships are compared with Monte Carlo simulation. B. Anbarasu proposed camera calibration parameter for microaerial vehicles [25]. Intrinsic parameters like focal length, skew, distortion coefficient and principal point are calculated for a sequence of frame images. After calculating intrinsic parameters, extrinsic parameters are estimated using MPU6050 camera sensor module. Using rotational and translation camera calibration vector, microaerial vehicle motion is estimated. Real-time camera calibration is done using a planar pattern.

Nowadays, there are high requirements and demand of systems which have more than one camera, utilized in applications like reality and 3D world, which requires calibration. Manual calibration is not practically possible and also it is a time-consuming work. To calibrate camera automatically, only a very few methods are available. OpenCV library is a well-known and computer vision archive, which provides the option to get chessboard patterns automatically in images via function known as findChessboardCorners(), which is an available inbuilt function. The technique determines the consecutive morphological operators till sequence of black and white area shapes are found and remaining four edges are searched from each shape. The patterns are identified only if all shapes, in this case rectangles, are similar or identical. In a connected network system, these constraints generate a desirable loss in number of image frames. It's infeasible every time to get all the rectangle parts of the chessboard. Using an array of fiducial markers, every pattern is a uniquely desired associated pattern. This method is vigorous to noise to a great extent and it does not at all require finding out the required calibration pattern. The next point to consider is that markers are complex at a certain level and requires to customize algorithms to recognize it. Another way to is to identify calibration points in terms of intersections of lines. The method utilizes a combination of pair of continuous Hough transformation to refine the collinear points of the pattern. Here the consideration is that points required are collinear and make the algorithm likely to distortion and limits its usability limited to cameras that have a low radial distortion.

Other identical method uses corner identification and sorting topologically available squares in a geometric network. The method has to find minimum three circles to find out the orientation of a given pattern. This method is more prone to noise and needs an empirical threshold. This method produces good results to the required part or features of the chessboard image.

Now a system for camera calibration describes automated detecting chessboard pattern. In the first step, specific fast and also x-shaped corner operators are performed to extract the initial point of interest. Delaunay triangulation is used to create geometric mesh with the help of all x-corners. Exploiting regularity of a pattern of a topological filter is proposed. The neighbor triangles and colors are analyzed and only matching pattern triangles are considered as valid. Other remaining points called as valid x-corners and refinement, which is required at a location, is performed locally. The complete calibration pattern does not require to be detected for the calibration process, with less number of points of a coordinated algorithm executed. The algorithm can be utilized in a complex background and is fast enough for online applications.

10.3 Methodology

10.3.1 Projection of a Camera Model

We convert 3D object points into 2D picture points when we project camera models. In order to get a high-quality outcome, the model is frequently based on estimates from a perspective. This pinhole camera can be viewed as a perspective projection from the eyes and

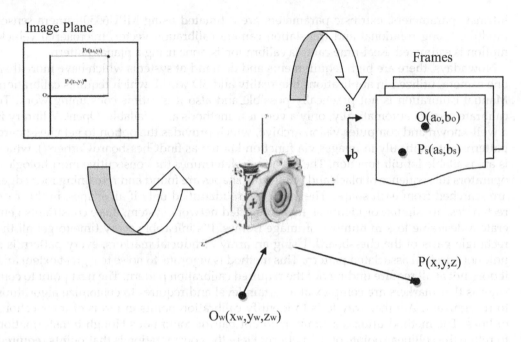

FIGURE 10.2
Camera experimental model.

camera. Now, we'll use the pinhole camera, with some distortion by lens, to show how an image is generated inside a camera and how it's formed.

We'll start by building an ideal pinhole camera model as shown in Figure 10.2.

The perspective transform to be described from the figure, where (x_w, y_w, z_w) is in the 3D world coordinate system, the coordinate of the target point P, and (x_c, y_c, z_c). In the 3D camera parameter system, is the coordinate of the target point P. The image coordinate that corresponds to it will be (a, b). So, the image of 3D points $P = [x_w, y_w, z_w, 1]T$ on the target of a camera $p = [a, b, 1]T$ is defined as the point of view projection of P on p through the optic center O_c, the distance to the image plain being the effective focal length f, which is appropriately given in the matrix equation in the form of homogeneous notation.

$$\lambda p = C[RT]p \tag{10.1}$$

Here λ will be the scale factor, R is the rotation matrix (3×3) and T is the translation vector (3×1), which denotes the relationship between relative and translation rotation parameters of the reference frame and the camera parameters of frame. M is indicated as the matrix of camera with intrinsic parameters and can be denoted as

$$M = \begin{bmatrix} A_x F & 0 & U_0 \\ 0 & A_y F & V_0 \\ 0 & 0 & 1 \end{bmatrix} \tag{10.2}$$

Row and column shows A_x and A_y pixels in numbers represented in per unit distance, and the principal point's coordinates in pixels are a_0 and b_0.

We may claim that the pinhole camera is simply the estimation of a true projection of a camera, but we can't say that it would be valid if great accuracy and zero error were required. Only radial distortion needs to be considered in industrial operations in machine vision applications since distortion is a critical factor that happens and has enormous influence on accuracy and it can be expressed in the following way:

$$x_s = x_d\left(1 + kr_2 s\right) \tag{10.3}$$

$$y_s = y_d\left(1 + kr_2 s\right) \tag{10.4}$$

where, coordinates of image are (x_s, y_s) and lens distortion radial parameters are (x_d, y_d) due to the radial lens distortion, k is denoted as distortion coefficient.

$$r_s^2 = x_s^2 + y_s^2 \tag{10.5}$$

10.3.2 Parameters

Extrinsic, intrinsic, and distortion coefficients are some of the parameters of a camera. To approximate the camera settings, 3-D world points and their corresponding 2-D picture points will be required. These correspondences may be created using many photographs of a calibration pattern, such as a chess board. The function of the parameters are shown in Figure 10.3.

The extrinsic parameters are used to convert the world points to camera coordinates. The intrinsic settings are used to convert the camera coordinates to the picture plane. The calibrating approach generates the matrix of a camera through both intrinsic and extrinsic characteristics. The extrinsic parameters represent a direct conversion from the world 3D ordered system to camera 3D ordered system. A projective translation from 3-D camera coordinates to 2-D picture coordinates is represented by the intrinsic parameters.

The extrinsic parameters are vectors of rotation and a translation. The system coordinate of the camera, which has the beginning on the optical center, define the picture plane. Among the inherent qualities are the focal lengths, optical center, also called as skew coefficient.

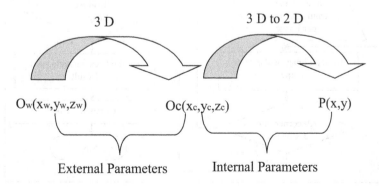

FIGURE 10.3
Function of parameters.

10.3.3 Methodology Used in Calibration

The Zhang technique was utilized to measure the camera in this case. To use the Zhang technique to measure the camera, we must capture a large number of sample photographs (at least 10–20) from different angles, distances, and locations while keeping the camera stable and modifying the test pattern. The main goal of camera measurement is to eliminate picture distortions; shown in Figure 10.4. Thus, the first step is to define our real-world linkages, which are the 3D coordinates of our image (using checkerboard), a computer library's OpenCV module, and statistics. Then we capture photos and read them using the 'imread ()' method, which saves the image to the chosen file and then returns it. The approach yields an empty matrix. ('Mat:: data == NULL')if the image can't be read (as a result of a missing file, incorrect permissions, or an unsupported or corrupt format). We may make our image grayscale by using OpenCV's 'cvtColor ()' function.

Next, we'll use Opencv's built-in 'findChessboardCorners ()' method to find the corners (Testing Board), which returns two values: True or False and a list of corners. True value indicates that we will receive corners, while false indicates that they will not be available. Image (gray), (pattern size), number of inner corners per chessboard line, and columns are among the contents (corners). A list of available corners is provided (flags). We can set you up with an egg or a series of values, like '.CALIB_CB_ADAPTIVE_THRESH ()' to make a picture dark, and utilize adaptive thresholding. There is a set limit level in both black and white (computerized from the central image brightness). 'CALIB CB FAST CHECK ()' 'CALIB CB FAST CHECK ()' 'CALIB C Perform a quick search of the chessboard corners, and if the phone isn't available, unplug it. In a worsening scenario when no chessboard is identified, this can considerably speed up the call. 'CALIB CB NORMALIZE IMAGE()' EqualizeHist adjusts the gamma of a picture before applying a fixed or variable threshold.

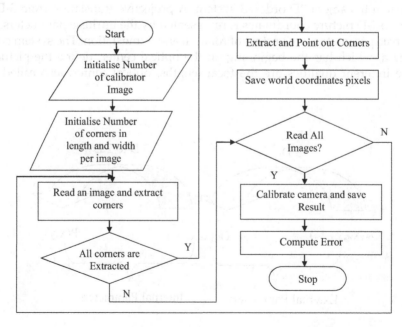

FIGURE 10.4
Calibration flowchart.

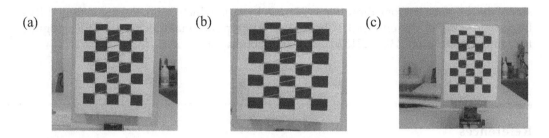

FIGURE 10.5
(a) Experimental representation 1, (b) Experimental representation 2, (c) Experimental representation 3.

When we find the desired number of angles, we process the pixel density and show them in the image termination of the repeated process of refining the corners. Then we use the opencv function 'drawChessboardCorners' that takes a picture, the number of inner corners with the chessboard line and columns, corners, the WasFound pattern, that is, true / false values to show the corners in the image. Finally, we do 3D bypassing points and parallel pixel integration of acquired angles. The 'CalibrateCamera' function from Opencv provides camera matrix, distortion parameter, rotating vector and translation vector.

Using arguments and the 'initUndistortRectifyMap ()' function. The function combines shared consistency with editing adjustments to produce #emap maps as the end result. The warped image seems to be real, as though it were taken with a camera that utilized the camera matrix = new Camera Matrix with less distortion. In a single-lens camera, the new camera matrix is normally the same as the camera matrix, or it can be computerized for better measurement using the # getOptimal New Camera Matrix. #stereo Rectify normally sets the new Camera Matrix to P1 or P2 computer in stereo camera mode.

We may utilize the 'undistort' function in OpenCV. #initUndistortRectifyMap (and R) and #remap are used to create the function (bilinear translation). Details of the adjustments being made can be found in earlier work. The destination picture's pixels that do not match the source image's pixels are filled with zero (black.color).new Camera Matrix can specify a percentage of the original image that will appear in the modified image. To compute the new CameraMatrix that best meets your needs, use # getOptimalNewCameraMatrix.

The #calibrateCamera command used to calculate the camera matrix and distortion characteristics. If the image rectification is different from the measurement resolution, they must be appropriately measured while the distortion coefficients stay the same. These are some of the experimental images we have taken and the corner points show which are used to remove distortion. Experimenting result is shown in Figure 10.5.

10.4 Conclusion

Through the process described above, the digital camera, Olympus 510 uz, was calibrated. The result of the experiment was the camera matrix that included the parameters values of a camera. The corners present in that chessboard pattern were detected successfully. The size of the dataset used for calibration is 52 megabytes in which 56 images are included. The images used are of dimension 3,072×2,304. The computational efficiency of the program for camera calibration is 0.2323153018951416 seconds.

References

1. A. Fetić, D. Jurić and D. Osmanković, "The procedure of a camera calibration using Camera Calibration Toolbox for MATLAB," 35th International Convention MIPRO, 2012, pp. 1752–1757.
2. Kalpana Kumbhar and Ketki P. Kshirasagar, "Comparative study of CCD & CMOS sensors for image processing", *International Journal of Innovative Research in Electrical, Electronics, Instrumentation andControl Engineering*, 194–196, 2015.
3. J. Sun, P. Wang, Z. Qin, and H. Qiao, "Overview of camera calibration for computer vision," 11th World Congress on Intelligent Control and Automation, 2014, pp. 86–92, doi: 10.1109/WCICA.2014.7052692.
4. R. Hartley, "Defending the 8-point algorithm", 5th International Conference on Computer Vision, pp. 1064–1070, June 1995. IEEE Computer Society Press, Boston, MA.
5. Q. Zhu and Y. Li, "A practical estimating method of camera's focal length and extrinsic parameters from a planar calibration image," Second International Conference on Intelligent System Design and Engineering Application, 2012, pp. 138–142, doi: 10.1109/ISdea.2012.505.
6. Y. Dong, X. Ye and X. He, "A novel camera calibration method combined with calibration toolbox and genetic algorithm," 2016 IEEE 11th Conference on Industrial Electronics and Applications (ICIEA), 2016, pp. 1416–1420, doi: 10.1109/ICIEA.2016.7603807.
7. R. I. Hartley, "Self-evaluation algorithm with a few views", IEEE Conference on Computer Vision and Pattern Recognition, Seattle, WA, pp. 908–912, June1994. IEEE.
8. I. Choi and J. Ha, "Easy calibration method for omni-stereo camera system," ICCAS 2010, pp. 2315–2317, doi: 10.1109/ICCAS.2010.5669912.
9. D. Liebowitz and A. Zisserman, "Matrix adjustment of aircraft viewing images", In Proceedings of the IEEE Conference on Computer Vision and Pattern Recognition, Santa Barbara, CA, pp. 482–488, June 1998. IEEE.
10. Z. Zhang, "Movement and structure from two perspectives: From critical boundaries to Euclidean movement through the basic matrix", *Journal of the Optical Society of America A*, 14 (11): 2938–2950,1997.
11. Q.-T. Luong, "Basic Mathematics and calibration vision in the United States:Verses in addition to the autonomous system of robotic systems", PhD Thesis, University de Paris-Sud, Center d'Orsay, Dec. 1992.
12. G. Wei and S. Ma, "Explicit and explicit camera measurement: Theory and testing", *IEEE Transactions on Pattern Analysis and Machine Intelligence*, 16 (5): 469–480,1994.
13. Q.-T. Luong and O. Faugeras, "Self-evaluation of the moving camera from textbook points and basic matrices", *International Journal of Computer Vision*, 22 (3): 261–289,1997.
14. J. More, "Levenberg–Marquardt algorithm, implementation and theory",InG.A. Watson, editor, *Numerical Analysis, Lesson Notes on Mathematics 630*. Springer-Verlag, Berlin,1977.
15. J. Weng, P. Cohen, and M. Herniou, "Measuring the camera with distorted models and checking accuracy", *IEEE Transactions on Pattern Analysis and Machine Intelligence*, 14 (10): 965–980, Oct. 1992.
16. S. J. Maybank and O. D. Faugeras, "Self-portrait of a moving camera", *International Journal of Computer Vision*, 8 (2): 123–152, Aug. 1992.
17. Wang Qi,Fu Li, and Liu Zhenzhong, "Review on camera calibration", 2010 Chinese Control and Decision Conference, 26–28 May 2010, IEEE Xplore,10.1109/CCDC.2010.5498574.

18. Y. M. Wang, Y. Li, and J. B. Zheng, "A camera calibration technique based on OpenCV", The 3rd International Conference on Information Sciences and Interaction Sciences, 23–25 June 2010, IEEE Xplore,10.1109/ICICIS.2010.5534797.

19. Jen-Hui Chuang, Chih-HuiHo, ArdianUmam, HsinYiChen, Mu-TienLu, Jenq-NengHwang, and Tai-AnChen, "A new technique of camera calibration: A geometric approach based on principal lines", 18 August 2019,arXiv:1908.06539.

20. Qian Zheng, Jinnan Chen Zhan Lu Boxin Shi, Xudong Jiangm Kim-Hui Yap, Ling-Yu Duan, and Alex C. Kot, "What does plate glass reveal about camera calibration?" CVPR 2020, Computer Vision Foundation, IEEE Xplore.

21. KaiGuo, HuYe, Junhao Gu, and Honglin Chen, "A novel method for intrinsic and extrinsic parameters estimation by solving perspective-three-point problem with known camera position", *MDPI,Appl. Sci.* 11: 6014, 2021.https://doi.org/ 10.3390/app11136014.

22. Dong-Ming Yan, Guo-Zun Men, and Ying-Kang Zhang, "A method of calibrating the intrinsic and extrinsic camera parameters separately for multi-camera systems", 2007 International Conference on Machine Learning and Cybernetics, 19–22 August 2007, 10.1109/ICMLC.2007.4370391.

23. Kun Yan, Hong Tian, Enhai Liu, Rujin Zhao,Yuzhen Hong, and Dan Zuo, "A decoupled calibration method for camera intrinsic parameters and distortion coefficients", *Hindawi Journal of Mathematical Problems in Engineering*, Dec 2016,doi.org/10.1155/2016/1392832.

24. Sunil Kopparapu and Peter Corke, "The effect of noise on camera calibration parameters", *Graphical Models*, 63(5):277–303, September 2001, https://doi.org/10.1006/gmod.2001.0551.

25. B. Anbarasu, "Camera calibration parameters: An estimation for navigation of micro aerial vehicle", *Research Articles*, 1(2)2021, https://doi.org/10.53659/shareit/2021/8.

11

Audio-Based Recognition of Bird Species Using Deep Learning

Arti Bang, Ambar Bidkar, Vishal Phulmante, and Yashkumar Mundada

CONTENTS

11.1 Introduction

Environmental concerns are now at the forefront of contemporary society's thinking. It is vital to gather information about the diversity of wildlife on a regular basis to analyze changes in our environment. Biodiversity includes all types of species residing on earth. Birds are an integral part of biodiversity. Birds are abundant on earth and are both generalists and specialists as well as locals and migrants. Birds aid in controlling insect population, act as plant dispersal agents, and play a vital role in pollination. Conservation of biodiversity is important for the existence of all the living beings. Some bird species are threatened and becoming extinct due to global climate change. Monitoring a region for presence of bird species is an important task required for the conservation of biodiversity. Birds are difficult to be sighted and they make their presence felt in the surrounding by their sounds. Therefore, surveying of birds is done efficiently through their sounds [1]. Traditionally, bird species identification was done by expert personnel, called as ornithologists. Visual inspection of bioacoustics tool, spectrogram, is also used for bird species identification. Monitoring the spectrograms continuously is a laborious task. Moreover, human decision is subjective. These limitations have

DOI: 10.1201/9781003342755-13

given rise to automatic recognition of bird species from their audio recordings. With the advent of machine learning algorithms, automated processes have opened various doors to recognition by auditory data. Processing of vast datasets containing various classes is challenging, but it definitely surpasses physical manual analysis of the same. Developing a system that can monitor birds through their audio poses many challenges. The basic objective among these issues is to be able to perform relatively well enough at bird species identification. The main goal is to develop a machine learning model that can identify bird species with higher accuracy on the unseen data. This chapter encapsulates classification and identification of bird species through their sounds using convolution neural network (CNN). Two different approaches are considered for the same CNN architecture to perform this task. The first approach is to extract mel spectrograms and the other one is to extract mel frequency cepstral coefficients (MFCC) plots from the audio files. These two different inputs were provided to the CNN model, which in turn gave impressive results.

11.2 Related Work

There is a long history of technical analysis of bird sounds. This field was greatly influenced by the advent of spectrograms in 1950s. Spectrographic bird sound analysis has been described in Thorpe's classic book [2]. Automatic recognition of bird species has been greatly influenced by the work done in other audio content classification [3], music classification [4], and speech recognition systems. Works by Anderson et al. [5] and Kogan and Margoliash [6] are considered to be the starting point for automatic recognition of bird species. They computed spectral features and implemented dynamic time warping (DTW) to classify two bird species. The presence of noise limits the ability of bird identification and at times it may also lead to misclassifications. In [5–7], the sound files are processed with a high pass filter, in order to remove the low-frequency noise. In [8], the broadband noise is reduced using bandpass filters. In [9], spectral subtraction algorithm is implemented to remove background noise. Somervuo et al. [10] classified 14 passerines by representing the bird sound with sinusoidal model, MFCC, and time and frequency parameters called as descriptive features (DF). Classifiers such as Gaussian mixture modeling (GMM) and hidden Markov model (HMM) were implemented and an accuracy up to 70% was reported. In [5], the authors applied a template matching algorithm called as DTW on the spectrograms of the bird species. Kogan and Margoliash [6] extracted linear predictive coefficients and MFCC and then used DTW and HMM for the recognition of two bird species. The method worked well in low-noise environment. The best results were obtained with MFCC and HMM. Selin et al. [11] applied wavelet packet decomposition to identify eight bird species with transient and inharmonic sounds. For feature extraction, wavelet packet decomposition was used and for recognition, self-organizing maps and multilayer perceptron was implemented. In yet another work [12], wavelet packet decomposition is applied and nearest neighbor was used as the classifier. Lopes et al. [13] applied artificial neural networks (ANN) and support vector machine (SVM) on various feature sets for classification of three bird species. In [14], the authors implemented three classification algorithms, viz, decision tree, linear discriminant analysis, and SVM, to accomplish automatic classification of calls of three bird species and nine frogs. Bang and

Rege [9] evaluated the performance of various feature sets such as MFCC, human factor cepstral coefficients, and perceptual linear prediction coefficients using classifiers such as GMM and SVM. Qian et al. [15] extracted acoustic features and applied ReliefF algorithm to accomplish reduction of features. For recognition purpose, a novel machine algorithm called as "extreme learning" was used. In [16], the authors used active learning (AL) and applied unsupervised recognition algorithm. AL is the approach in which few manually annotated samples are used during initial iterations. Stowell and Plumbley [17] derived 12 different feature sets from the mel spectrum and classified using a random forest classifier. These techniques are applied on four large databases of bird vocalizations. In [18], study of animal behavior is done using microphone backpacks, which are placed on the back of flying birds. Scene classification is done using feature learning and probabilistic latent component analysis is designed to perform event detection. Recently, deep learning is gaining immense popularity in pattern recognition. In [19] mel spectrograms of bird sound are used to train a CNN model to identify 24 species of birds and frogs. In [20], the authors have tested two color maps of spectrograms using CNN. In the past years, MFCCs have been extensively used in bird species recognition, audio content classification [21], and speech recognition. Hence, in this work, MFCCs and mel spectrograms are extracted and applied to CNN. The performance of mel spectrograms and MFCCs is compared applied to CNN.

11.3 Methodology

In this work, bird species identification from audio is done by two approaches: the first one is by extracting the spectrograms from the audio files and the second one is by plotting the MFC coefficients. Before extracting the spectrograms or plotting the MFCCs, the audio files need to be filtered, noise reduced, and sliced into equal audio length. After filtering, the spectrograms and MFCC plots are to be extracted. Then these image files are given as input to the CNN model in order to train the model [20] [22]. Input data from both the approaches are given to the same CNN architecture. This is done to compare the results between these two approaches.

11.3.1 Data Collection

The collection of data for the bird species was done from Xeno-Canto collaborative database website [23], which contains over 575,000 sound recordings from more than 10,000 species worldwide. All recordings come under Creative Common Licenses. The recordings are recorded by amateurs with non-professional equipment; hence it is bounded by environmental noises. The data sample duration is between under a second and up to 45 minutes. Every sample is labeled by a prominent species whose audio is clearly heard. In this work, audio files of 15 bird species as shown in Table 11.1 were downloaded from the website. To fasten this process of downloading the data set, a simple Python script was used. Most of the audio mp3 files are sampled at 44.1 kHz, 16 bits, mono channel having various durations. These audio files have significant noise at the background, which is to be taken care of in the prepossessing stage. For the final model, 1,200 samples for training, 300 samples for testing, and 672 samples for validation purposes were used.

TABLE 11.1

Bird Species

Common Name	Scientific Name	Sample Size
Black woodpecker	*Dryocopus martius*	194
Buzzard	*Buteo buteo*	132
Chiffchaff	*Phylloscopus collybita*	195
Crow	Corvus	124
House sparrow	*Passer domesticus*	128
Kingfisher	Alcedinidae	162
Long-eared owl	*Asio otus*	140
Common quail	*Coturnix coturnix*	125
Common rosefinch	*Carpodacus erythrinus*	172
Sandpiper	Scolopacidae	125
Scops owl	Otus	120
Toucan	Ramphastidae	120
Common whitethroat	*Sylvia communis*	175
Greater yellowlegs	*Tringa melanoleuca*	120
Yellow-throated bulbul	*Pycnonotus xantholaemus*	140

11.3.2 Data Pre-Processing

The data set comprising of more than 2,000 audio samples of 15 bird species were collected from Xeno-Canto collaborative database [23]. The data set had audio recordings with various duration from 4 s to over 40+ s. These audio files had a lot of background noises and even some of the audio files had other bird species in the background. The audio files are not time coded to the point where the bird is actually calling/singing. The collected audio samples were in MP3 file format. The conversion of these MP3 files into the .WAV format was done by free to use "Any Audio Converter" software. The .WAV files were then processed for any distortion, noise, or any unwanted audio components using noise reduce Python library. Then to filter these noise-reduced audio files, a fourth order high pass Butterworth filter was used. Since most of the birds have sound frequencies over 500 Hz, the cut-off frequency was selected as 500 Hz for the Butterworth filter.

Later on multiple audio chunks of length 9 s were created from a long audio file. A long audio file resulted in cluttered spectrograms, which made it harder for the model to train and test the data, which in turn reduced the accuracy. Whereas in the case of chunks of audio data, the features were clearly visible and evenly distributed, which ensured that the model was trained and tested efficiently. Figure 11.1 shows the difference between the spectrogram of raw and filtered audio files of the bird species. The raw file has distortion but its filtered version shows little to no distortion and has a sharper pattern.

The data collection was done for the 15 bird species. For each bird species more than 100 samples were collected. Then from these samples of each species, 80 samples were chosen randomly for training, 20 samples were chosen for testing and remaining samples of each species was used for evaluation. Hence there were more than 650 samples in the evaluation set.

11.3.3 Spectrograms

Spectrograms are images that represent the frequency content of a signal, which varies with time. In a spectrogram, the X-axis denotes time, Y-axis denotes frequency, while intensity of color is used to represent the magnitude of a specific frequency at specific time in a color-coded format [24]. The spectrogram images of 1,440 × 720 pixels were used

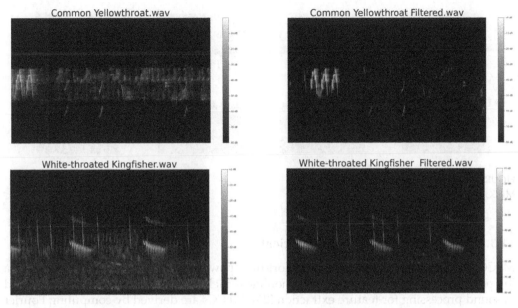

FIGURE 11.1
Spectrograms of RAW and filtered audio files.

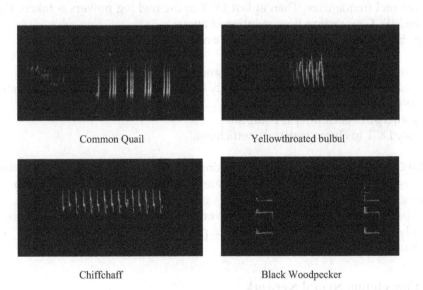

FIGURE 11.2
Spectrograms of bird sounds.

to represent the filtered audio file. The spectrograms were obtained using the built-in function of librosa library of Python. The features were extracted from the audio file by using 250 numbers of mels with min frequency of 500 Hz, the sampling rate is set to 22,050 Hz and max frequency to half of sampling rate. The number of FFT were set to 1,024 with hop length of 256. Hanning window is used keeping its length same as number of FFT. Figure 11.2 shows the spectrograms of four bird sounds.

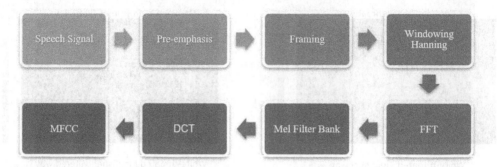

FIGURE 11.3
MFCC extraction flow.

11.3.4 Mel Frequency Cepstral Coefficient

MFCC is an illustration of a sound's short-time power spectrum. Cosine transform of a log power spectrum is computed on a nonlinear mel scale of frequencies, which is used in sound processing for feature extraction [25]. MFCCs are derived by computing Fourier transform of a windowed portion of a signal. It maps these spectrums on the mel scale using triangular overlapping or cosine overlapping windows. Log of the power is taken at each of the mel frequencies. Then at last DCT of the mel log powers is taken. Figure 11.3 shows the MFCC extraction flow mentioned above.

The steps involved in extracting MFCCs are as follows:

- Segment the signal into short frames and apply windowing like Hanning.
- For each frame, find its spectral density by characterizing it in the frequency domain.
- Apply Mel filterbank.
- Log energy of each filter is computed.
- Apply DCT to obtain cepstral coefficients.

The MFC coefficients were extracted using the inbuilt feature of librosa library. The parameters used for extracting MFCC were: Number of MFCCs = 13, Fmin = 500Hz, Number of FFT = 1024, Hop length = 256.

Using the librosa library, these MFCCs were plotted into logarithmic scale as shown in Figures 11.4 to 11.7. The parameters used to plot the MFCCs: X_axis = time, Y_axis = log, Fmax = Sample_rate / 2.

11.3.5 Convolution Neural Network

Deep learning networks are multiple layers of artificial neural networks. It helps to develop, train, and use these neural networks on large datasets [20, 22] There is a huge room for tweaks to current existing models. Convolutional neural networks (CNN) are an important class of deep neural networks.

11.3.6 Model Architecture

As spectrograms and MFCC plots are in image format, CNN architecture is chosen to perform the task. Five conv2D layers are used. The 3×3 kernel size is chosen with Relu as an

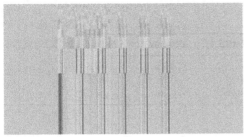

FIGURE 11.4a
MFCC plot of common quail.

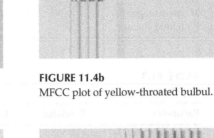

FIGURE 11.4b
MFCC plot of yellow-throated bulbul.

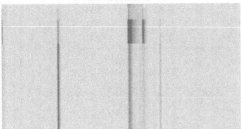

FIGURE 11.4c
MFCC plot of black woodpecker.

FIGURE 11.4d
MFCC plot of chiffchaff.

activation function and keeping the padding to 'same'. With each convolution layer, a max pooling layer and batch normalization is implemented. At last, the flatten layer is used followed by a dense layer of 512 units. To generalize the model properly and to prevent the model from overfitting, one dropout layer is used with a shut off probability of 0.3.

The model is later trained for more than 50 epochs with batch size of 32 using an Adam optimizer. The model is then fine-tuned for another 30 epochs keeping lower learning rate (0.0001). The early stopping is used to get the best performance and to overcome overfitting. For early stopping, 'model checkpoint callback' function is used. The entire training of the model is done on the Google colab platform as it provides the adequate GPU and memory resources for smooth operations. Using the GPU resources for training the model significantly decreases the training time as compared to normal training procedures on the CPU.

11.4 Results and Discussion

11.4.1 Spectrogram Model

The model based on the spectrograms of the audio files gave an impressive result. This model performed very well on the evaluation dataset with an accuracy of 96% as shown in Table 11.2 and 97% as shown in Table 11.3 on the test dataset. For this model, almost 13 birds showed F1 score of more than 0.90 while only two birds had F1 score of around 0.85 (Figures 11.8 and 11.10). Figures 11.9 and 11.11 show the confusion matrix. From Figures 11.8 and 11.10, it can be seen that the identification of bird 'yellowthroat' is found

TABLE 11.2
Results of Evaluation Dataset

Parameter	Precision	Recall	F1 score	Support
Accuracy			0.96	672
Macro average	0.96	0.97	0.96	672
Weighted average	0.96	0.96	0.96	672

TABLE 11.3
Results of Test Dataset

Parameter	Precision	Recall	F1 score	Support
Accuracy			0.97	300
Macro average	0.97	0.97	0.97	300
Weighted average	0.97	0.97	0.97	300

	precision	recall	f1-score	support
Black Woodpecker	1.00	0.95	0.97	94
Buzzard	0.91	0.97	0.94	32
Chiffchaff	0.98	0.96	0.97	95
Crow	1.00	0.96	0.98	24
House Sparrow	0.82	1.00	0.90	28
Kingfisher	1.00	1.00	1.00	62
Long eared Owl	0.93	1.00	0.96	40
Quail	1.00	1.00	1.00	25
Rosefinch	0.93	0.97	0.95	72
Sandpiper	1.00	1.00	1.00	25
Scops Owl	1.00	1.00	1.00	20
Toucan	1.00	1.00	1.00	20
Whitethroat	0.90	0.88	0.89	75
Yellowlegs	0.95	1.00	0.98	20
Yellowthroat	0.91	0.80	0.85	40
accuracy			0.96	672
macro avg	0.96	0.97	0.96	672
weighted avg	0.96	0.96	0.96	672

FIGURE 11.5a
Statistics of the evaluation dataset.

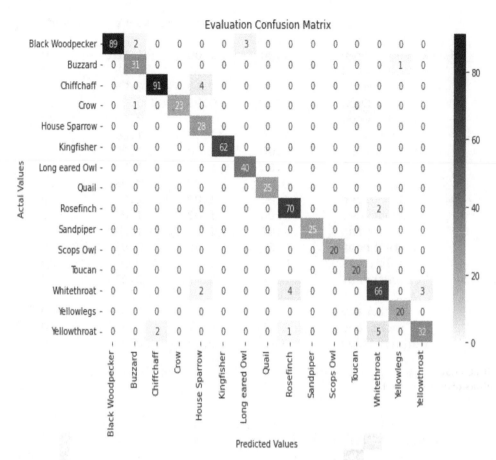

FIGURE 11.5b
Evaluation confusion matrix.

to be slightly less accurate when compared to other birds with a F1 score of 0.85. The parameters like accuracy, macro average, and weighted average have a value of 0.96 as shown in Table 11.3.

11.4.2 MFCC Model

The results for the MFCC model were also equally good with over 95% accuracy on the evaluation dataset as shown in Table 11.4 while 96% on the test dataset as shown in Table 11.5. Similar to the first model, this model also showed a F1 score of more than 0.90 for 13 birds and 0.84+ for remaining two birds as shown in Figures 11.12–11.15. The values of accuracy, macro average, and weighted average for evaluation dataset were 0.95, 0.94, and 0.95 respectively as shown in Table 11.5.

	precision	recall	f1-score	support
Black Woodpecker	1.00	1.00	1.00	20
Buzzard	0.95	0.95	0.95	20
Chiffchaff	0.91	1.00	0.95	20
Crow	1.00	0.95	0.97	20
House Sparrow	0.95	1.00	0.98	20
Kingfisher	1.00	1.00	1.00	20
Long eared Owl	1.00	1.00	1.00	20
Quail	1.00	1.00	1.00	20
Rosefinch	0.95	1.00	0.98	20
Sandpiper	1.00	1.00	1.00	20
Scops Owl	1.00	1.00	1.00	20
Toucan	1.00	1.00	1.00	20
Whitethroat	0.85	0.85	0.85	20
Yellowlegs	0.95	1.00	0.98	20
Yellowthroat	0.94	0.75	0.83	20
accuracy			0.97	300
macro avg	0.97	0.97	0.97	300
weighted avg	0.97	0.97	0.97	300

FIGURE 11.5c
Statistics of the test dataset.

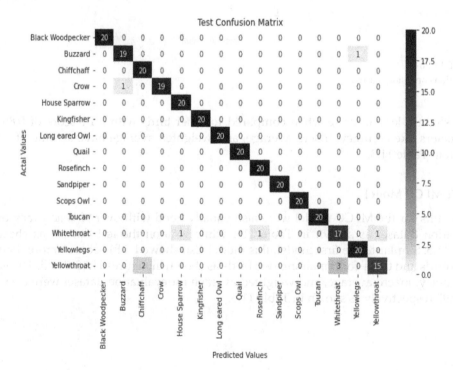

FIGURE 11.5d
Test dataset confusion matrix.

	precision	recall	f1-score	support
Black Woodpecker	0.96	0.84	0.90	95
Buzzard	0.96	0.78	0.86	32
Chiffchaff	1.00	0.99	0.99	95
Crow	0.89	1.00	0.94	24
House Sparrow	1.00	1.00	1.00	28
Kingfisher	0.98	0.98	0.98	62
Long eared Owl	0.97	0.90	0.94	40
Quail	1.00	1.00	1.00	25
Rosefinch	0.83	1.00	0.91	72
Sandpiper	0.77	0.92	0.84	25
Scops Owl	0.95	0.95	0.95	20
Toucan	1.00	0.95	0.97	20
Whitethroat	1.00	0.95	0.97	75
Yellowlegs	0.87	1.00	0.93	20
Yellowthroat	0.95	0.97	0.96	40
accuracy			0.95	673
macro avg	0.94	0.95	0.94	673
weighted avg	0.95	0.95	0.95	673

FIGURE 11.6a
Evaluation dataset statistics.

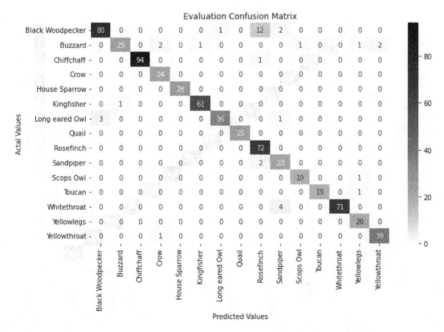

FIGURE 11.6b
Evaluation dataset confusion matrix.

	precision	recall	f1-score	support
Black Woodpecker	0.94	0.85	0.89	20
Buzzard	0.94	0.85	0.89	20
Chiffchaff	1.00	1.00	1.00	20
Crow	1.00	1.00	1.00	20
House Sparrow	1.00	1.00	1.00	20
Kingfisher	0.95	0.95	0.95	20
Long eared Owl	1.00	0.90	0.95	20
Quail	1.00	1.00	1.00	20
Rosefinch	0.87	1.00	0.93	20
Sandpiper	0.95	1.00	0.98	20
Scops Owl	0.95	0.95	0.95	20
Toucan	1.00	0.95	0.97	20
Whitethroat	1.00	1.00	1.00	20
Yellowlegs	0.87	1.00	0.93	20
Yellowthroat	1.00	1.00	1.00	20
accuracy			0.96	300
macro avg	0.97	0.96	0.96	300
weighted avg	0.97	0.96	0.96	300

FIGURE 11.6c
Test dataset statistics.

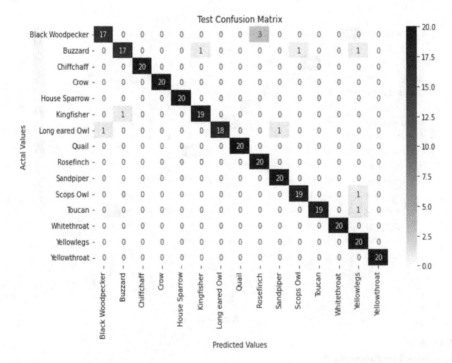

FIGURE 11.6d
Test dataset confusion matrix.

TABLE 11.4
Results of Evaluation Dataset

Parameter	Precision	Recall	F1 score	Support
Accuracy	-	-	0.95	673
Macro average	0.94	0.95	0.94	673
Weighted average	0.95	0.95	0.95	673

TABLE 11.5
Results of Test Dataset

Parameter	Precision	Recall	F1 score	Support
Accuracy	-	-	0.96	300
Macro average	0.97	0.96	0.96	300
Weighted average	0.97	0.96	0.96	300

11.5 Conclusion and Future Work

In the recent years, there has been steady increase in the field of bird species recognition using audio and machine learning. Spectrogram and MFCC feature extraction methods found to be extremely useful for audio data classification. This also showed the performance benefit of machine learning algorithms for real-world problems. The CNN architecture performed excellently on this type of dataset. For future work, the dataset can be tested on different neural network architectures like RCNN and more. Recognizing different audio patterns like singing, calling, distress, and mating calls of the birds can be done, but it could be challenging considering the dataset availability and neural network limitations.

References

1. T. S. Brandes, "Automated sound recording and analysis techniques for bird surveys and conservation", *Bird Conservation International*, 18: 163–173, 2008.
2. W. H. Thorpe, "The process of song-learning in the chaffinch as studied by means of the sound spectrograph", *Nature*, 173: 465–469, 1954.
3. E. Wold, T. Blum, D. Keislar, and J. Wheaton, "Content based classification, search, and retrieval of audio", *IEEE Multimedia* 3: 27–36, 1996.
4. M. F. McKinney, and J. Breebaart, "Features for audio and music classification", *Proceedings of the Int. Symposium on Music Information Retrieval*, 2003.
5. S. E. Anderson, A. S. Dave, and D. Margoliash, "Template-based automatic recognition of birdsong syllables from continuous recordings", *Journal of Acoustical Society of America*, 100(2): 1209–1219, 1996.
6. J. Kogan and D. Margolash, "Automated recognition of bird song elements from continuous recordings using dynamic time warping and hidden Markov models: A comparative study", *Journal of Acoustical Society of America*, 103(4): 2187–2196, 1998.

7. V. M. Trifa, A. N. G. Kirschel, and C. E. Taylor, "Automated species recognition of antbirds in a Mexican rainforest using hidden Markov models", *Journal of Acoustical Society of America*, 123(4): 2424–2431, 2008.
8. A. Selin, J. Turunen, and J. T. Tanttu, "Wavelets in recognition of bird sounds", *EURASIP Journal on Advances in Signal Processing*, Article ID 51806, 9 pages, 2007. doi:10.1155/2007/51806
9. A. V. Bang and P. P. Rege, "Evaluation of various feature sets and feature selection towards automatic recognition of bird species", *International Journal of Computational Applications and Technology*, 56(3): 172–184, 2017.
10. P. Somervuo, A. Harma, and S. Fagurland, "Parametric representations of bird sounds for automatic species recognition", *IEEE Transactions on Audio, Speech and Language Processing*, 14(6): 2252–2263, 2006.
11. A. Selin, J. Turunen, and J. Tanttu, "Wavelets in recognition of bird sounds", *EURASIP Journal on Advances in Signal Processing*, 9 : 2007.
12. A. Bang and P. Rege, "Classification of bird species based on bioacoustics", *International Journal of Advances in Computer Science and Its Applications*, 4(1): 184–188, 2014.
13. M. Lopes, A. Koerich, C. Cilla, and C. Kaestner, "Feature set comparison for automatic bird species identification," *Proceedings of the IEEE International Conference on System, Man, Cybernetics, and Anchorage*, 965–970, 2011.
14. M. Acevedo, C. Bravo, H. Bravo, L. Rivera, and T. Aide. 2009. "Automated classification of bird and amphibian calls using machine learning: A comparison of methods", *Ecological Informatics*, 4: 206–214.
15. K. Qian, Z. Zhang, A. Baird, F. Ringeval, and B. Schuller, "Bird sounds classification by large scale acoustic features and extreme machine learning", Proc. of GlobalSIP, Orlando, Florida, USA, 1317–1321, 2015. DOI: 10.1109/GlobalSIP.2015.7418412
16. K. Qian, Z. Zhang, A Baird, and B. Schuller, "Active learning for bird sounds classification," *Journal of ActaAcustica United with Acustica*, 361–364: 2017. DOI 10.3813/AAA.919064
17. D. Stowell and M. D. Plumbley, "Automatic large-scale classification of bird sounds is strongly improved by unsupervised feature learning", *PeerJ*, 2:e488, 31, 2014, DOI 10.7717/peerj.488.
18. D. Stowell, E. Benetos, and L. Gill, "On-bird sound recordings: automatic acoustic recognition of activities and contexts", *ACM Transactions on Audio, Speech, and Language Processing*, 25(6): 1193–1206, 2017.
19. J. LeBien et al., "A pipeline for identification of bird and frog species in tropical soundscape recordings using a convolutional neural network", *Ecological Informatics* 59: 101113, 2020.
20. Á. Incze et al., "Bird sound recognition using a convolutional neural network", IEEE 16th International Symposium on Intelligent Systems and Informatics, 2018, pp. 295–300, doi: 10.1109/SISY.2018.8524677.
21. P. Dhanalaxmi, S. Palanivel, and V. Ramalingam, "Classification of audio signals using SVM and RBFNN", *Expert System with Applications*, 36(3): 6069–6075, 2008.
22. G. Chen, et al., "Deep convolutional neural network based species recognition for wild life monitoring", IEEE International Conference on Image Processing (ICIP), 2014, pp. 858–862. doi: 10.1109/ICIP.2014.7025172
23. www.zeno-canto.org
24. D. Lucio, Y. Maldonado, and G. da Costa, "Bird species classification using spectrograms", Latin American Computing Conference, 2015, pp. 1–11. doi: 10.1109/CLEI.2015.7359990.
25. Arti Bang and Priti Rege, "Recognition of bird species from their sounds using data reduction technique", 7th International Conference on Computer and Communication Technology, ACM digital library, November 2017, doi:10.1145/3154979.3155002.

Section III

Data Science and Analysis for Intelligence and Enterprise

12

Development of a Mathematical Model for Milk Evaporation Process

Vijaya N. Aher and Ganesh S. Sable

CONTENTS

12.1 Introduction

India is known throughout the world for its agriculture base, and dairy industry is one of the key industries based on agricultural produce called raw milk. Milk production in India increased from 17 million tons in 1950–51 to 84.6 million tons in 2001–02. In the 1960s, India has rapidly positioned itself as the world's largest producer of milk. Although per capita consumption in India is lowest by developing country standards, it is one of the lowest in the world. Consumption of 280 grams of milk per day is recommended by the Indian Council of Medical Research (ICMR).

In India, milk production is increased to 208 million tons (MT) in 2021 from 198 MT in 2020 and 187.7 MT in 2019. With increase in milk production, per capita availability went up to 428 g per day in 2021.

The performance of the Indian dairy sector during the past three decades has been truly impressive. Milk production grew at an average annual rate of 4.6% during the 1970s, 5.7% during the 1980s, and 4.2% during the 1990s. Until 1991, the Indian dairy industry

DOI: 10.1201/9781003342755-15

was highly regulated and protected [55]. On the basis of the experience of a visit paid to dairy industries such as National Dairy Research Institute (NDRI), Arey milk schemes, it is observed that hardly any instrumentation exists in dairy industry and lot of scope exists for the improvement of process techniques, optimization, and efficiency at every stage of the process. Through behavioral and deterministic modeling techniques, one can achieve proper and optimal control action, as controller design is totally based on process modeling and analysis. In short, process modeling provides a platform for optimal control actions in terms of minimization of process timings, thereby saving the useful energy resources, efficient control of process parameters in closure limits to deliver maximum output in a short span of time to achieve efficiency in milk evaporation process. The evaporated milk at higher density makes it preservable and hence the milk evaporation process in dairy industry assumes great importance due to the importance of the final product. Hence the process of milk evaporation is considered for this research.

12.2 Literature Review

The purpose of this research is to control milk evaporation by developing a mathematical model. Hence, research work involves process studies, identification of variables, process characterization, system identification, process modelling, and controller design for the process based on model development and simulation.

The area of work lies in the domain of industry and specific area is dairy industry. The global overview of dairy sector in developing countries is given by Vivien Knips in his report "Living from Livestock" [1]. The dairy manufacturing process steps are covered in a report [2] called Fact Sheet: Food Manufacturing series brought out by the United Nations Environmental Program. Many books are available in the area of milk and milk processes and four books have been referred in this research proposal. The milk components and related processes are well described by [3] and same reference also covers the process of milk concentration by evaporation. The technology aspects of dairy products (technology of concentrated milk product manufacture) [4] are covered in a book edited by Ralph Early. We are particularly interested in products related to evaporated milk from the angle of utility of evaporated milk. Milk and milk products [5] are covered in a book written by Alan H. Varnam. The last reference in this area of dairy related information covers Indian milk products [6]. The concept of evaporated milk was first reported in *Scientific American* in 1857–1860. The three articles [7–] written by Borden Gail revolutionized the manufacturing of evaporated milk and related milk products from the point of milk preservation. Since the proposed work focuses on the evaporated milk process, a reference has been made to these documents. More detailed information about milk concentration and evaporation [10] can be found in book written by Dr.-Ing. Pieter Walstra.

Christian Kiesner et al. describe the concentration process for milk by multistage flash evaporation [11]. A journal article [12] and patent [13] also describe milk evaporation and a process for the preparation of evaporated milk. Detailed treatment for milk evaporation in commercial equipment [14] is described in a report of Agriculture Research Service (ARS) of United States Department of Agriculture (USDA), Eastern Regional Research Centre.

The commercial equipment [15–17, 18] for carrying out milk evaporation has great significance from the angle of determination of various constants to be used in mathematical equations for modeling. Process modeling requires the identification of number of process variables those are required to control that particular process based on the degree of freedom. Degree of freedom for liquid, solid, and vapor phase systems can be judged by degree of freedom equation [19] based on Gibbs phase rule [20]. A detailed study of process and equipment used for carrying out the process gives an idea of variables affecting that particular process. The number of control variables can be limited to the degree of freedom of the process and are chosen from the variables that affect the process. We intend to develop a behavioral model [21] of the process suitable for the control of process under consideration. Models can be developed by using theoretical as well as practical methods [22]. The theoretical model building for most of the industrial processes proceeds with process studies. Process studies deal with material balance, energy balance, volume, pressure, and temperature, which are most common in every industrial process. In case of practical model building, one can obtain the process models using practical measurements [23, 24] on the dynamic processes. System identification is a general term to describe mathematical tools and algorithms that build dynamical models from the measured data. The specific case of system identification for falling film vacuum evaporators [25] is described in a reference by Peter Cunningham et al. Many industrial processes are multi-input and multi-output (MIMO) processes [26], which are complex in nature where every output variable is affected by multiple input variables. Such processes are also referred as cross-coupled processes, which are extremely difficult to control as set point changes related to one variable gets reflected in to other. MIMO processes and their dynamics play an important role in understanding the behavior of the processes. There are number of reference for process dynamics; however, the reference is made to about eight relevant papers. The various articles by various authors such as papers by Dutton et al., Spano et al., Javalagi et al., and Gupta et al. cover general modelling and system dynamics [27–30], Mc Coy et al. consider various aspects [31] of planning, modelling and dynamics, Horvath et al. worked on multilevel modeling [32] using object oriented approach while Biao Huang at al. mainly focused on the online control performance monitoring [33] of MIMO control systems.

As we know that there are theoretical and practical approaches for model building related to processes or controllers, identification pertains to practical modeling case where from measurements [34] related to process or control action or system (both process and controller together) lead to model development. Prominent identification techniques employ online methods [34], least square [36, 37], methods and perception [38] based methods. Isik et al. worked on an identification of feed-forward systems [39].

Many researchers also worked for process dynamics estimation [40] and optimization [41] before process models are subjected to control action using controllers. Optimization of dynamics is also applicable to processes [42], controllers, and systems [43] as a whole. It is imperative that behavior of the process is to be predicted [44] that enables the researcher to design the suitable controller for the process under consideration.

There are many research papers in the area of controllers and many researchers have attempted the design of controllers based on many different aspects such as control laws [45], design for MIMO systems [46, 47], and controllers for time delay [48,49] components. Yet another class of controllers are designed for taking care of time-varying process dynamics called adaptive control [50] systems.

Design of controllers for complex cross-coupled industrial processes is a major issue and people have attempted to design controllers for such processes so that set points can only be used to control related output variable without disturbing other variable. Such controllers have been often called decoupled controllers [51,52,53].

Since not much work is done in the area of decoupling control aspects of milk evaporation process, it has been difficult to locate specific papers related to the control of
milk evaporation process used in dairy industry. However, general paper related to
evaporation process [54] control titled "Simulation and Control of a Multiple Effect
Evaporator" has been referred, which seems to be more closer for the type of work we are
perusing.

12.3 Gaps in Existing Research

The research problem pertains to design of controllers for complex cross-coupled MIMO
milk evaporation process used in dairy industry. This specific industrial problem has been
chosen because of the importance and role of evaporated milk in producing other milk
products. The evaporated milk is preservable and can be used as base product for other
milk products and it is used as an ingredient for traditional Indian milk products.

From the existing literature, we have not come across any significant work on the behavioral process model development for milk evaporation process that can characterize the
process of milk evaporation. Hence the development of behavioral model for the milk
evaporation process is proposed that can ultimately be used for designing the controller.
Milk evaporation is MIMO complex cross-coupled process and it is a challenging to design
the controller for such process that will lead to decoupling of overall controlled process.

Although some work has been done on the general decoupling concept, only few references
[52, 53, 54] exist in these areas. In some cases, the combination of Proportional Integral
Derivative (PID) control algorithms is used to reduce the effects of coupling while in other
cases adaptive control algorithms are used, leading to more complex solutions and techniques.

To bridge the above gaps, we have planned to work on decoupling mechanism that can
achieve dead-bit response by transfer function adjustments in the overall system model.

12.4 Milk Evaporation Process

The typical steps involved for characterization of milk evaporation process is to identify
output control and input manipulation variables required for the milk evaporation process and to develop the mathematical relations between these variables to form a model of
the process, which ultimately characterizes the milk evaporation process falling film milk
evaporator is as shown in Figure 12.1.

12.4.1 Falling Film Heat Exchanger

The milk to be targeted is allowed to flow through the pinnacle of the heating tubes and
allotted in this type of manner as to float down the inside of the tube walls as a thin film. The
liquid film starts to boil due to the outdoor heating of the tubes and is in part evaporated as
a result. The milk downward goes together with the glide, precipitated initially by means
of manner of gravity, which is superior through the parallel, downward flow goes with
the flow of the vapor.

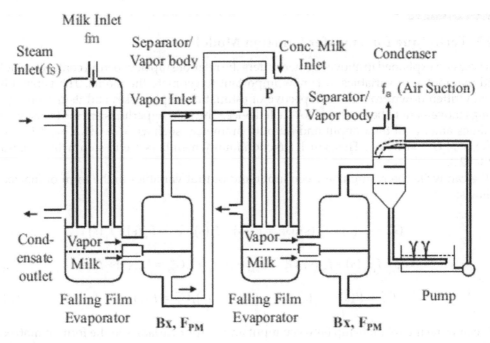

FIGURE 12.1
Falling film milk evaporator.

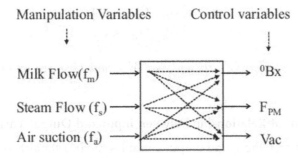

FIGURE 12.2
Milk evaporation process models.

12.4.2 Vapor Separator

In this stage, liquid is separated from the vapor. This is again used for the next evaporation level.

12.4.3 Condenser

This is the last stage of falling film evaporator. In this stage, sucked and condensed vapors are generated. Vacuum is created by cold water spray and hence boiling temperature is reduced.

The system of milk evaporation is finished in vacuum evaporators as established in Figure 12.2.

12.5 Technique for Transfer Function Model

The version explained in above segment offers the relationship between all control variables and manipulation variables. It is now important to estimate the model. The version has been written down from the perspective of estimation of processes and its use on top of things movement to be provided for such device. The pass hyperlinks are the transfer capabilities among all three input and output parameters such as G^P_{11}, G^P_{12}, G^P_{13}; G^P_{21}, G^P_{22}, G^P_{23}; G^P_{31}, G^P_{32} and G^P_{33}. The switch function family members are in step with Equations 12.1–12.3.

We can write the relation between input and output variables in the form of matrix as follows:

$$G^P_{11} = B_x(s) \div f_m(s), G^P_{12} = B_x(s) \div f_s(s), G^P_{13} = B_x(s) \div f_a(s) \tag{12.1}$$

$$G^P_{21} = F_{PM}(s) \div f_m(s), G^P_{22} = F_{PM}(s) \div f_s(s), G^P_{23} = F_{PM}(s) \div f_a(s) \tag{12.2}$$

$$G^P_{31} = P(s) \div f_m(s), G^P_{32} = P(s) \div f_s(s), G^P_{33} = P(s) \div f_a(s) \tag{12.3}$$

We can write the relationship between input and output variables in the form of matrix as follows:

$$G^P = \begin{pmatrix} G^P_{11} & G^P_{12} & G^P_{13} \\ G^P_{21} & G^P_{22} & G^P_{23} \\ G^P_{31} & G^P_{32} & G^P_{33} \end{pmatrix} \tag{12.4}$$

where G^P_{11}, G^P_{12}, G^P_{13}; G^P_{21}, G^P_{22}, G^P_{23}; G^P_{31}, G^P_{32}, and G^P_{33} are as given in Equations 12.1–12.3.

12.5.1 Development of Relationship between Input and Output Variables

The relationship between input and output variables can be established by applying input step function and the response can be plotted. The milk has diverse components including fats (f), solid non fats (snf), and water (w). As a result, Brix and fats purity (FP) are written inside the shape of their person hundreds, which include M_f, M_{snf}, and M_w as proven in Equations 12.5 and 12.6.

$$B_X = (M_f + M_{snf}) / (M_f + M_{snf} + M_w) \tag{12.5}$$

$$FP = (M_f) / (M_f + M_{snf}) \tag{12.6}$$

We have boiled milk in a vessel, which is closed vessel and pressure is reduced and hence it reduces the boiling temperature also. Normally the boiling is done at 600°C by way of keeping a vacuum of 25 inches of Hg. Considering the fact that boiling is suffering from strain (P), this is our third control variable.

12.5.2 Relationship between Bx, FP, and f_m

The reaction of Bx is acquired by using mass stability equations

$$M_m = M_{mi} + M_{ma} \tag{12.7}$$

The component's initial value of milk in vessel is obtained by

$$M_{fi} = (FP_{mi} \div 100)*(Bx_{mi} \div 100)*(M_{mi}) \tag{12.8}$$

$$M_{wi} = [1-(Bx_{mi} \div 100)]*(M_{mi})]M_{snfi} = [1-(FP_{mi} \div 100)]*(Bx_{mi} \div 100)*(M_{mi}) \tag{12.9}$$

$$M_{fa} = (FP_m \div 100)*(Bx_{mi} \div 100)*(f_m \Delta T) \tag{12.10}$$

Mass of milk introduced is $(f_m \Delta T)$. as a result, we get the subsequent equations:

$$M_{fa} = (FP_m \div 100)*(Bx_{mi} \div 100)*(f_m \Delta T) \tag{12.11}$$

$$M_{wa} = [1-(Bx_{mi} \div 100)]*(f_m \Delta T)M_{snfa} = [1-(FP_m \div 100)]*(Bx_{mi} \div 100)*(f_m \Delta T) \tag{12.12}$$

$$M_{fa} = (FP_m \div 100)*(Bx_{mi} \div 100)*(M_{mi}) \tag{12.13}$$

It is increasing by successive additions and they are computed as follows:

$$M_f = M_{fP} + M_{fa} \tag{12.14}$$

$$M_{snf} = M_{snfP} + M_{snfa} \tag{12.15}$$

$$M_w = M_{wP} + M_{wa} \tag{12.16}$$

Every time the C++ application has been written responses are received with respect to time. The reaction of milk has been received. For calculating (FPm) values, we've taken into consideration the values of input milk (Bxm) to the evaporator as constant and hence fat purity (FP) values stay constant (as it's far a ratio of mass of fats component with respect to overall stable component in the milk). But the fat component will change immediately if Brix of input milk (Bxm) goes on converting due to fact that the milk received could have unique fat contents. Applying curve-becoming techniques to various parameters to above stated statistics, deterministic members of the family can be hooked up to update τ_{Bxfm} as a feature of M_{mi}. The equation as a consequence can be written as follows:

$$\tau_{Bxfm} = (-2.4) \times 10^{-9} * M_{mi}^2 + (1.1717) \times 10^{-4} * M_{mi} + 0.248 \tag{12.17}$$

12.5.3 Relationship among Milk Concentration (Bx), FP, and f_s

Relation of Bx is obtained by

$$M_m = M_{mi} - Mw_{ev} \tag{12.18}$$

The evaporated water is now calculated using energy balance equation:

$$H_{in} = H_c + H_{out} \tag{12.19}$$

$$f_s * L_s = M_m * C_m * T_m + f_v * L_v \tag{12.20}$$

$$f_v = \left(f_s * L_s - M_m * C_m * T_m \right) \div L_v \tag{12.21}$$

The water evaporated in time ΔT is given by equation as $M_{wev} = f_v \Delta T$.

12.5.4 Relationship of Time Constant (τ_{Bxfs}) and M_{mi}

The statistics regarding relation of time constant (τ_{Bxfs}) and (M_{mi}) is decided.

$$\tau_{Bxfs} = (1.248) \times 10^{-10} \times M_{mi}^3 - (1 \cdot 949) \times 10^{-6} * M_{mi}^2 + 0.01343 * M_{mi} - 13.62 \tag{12.22}$$

The fat purity (FP) again remains constant because it is the ratio of two solid quantities.

12.5.5 Relationship between Pressure (P) and f_a

Evaporation of milk is done under vacuum that is generated by way of sucked and condensed air. The amount air in vessel at specific time is given by

$$M_a = M_{ai} + M_{aev} \tag{12.23}$$

The equation for air removed is

$$M_{aev} = f_a * \Delta t \tag{12.24}$$

Pressure is given by

$$P = P_{prev} - \Delta P \tag{12.25}$$

The subsequent equation indicates relation between P and f_a for falling film evaporator.

$$G_{33}^P (s) = (4.4 * 0.075 * s) \div (1 + 0.075 * s) \tag{12.26}$$

12.6 Conclusion

Evaporation being one of the crucial device steps in a Dairy Corporation from the point of view of preservation, it was taken up for research in this chapter considering several factors controlling this method. As a way to manipulate the method, mathematical modeling plays an important role and is to be derived from the previous examples. Therefore, in this work, attempts had been made to derive the switch elements of standard switch matrix of the method of milk evaporation and the steps involved in the reaction are also factored in the model. The model presented right here is based totally on recursive calculations of several components of the method in real time. The mathematical expressions are derived to predict the way dynamics, which in the long run, lead us to format the controller in the way we desire. It's also highlighted that the process is a complex and move coupled, Usually, the controllers for such strategies are designed by decoupling elements. The evaporation process can thus be controlled using our model.

References

1. Vivien Knips, *Developing Countries and the Global Dairy Sector Part I: Global Overview*. Pro-Poor Livestock Policy Initiative (PPLPI) Website: www.fao.org/ag/pplpi.html Working Paper: www.fao.org/ag/againfo/projects/en/pplpi/docarc/wp30.pdf
2. Dairy Manufacturing, Fact Sheet: Food Manufacturing Series, United Nations Environmental Program (UNEP), 1997.
3. T. J. Geurts, A. Jellema, A. Noomen, P. Walstra, and M. A. J. S. van Boekel, *Dairy Technology: Principles of Milk Properties and Processes*, pp. 265–320, 1999.
4. Ralph Early (Editor), *The Technology of Dairy Products* (2nd edition), Blackie Academic and Professional, an imprint of Thompson Science, London.
5. Alan H. Varnam Jane P. Sutherland, *Milk and Milk Products: Technology, Chemistry and Microbiology* (Food Product series, Vol. 1), Aspen (originally published by Chapman & Hall in 1994), 2001.
6. R.P. Aneja, B.N. Mathur, R.C. Chandan, and A.K. Banerjee, *Technology of Indian Milk Products* (ISBN 81-901603-0-3), Dairy India Yearbook Publications, New Delhi, 2002.
7. Borden Gail, Concentrated milk (sweet milk), *Scientific American*, 11(51): 405, 30 Aug 1856.
8. Borden Gail, Concentrated milk, *Scientific American*, 12(49): 387, 5 Aug 1857.
9. Borden Gail, Milk and its preservation, *Scientific American*, New Series, 3: 2–3, 2 Jul 1860.
10. Pieter Walstra, *Dairy Technology: Principles of Milk Properties and Processes* (Food Science and Technology), (9780824702281), Marcel Dekker, New York, 1999.
11. Christian Kiesner and Rudolf Eggers, Concept of a sterile concentration process for milk by multistage flash evaporation, *Chemical Engineering and Technology*, 17(6): 374–381, Wiley-VCH Verlag GmbH & Co. KGaA, Weinheim.
12. Frank E. Rice, Evaporated Milk Associated, Chicago, IL, , *Ind. Eng. Chem.*, 22(1): 45–48, 1930.
13. Cornelis Glas and Hans Niewenhuyse, A process for the preparation of evaporated milk, European Patent EP0627169, 17 May 1994.
14. Leland C. Dickey, James C. Craig, Jr., E. Richard Radewonuk, Andrew J. Mcaloon, and Virginia H. Holsinge, Our industry today: vacuum evaporation, USDA, *Journal of Dairy Science*, 78: 1369–1376, 1995.
15. Liquid milk processing plant, SSP Pvt Ltd., 13 Milestone, Mathura Road Faridabad, Haryana – 121 003 (India), www.sspindia.com/liquid-milk-processing-plant.html
16. Sweetened Condensed Milk Plant, SSP Pvt Ltd., 13 Milestone, Mathura Road Faridabad, Haryana – 121 003 (India), www.dairy-equipments.com/sweetened-condensed-milk-plant.html
17. Evaporated Milk Plant, SSP Pvt Ltd., 13 Milestone, Mathura Road Faridabad, Haryana – 121 003 (India), www.dairy-equipments.com/sweetened-condensed-milk-plant.html
18. Evaporated Milk, Hyfoma, Heggerenkweg, 8171 PD Vaassen, Netherlands (www.hyfoma.com/en/content/food-branches-processing-anufacturing/dairy/milk/condensed-milk/)
19. *Proceedings of 13th ISSCT*, Taiwan, Elsevier Publishing Company, Amsterdam, 1968.
20. W.C. Carter, Gibbs phase rule and its applications, Lecture 26, MIT, 3.0 Fall 2002.

21. V.L. Patil, Mathematical modelling of process plants, Technical Report No. CEERI/ES/TR-8/ 88, 1988.
22. Ernest O. Doebelin, *System Modelling and Response: Theoretical and Experimental Approaches*, John Wiley and Sons, New York.
23. Joroslav Pachner, *Handbook of Numerical Analysis and Applications*, McGraw Hill Company, New York, 1972.
24. R.W. Southworth and S.L. Deleer, *Digital Computations and Numerical Methods*, Mc-Graw Hill Company, New York, 1965.
25. Peter Cunningham, Niel Canty, Tom O'Mahony, Barry O'Connor, and Donal O'Callaghan, System Identification of a Falling-Film Evaporator in the Dairy Industry, International Control Conference (ICC2006), Glasgow, Scotland, United Kingdom, 30 August to 1 September 2006.
26. Bela G. Liptak *Instrument Engineers Handbook: Process Control and Optimization*, Liptak Associates, Stamford, Connecticut, USA. ISA and CRC Press, Taylor & Francis Group, 2006.
27. J.E. Dutton, Commonsense approach to process modeling, *Software, IEEE* 10(4): 56–64, 1993.
28. C. Spano and G. May, Process modeling, IEEE Book chapter, 2006, pp. 272–332.
29. C.M. Javalagi and E.M. Bhushi, An overview of application of system dynamics modeling for analysis of Indian sugar industry, IEEE *International Conference*, 2007, pp. 1828–1832.
30. M. Gupta, On the characteristics of parameters perturbation process dynamics, *IEEE Journal*, 14(5): 540–542, 1969.
31. W.L. McCoy, Interfacing 3 complimentary tech.: Strategic planning, process modelling and system dynamics, *IEEE Conference*, Vol. 3, 1998, pp. 2620–2624.
32. L. Horvath and I.J. Rudas, Multilevel modeling of manufacturing processes using object-oriented Petri nets and advanced knowledge representation, Industrial Electronics, Control, and Instrumentation, 1995, *Proceedings of the 1995 IEEE IECON 21st International Conference*, Vol. 1, 1995, pp. 133–137, DOI: 10.1109/IECON.1995.483346.
33. Biao Huang, S.L. Shah, and E.K. Kwok, Online control performance monitoring of MIMO processes, *Proceedings of American Control Conference*, Vol. 2, 1995, pp. 1250–1254.
34. K.E. Huff, Process measurement through process modeling and simulation, Proceedings of the 10th International Software Process Workshop, Process Support of Software Product Lines, 1996, pp. 83–85, DOI:10.1109/ISPW.1996.654378
35. E.B. Doblin, Online identification of process dynamics, *IBM Journal of Research and Development*, 11(4): 406–426, 1967.
36. R. Hastings-James, and M.W. Sage, Recursive generalized least square procedures for online identification of process parameters, Proceedings of the Institution of Electrical Engineers, Vol. 116(12): pp. 2057–2062, 1969. DOI: 10.1049/piee.1969.0378
37. H.W. Bode and C.E. Shannon, A simplified derivation of linear least square smoothing and prediction theory, *Proceedings of the IRE*, 38(4): 417–425, 1950.
38. J.M. Douglas and D.E. Cormack, Application of the recurrent multilayer perception in modeling complex process dynamics, process dynamic and control, Vol. 1: analysis of dynamic systems, Vol. 2: control system synthesis, *IEEE Journal*, 7(6): 495, 1977.
39. C. Isik and A.M. Calmakci, Identification of a non-linear multivariable dynamic process using feed forward networks, IEEE Conference, Vol. 1, 1993, pp. 564–567.
40. O.L.R. Jocobs, Process dynamics estimation and control, *IET Journal*, 113(6), 1986.
41. P. Eykhoff and O. Smith, Optimalizing control process dynamics identification, *IRE Transaction on Automatic Control*, 7(2): 140–155, 1962.
42. D.J. Sandoz, Description of linear multivariable process dynamics using continuous and discrete output equations, Proc. IEE, 120(12): 1541–1544, 1973.
43. D.J. Sandoz, Optimal control of linear multivariable system based upon discrete output feedback, Proc. IEE, 120(11): 1439–1444, 1973.
44. D.J. Sandoz and P.A.W. Walker, Output–prediction equation with minimum-time control of linear multivariable systems, Proc. IEE, 120(3): 385–389, 1973.
45. D.J. Sandoz and P.G. Appleby, Further analysis of a discrete single-stage control law, Proc. IEE, 119(8): 1201–1204, 1972.

46. K.H. Johansson, A. Horch, Wijk Olle, and A. Hanssom, Teaching multivariable control using the quadruple tank process, IEEE Conference on Decision and Control, Vol. 1, 1999, pp. 807–812.
47. Y. Kouhi, R. Adlgostar, B. Labibi, A. Fatehi, and S. Fakhimi, Multivariable Control Design for MIMO Flow-Level Control Plant, EUROCON, 2007. The International Conference on "Computer as a Tool", 2007, pp. 725–730. DOI: 10.1109/EURCON.2007.4400241.
48. P. Atkinson, P.B. Fellgett, and T.G. Swann, An approach to the control of processes with pure time delay, *Radio and Electronic Engineer*, 43(3): 219–223, 1973. DOI: 10.1049/ree.1973.0032.
49. M. Gil-Martinez and J. Rico, A course on MIMO time delay process control from practice emerging technologies and factory automation, IEEE Conference on ETFA 2009, 2009, pp. 1–8, DOI: 10.1109/ETFA.2009.5347161
50. H.K. Song, D.G. Fisher, and S.L. Shah, Experimental evaluation of adaptive control methods on a pilot plant evaporator, American Control Conference, 1984, pp. 1843–1849.
51. K.J. Astrom, K.H. Johansson, and Q.-G. Wang, Design of decoupled PI controllers for two-by-two systems, IEE Proc. Control Theory and Applications, Vol. 149, Part 1, 2002, pp. 74–81.
52. Geng Liang and Guotian Yang, A kind of MIMO decouple control system based on double-neuron adaptive predictive and static decouple algorithm, computational intelligence and industrial application, PACIIA '08. Pacific-Asia Workshop, Vol. 2, 2008, pp. 360–364, DOI-10.1109/PACIIA.2008.56
53. Hua Mei, Shaoyuan Li, Wen-Jian Cai, and Qiang Xiong, Decentralized closed-loop parameter identification for multivariable processes from step responses, *Mathematics and Computers in Simulation*, 68(2): 171–192, 2005.
54. K.M. Nielsen, T.S. Pedersen, and J.F.D. Nielsen, Simulation and control of a multiple effect evaporator, Control '96, UKACC International Conference on (Conf. Publ. No. 427), Vol. 2, 1166–1171, 1996.
55. Christopher Delgado (IFPRI), Clare Narrod (FAO), and Marites Tiongco (IFPRI), Growth and Concentration in India, FAO Corporate Document Repository, and report is submitted to the Food and Agricultural Organization of the United Nations by IFPRI in fulfillment of Letter of Agreement PR20803, 24 July 2003.

13

Hate Speech Detection and Analysis Using Machine Learning

Pratik Patil and Deepali Nilesh Naik

CONTENTS

13.1 Introduction

In the last several years, modern life and society have been affected by the development of technology in the world. Access to education, medication and transportation has been abridged due to modern-day technology. Social media platforms are also part of these technologies by offering humans the privilege to communicate with people across the planet. The misuse of evolving technology leads to an unstable and disturbing environment in society. The objective of the hate communities is to broadcast the substance that comprises objectionable information apart from that to produce similar material as a regular part of the community. To secure peaceful and persistent surroundings, we ought to diminish the hate speech around us.

If the public can recognize the public's repulsive post as just another opinion, such messages can be freely expressed. The goal is to form "public acceptability" about the hate speech comments. Social media platforms need to advance user experience and care for the users who belong to minority groups to not come upon abusive and hate content.

DOI: 10.1201/9781003342755-16

Consequently, it is customary to have administrators spot offensive posts and attacks or check posts informed by the users on many platforms and forums.

The main contribution of this article is to design text analysis technique using a natural language processing (NLP) approach. Authors have implemented TF-IDF, Doc2Vec, sentiment analysis, and also the combination of these approaches (TF-IDF + Doc2Vec Doc2Vec + sentiment analysis TF-IDF + sentiment analysis TF-IDF + Doc2Vec + sentiment analysis) to understand sentiments of the provided tweet. Moreover, authors trained linear regressing, random forest, naïve Bayes and support vector machines classifiers to categorize tweets in "hate speech", "offensive" and "neither" groups. The performance of the classification is evaluated considering accuracy, precision, recall and F1-score.

This chapter is outlined in the following sections: Section 13.2 focuses on the existing literature. Section 13.3 describes the methodology used for experimentation. Section 13.4 clarifies the experimental setup; results are shown in Section 13.5 and elaborated in Section 13.6, respectively. In addition, Section 13.7 examines limitations, future directions and concluding remarks.

13.2 Related Works

Nowadays, on social media, hate speech is familiar to us. Many researchers have used different types of feature extraction methods such as dictionary-based (Gitari, Zuping, Damien, & Long, 2015) (Tulkens, Hilte, Lodewyckx, Verhoeven, & Daelemans, 2016) (Greevy & Smeaton, 2004), TF-IDF-based (Liu & Forss, 2014) and deep-learning-based (Köffer, Riehle, Höhenberger, & Becker, 2018).

Burnap and Williams (2016) employed a dictionary-based method to recognize hate speech on Twitter. An N-gram feature extraction approach makes the digital vectors out of the established in advanced dictionary or lexicon of hateful statements. The authors nourished the produced digital vector to the support vector machine, a machine learning algorithm, and achieved a 67% F1-score. To catch racism automatically in Dutch social media platforms, Tulkens et al. (2016) utilized a dictionary-based technique. In this research, the authors employed three dictionary features in the circulation of words.

To categorize hate speech in web forums and blogs, Gitari et al. (2015) used a machine learning-based classifier. The authors produced a master feature vector to exercise a dictionary-based method. On sentiment terminologies using subjectivity features and semantic features, the features were placed. In the research study (Gao, Wang, Lin, Xu, & Qi, 2017), a ULMFiT model was proposed for text classification purposes. The authors applied three deep neural network models on Twitter messages data to detect hate words and assessed the performance to claim the efficiency of the proposed model. ULMFiT can furnish 97.5% and 96% and F1 score on publicly available and recently established dataset. Badjatiya, Gupta, Gupta and Varma (2017) researched the application of deep neural network (DNN) architectures to perform hate speech identification. The researchers established the methods extensively performed better than the present methods. Agrawal and Awekar (2018) have revealed that DNN techniques are feasible for finding cyberbullying on several subjects throughout numerous social media platforms using DNN models. Salminen et al. (2020) noticed the most satisfactory result with feature extraction using BERT followed by the classifier as XGBoost. They tested numerous machine learning classification algorithms and neural networks for hate detection. The outcome of the suggested approach for various social media is decent, although it differs somewhat amid the platforms.

In recent times, some researchers exercised machine learning approaches to detect hate speech. Deep learning-based classification techniques are also used in the current time to categorize hate speech statements. Köffer et al. (2018) obtained a 0.67 F1-score by exercising word2vec features and classifier as support vector machine (SVM) to detect German posts of hateful statements. Many scholars from around the world are researching hate speech detection, which is available in diverse languages. We equated machine learning classifier models and three feature extraction methods to assess which technique works better on hate speech datasets.

13.3 Methodology

The section describes the methods used to categorize within three groups: "hate speech, offensive, and neither of them". This research methodology has six key phases: data acquisition, data preprocessing, feature extraction, data splitting, classifier model and model evaluation. In the following section, these methods are described.

13.3.1 Data Acquisition

The dataset used in this research is acquired from the openly accessible hate speech comments dataset. Then, collected datasets were compiled and labeled. The comments were labeled into three definite categories in this dataset: hate speech, offensive, and neither. In this dataset, there are 24,783 posts. From the total number of posts, 1,430 posts are from the class hate speech, 19,190 posts are from the offensive class and the remaining 4,163 posts are from the type of offensive speech but not hate speech.

13.3.2 Data Preprocessing

The data preprocessing methods inspire better results in the classification of hate speech (Shaikh & Doudpotta, 2019). Thus, there is a need to preprocess data by applying the following techniques: retweet removal, lemmatization, tokenization, text cleansing, lowercasing, spell correction, negation handling and stop word removal.

13.3.3 Feature Extraction

Feature extraction is the process or mechanism used to derive unique characteristics (features) based on the input text data. Feature extraction also helps to collect illuminating, unambiguous and non-redundant data to enhance the performance of learning models (Guilherme & De Sousa, 2019). The feature extraction technique separates the essential features from the text file dataset and shows the features in numerical form. TF-IDF (Ramos, 2003), sentiment analysis using polarity scores and Doc2vec (Le & Mikolov, 2014), the three different features engineering techniques, are used in this research.

13.3.4 Data Splitting

Table 13.1 presents the training and testing instances from the dataset (i.e., training set and test set) class-wise. Our research used the 80–20 split ratio to split the preprocessed data

TABLE 13.1
Data Splitting

	Class	Training Instances	Testing Instances
0	Hate speech	1160	290
1	Offensive	14128	3832
2	Neither	3340	835
	Total	**18628**	**4957**

(i.e. 80% for training of the data and 20% for testing of the data). Training instances are used to train the classifiers. Testing instances are used to examine the data.

13.3.5 Machine Learning Models

In accordance with the "no free lunch theorem", it is highly recommended to use multiple and different classification models on the master feature vector to evaluate the best results (Ho & Pepyne, 2001). The probability of a single classifier working better for a particular dataset is less. Hence, we selected different classifiers such as logistic regression, random forest (Xu, Guo, Ye, & Cheng, 2012), naïve Bayes (Lewis, 1998) and support vector machine (Inglehart, 2019).

13.3.6 Evaluation Metrics

Using testing instances, the assembled classification model calculates which posts belong to a dataset class (i.e., "hate speech, offensive, neither"). The performance of classification models is evaluated based on true negative, false positive, false negative and true positive values.

1. *Precision:* Precision gives the number of correct predicted results divided by the number of predictions derived from the classifier (M & M.N, 2015). Precision can be calculated as follows.

$$Precision = \frac{True\ Positive}{True\ Poitive + False\ Positive}$$

2. *Recall:* Recall provides the number of correct predicted results divided by a number of all applicable instances (M & M.N, 2015). It can be calculated as follows:

$$Recall = \frac{True\ Positive}{True\ Poitive + False\ Negative}$$

3. *F1 Score:* F1-measure / F1-Score: The harmonic mean is derived by combining both the precision and recall values (Liu, Zhou, Wen, & Tang, 2014). F1-measure can be calculated as follows:

$$F1\ Score = 2 * \frac{Precision*Recall}{Precision + Recall}$$

13.4 Experimental Settings

As described in Section 13.3.3, the authors have applied three feature extraction techniques: TF-IDF, Doc2vec and sentiment analysis. Additionally, the combination of those feature extraction techniques is also evaluated.

13.5 Results

Table 13.2 shows the accuracy of all investigations. The numbers in the table are F-scores of respective feature extraction techniques and classification algorithms. Moreover, the highest accuracy (90%) were obtained by SVM using TF-IDF features representation. In feature extraction, TF-IDF received better results as compared to sentiment analysis and Doc2vec. In-text classification models, support vector machine classifier best performed within all the algorithms. Although, the random forest classifier results were almost identical to SVM results and were better than logistic regression and naïve Bayes results. The amalgamation of TF-IDF, Doc2Vec and sentiment analysis using polarity scores feature combination gave a better outcome for logistic regression and the same result for random forest, naïve Bayes and SVM algorithm.

13.6 Discussion

As shown in Figure 13.1, we have assessed seven classifiers with three different feature extraction methods, providing examination on top of the hate speech dataset covering three classes in the experimental setup. The combination of TF-IDF feature extraction techniques with the SVM algorithm displayed better experimental results. The following sections describe theoretical analyses.

TABLE 13.2

Accuracy of Analyses

Features	LR	RF	NB	SVM
TF-IDF	0.89	0.90	0.65	0.89
Doc2Vec	0.80	0.79	0.78	0.80
Sentiment analysis	0.78	0.76	0.70	0.77
TF-IDF + Doc2Vec	0.90	0.89	0.64	0.89
Doc2Vec + Sentiment analysis	0.82	0.81	0.78	0.82
TF-IDF + Sentiment analysis	0.90	0.89	0.65	0.89
TF-IDF + Doc2Vec + Sentiment analysis	0.90	0.89	0.65	0.89

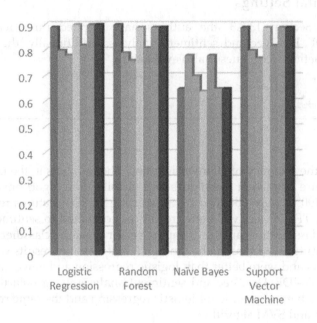

FIGURE 13.1
Accuracy analysis of various models.

13.6.1 Feature Extraction

The feature extraction techniques, that is, TF-IDF, sentiment analysis features and doc2vec, are compared in this study. TF-IDF gave the best results comparing the other feature extraction techniques. Conversely, sentiment analysis using polarity scores and the Doc2vec showed lower results. For text classification, the selection of feature extraction has tremendous importance.

Doc2Vec performed poorly in the experimental results. Because of that reason (Wang, Zhou, Jin, Liu, & Lu, 2017) short-length documents lower the performance of Doc2Vec. Though, to train the data commendably, the dataset we use might not be sufficient.

13.6.2 Classification Models

The SVM classifier achieved the best performance shown by the experimental results because of the threshold functions used by the SVM to separate the data and not the number of features. The results indicate that the SVM is independent of the number of features in the data (Min-Ling Zhang & Zhi-Hua Zhou, 2005).

13.6.3 Class-wise Accomplishment

As we discussed in Section 13.3, we have three classes: "hate speech", "offensive", and "neither of them". All classifier models and the features performed well for two classes, that is, offensive and neither of them. For the class hate speech, the combinations performed not so well. The "hate speech" class has a smaller number of training data points compared to other classes.

13.7 Conclusion

Through the immense use of social media and the internet, the growth of hate against minorities in modern societies led to the wild spread of hate speech messages through social media platforms. The human factor has been tremendously unproductive because of the enormous amount of hate speech data shared around the internet. Hate speech detection tools are essential to eradicate hate speeches. In this research, various extraction techniques and classification algorithms are compared. Therefore, we found whether feature combination works well and better classification algorithms and the features by executing the classification algorithms and feature extraction techniques. The selection of features is momentous in text processing. We studied three definite feature extraction approaches during experimentations: TF-IDF, sentiment analysis using polarity scores, and doc2vec.

In the experimentation following results are recorded: (1) TF-IDF technique outperformed binary and term frequency representation methods. (2) Doc2vec lowers performance due to minimal length documents.

References

Agrawal, S., & Awekar, A. (2018). Deep learning for detecting cyberbullying across multiple social media platforms. *Lecture Notes in Computer Science (Including Subseries Lecture Notes in Artificial Intelligence and Lecture Notes in Bioinformatics)*, *10772 LNCS* (Table 2), 141–153. https://doi.org/10.1007/978-3-319-76941-7_11

Badjatiya, P., Gupta, S., Gupta, M., & Varma, V. (2017). Deep learning for hate speech detection in tweets. *26th International World Wide Web Conference 2017, WWW 2017 Companion* (2), 759–760. https://doi.org/10.1145/3041021.3054223

Burnap, P., & Williams, M. L. (2016). Us and them: identifying cyber hate on Twitter across multiple protected characteristics. *EPJ Data Science*, *5*(1), 1–15. https://doi.org/10.1140/epjds/s13688-016-0072-6

Gao, J., Wang, B., Lin, Z., Xu, W., & Qi, Y. (2017). Deep Cloak: Masking deep neural network models for robustness against adversarial samples. *2019 International Conference on Intelligent Computing and Control Systems (ICCS)*, 2014, 1–8.

Gitari, N. D., Zuping, Z., Damien, H., & Long, J. (2015). A lexicon-based approach for hate speech detection. *International Journal of Multimedia and Ubiquitous Engineering*, 10(4), 215–230. https://doi.org/10.14257/ijmue.2015.10.4.21

Greevy, E., & Smeaton, A. F. (2004). Classifying racist texts using a support vector machine. *Proceedings of Sheffield SIGIR – Twenty-Seventh Annual International ACM SIGIR Conference on Research and Development in Information Retrieval*, 468–469. https://doi.org/10.1145/1008992.1009074

Guilherme, J., & De Sousa, R. (2019). *Faculdade de Engenharia da Universidade do Porto: Feature extraction and selection for automatic hate speech detection on Twitter.*

Ho, Y. C., & Pepyne, D. L. (2001). Simple explanation of the No Free Lunch Theorem of Optimization. *Proceedings of the IEEE Conference on Decision and Control*, 5, 4409–4414. https://doi.org/10.1109/cdc.2001.980896

Inglehart, R. (2019). Chapter 10. From elite-directed to elite-directing politics: The role of cognitive mobilization, changing gender roles, and changing values. *Culture Shift in Advanced Industrial Society*, 335–370. https://doi.org/10.1515/9780691186740-014

Köffer, S., Riehle, D. M., Höhenberger, S., & Becker, J. (2018). Discussing the value of automatic hate speech detection in online debates. *MKWI 2018 – Multikonferenz Wirtschaftsinformatik*, 2018 March, 83–94.

Le, Q., & Mikolov, T. (2014). Distributed representations of sentences and documents. *31st International Conference on Machine Learning, ICML 2014*, 4, 2931–2939.

Lewis, D. D. (1998). Naive (Bayes) at forty: The independence assumption in information retrieval. *Ecml*, (x), 16.

Liu, S., & Forss, T. (2014). Combining N-gram based similarity analysis with sentiment analysis in web content classification. *KDIR 2014 – Proceedings of the International Conference on Knowledge Discovery and Information Retrieval*, pp. 530–537. https://doi.org/10.5220/0005170305300537

Liu, Y., Zhou, Y., Wen, S., & Tang, C. (2014). A strategy on selecting performance metrics for classifier evaluation. *International Journal of Mobile Computing and Multimedia Communications*, 6(4), 20–35. https://doi.org/10.4018/IJMCMC.2014100102

Hossin, M., & Sulaiman M.N. (2015). A review on evaluation metrics for data classification evaluations. *International Journal of Data Mining & Knowledge Management Process*, 5(2), 1–11. https://doi.org/10.5121/ijdkp.2015.5201

Min-Ling Zhang, & Zhi-Hua Zhou. (2005). A k-nearest neighbor based algorithm for multi-label classification. *IEEE International Conference on Granular Computing (GRC)* 2, 718–721. https://doi.org/10.1109/grc.2005.1547385

Ramos, J. (2003). Using TF-IDF to determine word relevance in document queries. *Proceedings of the First Instructional Conference on Machine Learning*, 242(1), 29–48.

Salminen, J., Hopf, M., Chowdhury, S. A., Jung, S. gyo, Almerekhi, H., & Jansen, B. J. (2020). Developing an online hate classifier for multiple social media platforms. *Human-Centric Computing and Information Sciences*, 10(1), 1–34. https://doi.org/10.1186/s13673-019-0205-6

Shaikh, S., & Doudpotta, S. M. (2019). Aspects based opinion mining for teacher and course evaluation. *Sukkur IBA Journal of Computing and Mathematical Sciences*, 3(1), 34–43. https://doi.org/10.30537/sjcms.v3i1.375

Tulkens, S., Hilte, L., Lodewyckx, E., Verhoeven, B., & Daelemans, W. (2016). A dictionary-based approach to racism detection in Dutch social media. Retrieved from http://arxiv.org/abs/1608.08738

Wang, Y., Zhou, Z., Jin, S., Liu, D., & Lu, M. (2017). Comparisons and selections of features and classifiers for short text classification. *IOP Conference Series: Materials Science and Engineering*, 261(1). https://doi.org/10.1088/1757-899X/261/1/012018

Xu, B., Guo, X., Ye, Y., & Cheng, J. (2012). An improved random forest classifier for text categorization. *Journal of Computers (Finland)*, 7(12), 2913–2920. https://doi.org/10.4304/jcp.7.12.2913-2920

14

Bibliometric Survey on Personality Detection for Resume Filtration Using Artificial Intelligence

Hridyesh Singh Bisht, Kavya Suthar, Sejal Shrestha,
Ambika Vishal Pawar, and Deepali Arun Bhanage

CONTENTS

14.1 Introduction

With the arrival of online job portals and social media, there is a burst of job opportunities available to the unemployed youth at the tip of their thumbs. For an applicant, the job platforms have provided them with accessibility to several previously hidden job profiles. The online job portal has opened the applicant to new talent and skills that they can harness to further their vision for the companies. The existing approach also brings a massive drawback to the recruitment scene. Thus, researchers are seeing a surge of job applicants: freshers and those with previous job experience. Now the companies have a whole slew of talent to sieve.

DOI: 10.1201/9781003342755-17

Automated resume-scanning software automatically rejects candidates with gaps of longer than six months in their employment history, without ever asking the cause of this absence.

As time goes on, formats for applications and resumes are ever-changing and evolving. Therefore, it can be a bit blind sighting for the aspirant and the company to determine the de facto format and procedure to streamline the process. The proposed approach is to perform a filter based on which applicants can be segregated and clubbed together to simplify the hiring process. We found a few interesting approaches during our study, and a majority of the publications were using an algorithm or a collection of algorithms such as SVM classifier, CNN-based models, naive Bayes, etc. based on different parameters such as stress, sentiments and emotions and a correlation between them. Some publications even proposed architecture or a framework for approaching personality prediction.

The bibliometric analysis is suitable for understanding and capturing a survey of the research, "Personality Detection for Resume Filtration Using Artificial Intelligence." We conducted a study of the contribution of different researchers, subject areas, and nations, and awareness of around the world research in the given area. Statistical analysis of the extracted relevant documents assists in pursuing technological growth till now in a selected research domain [1]. This chapter conveys a bibliometric analysis to better conceive compelling research trends in resume filtration by predicting personality using artificial intelligence. This research will provide us with a baseline solution and will try to form an integrated explanation of many of the problems applicants and employers face using traditional online job portals.

14.2 Literature Review

In the literature, Ahmad et al. [2] proposed a deep learning architecture to extract psychometric dimensions such as trust, anxiety, literacy ratings, etc., from messages or texts. On similar grounds, Mazni, Syed-Abdullah and Hussin [3] presented research to understand the permutation and combination of personality types, temperament, team diversity, and team performance. Chen et al. [4] conducted a sentiment analysis to enumerate emotion compositions as ratios and sentiment polarity. Diversity of emotions across contexts were scrutinized through analysis of variance (ANOVA) tests and visualized for better understanding. Correspondingly, Moraes et al. [5] aimed to automate the personality assessment by analyzing the text extracted from tweets and suggesting suitable job roles.

Piedboeuf, Langlais, and Bourg [6] examined an SVM classifier with a feature or characteristics ranking algorithm and optimizer. They introduced a possibility of bringing out the personality of a LinkedIn user based on the texts on LinkedIn. At the same time, Yan et al. [7] created a model to collect clear social validation from LinkedIn as we can know how they will treat other people by validating social skills. Krommyda et al. [8] provided a methodology for collecting and annotating tweets into eight categories. They have also utilized the machine learning classification technique to classify these short text messages. Amirhosseini and Kazemian [9] developed personality type prediction based on the Myers Briggs Type Indicator (MBTI). Moreover, the authors claimed that the results show finer accuracy and reliability than the other methods that are existing.

Keh and Cheng [10] trained a language model on the scraped texts for each personality type, computed the loss after each epoch, and summed up the final losses. Salloum et al.

[11] presented a methodology for data collection and preprocessing to extract information from the collected articles using text mining techniques. Putri, Puji, and Razaq [12] used a questionnaire to collect and analyze undergraduate students' data. They demonstrated that introverted students and extroverted personality traits balance each other. Similarly, Makwana and Dave [13] designed a survey to generate the personality profile of management students while validating and confirming the scale of personality assessment.

Khan et al. [14] provided the basis for developing a personality identification system that could assist in recruiting personnel by knowing their personality and preference. Salminen et al. [15] developed a deep learning classifier by means of openly accessible datasets to look over how each person varies by their identified personality traits and how personality traits could be carried out in profiles driven by data. Stachl et al. [16] discussed the estimate of personality scales attained using machine learning (ML) algorithms along with highlighting some of the key issues that emerge from the use of latent variables in the modeling process. At the same time, Ahmad et al. [17] presented a scrutiny on by what means particular personality can be identified using online content through natural language processing (NLP). Li et al. [18] built the correlation between personality and emotional behaviors and proposed a novel multitask learning framework. They implemented a CNN-based model across numerous personality and emotion datasets, even outperforming language model-based models. Similarly, Alexander, Mulfinger, and Oswald [19] provided a framework for approaching big data in personality science, along with ideas and intentions that link psychometric reliability and validity.

Plenty of research has been done in the area of artificial intelligence, but not much focus has been given to the area of personality detection using artificial intelligence. Various machine learning algorithms such as Long Short-Term Memory (LSTM) network, SVM classifier, random forest with AdaBoost, and naive Bayes were studied. However, the majority of the algorithms still have to focus on various parameters and tasks to perform personality prediction with accuracy. Going to more depth of the research done, as per our research, it could be concluded that no comprehensive bibliometric survey has been carried out in this field from 2008 to 2021 via the Scopus database. Due to this, one of the reasons for conducting a bibliometric analysis covering the significant keywords used for data collection, distribution of research output based on language, type-wise distribution of research output, growth in literature in recent years, publications sources by subject, affiliation, authors, geographical, citation attributes, network, etc. This bibliometric survey was implemented with the following four aims in mind:

1. Determine statistical data of keywords that are frequently used, authors and their contributions, categorization of the subject area, affiliation, and publications sources per year.
2. Present analysis in light of geographical locations, citations, documents, and network of co-occurrence of author's keywords, the relation between documents and citations, and bibliographic coupling and sources; and present a conclusion that can assist other researchers working in this particular field.
3. Understand the research ramifications of personality detection for resume filtration using artificial intelligence.
4. Understand the gaps and problems faced in resume filtration using artificial intelligence.

The following are the sections that make up this chapter: Data acquisition for bibliometric analysis is covered in Section 14.3. The statistical and network data results of the bibliometric investigation are presented in Section 14.4. The research implications of our findings are presented in Section 14.5. Following our bibliometric study, we arrived at our results in Section 14.6.

14.3 Data Collection

The study was conducted by referring to the majority of publications from peer-reviewed journals. Most publications for the study of personality detection for resume filtration using artificial intelligence were collected using Scopus, an extensive database with citations and abstracts from journals, books, conferences, and patents utilized to extract relevant publications. This chapter was intended to get a broader outline along with visualization and analysis of the search results to give an analytical view of the research done in personality detection for resume filtration using artificial intelligence.

14.3.1 Significant Keywords

In this bibliometric analysis of personality detection for resume filtration using artificial intelligence, the keywords are determined by keeping in mind the expert opinion. The keywords are split into two categories: a series of keywords used and a search query utilized during the search. Some suitable keywords following selected topics are mentioned in Table 14.1.

14.3.2 Initial Search Results

After preparatory exploration applying a search query, a total of 417 documents were retrieved from the Scopus repository. Table 14.2 displays the distribution of research

TABLE 14.1

Significant Keywords for Data Collection

Keywords	Recruitment system, predicting personality type, psychometric dimensions, MBTI test, questionnaire form
Search query	("Recruitment system" or "Personality Prediction") and ("Artificial Intelligence" or "Machine Learning" or "Deep Learning") and ("Social Media" or "Facebook data" or "Tweeter data")

TABLE 14.2

Distribution of Research Output Regarding the Language

No.	Language of Publication	Number of Publications
1	English	407
2	Chinese	5
3	Russian	2
4	Turkish	2
5	Japanese	1
6	Spanish	1

Source: Accessed on 30 July 2021 with the assistance of www.scopus.com

TABLE 14.3

Source Type-wise Distribution of Research Output

No.	Type of Publication	Number of Publication
1	Conference paper	218
2	Article	175
3	Review	14
4	Book chapter	7
5	Conference review	2
6	Note	1

Source: Accessed on 30 July 2021 with the assistance of www.scopus.com

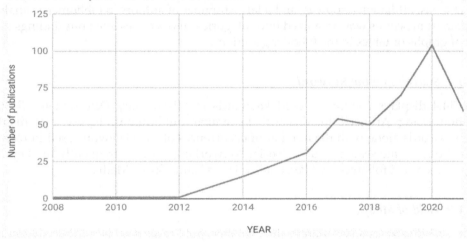

FIGURE 14.1

Yearly growth in publications.

Source: Accessed on 30 July 2021 with the assistance of www.scopus.com.

output based on language reference. Out of 417 papers, 407 were in the English language, five documents were in the Chinese language, followed by two in the Russian language. Hence, the majority of articles were issued in the English language, which then is followed by the Chinese language.

Table 14.3 displays the distribution of research output concerning publication. Out of the total 417 publications, 218 are conference papers, 175 are articles, and 14 are reviews. More than 50% of publications were conference papers. Figure 14.1 displays the yearly growth in publications of research output. It indicates that there has been an upsurge in the quantity of publications in years.

14.4 Analysis of Bibliometric Data

The bibliometric analysis of publications gathered from the Scopus database is displayed in this segment. Our analysis was carried out using the following methods:

1. Analysis of keywords, subject areas, affiliations, sources, and author qualities using statistical techniques.
2. Examination of geographic locations, citations, and network diagrams using analytical techniques.

14.4.1 Statistical Methods

Searching the Scopus database for search results can yield statistical data on keywords, subject areas, affiliations, sources, and a large number of authors in bibliometric analysis. The data from Scopus was organized into categories, and we presented our findings in the form of graphs or tables in the following sections.

14.4.1.1 Statistics on the Keyword

Table 14.4 displays commonly used keywords in "Personality Detection for Resume Filtration Using Artificial Intelligence" in similar publications. Figure 14.2 displays these keywords along with the number of occurrences of each keyword used in research publications. In the search results, "Social Networking" is very frequently the keyword that gets recorded followed by "Personality Traits" and "Social Media."

14.4.1.2 Field of Study

Figure 14.3 illustrates a selection of the extracted publications related to the subject area in which the document is published. Approximately 64% of research is conducted in the fields of computer science, engineering, and mathematics along with a little amount of

TABLE 14.4
Top 11 Keywords

Sr. No.	Keywords	Number of Publications
1	Social Networking (online)	165
2	Personality traits	106
3	Social media	101
4	Forecasting	86
5	Personality predictions	79
6	Machine learning	78
7	Behavioral research	76
8	Learning systems	69
9	Data mining	56
10	Big five	50
11	Personality prediction	50

Source: Accessed on 30 July 2021 with the assistance of www.scopus.com

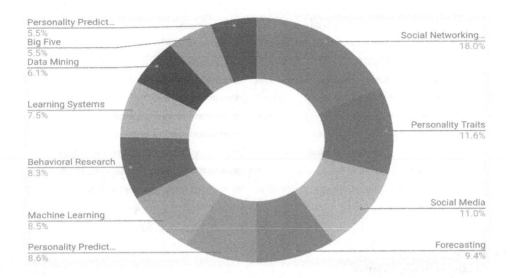

FIGURE 14.2

Top 11 keywords graph.

Source: Accessed on 30 July 2021 with the assistance of www.scopus.com.

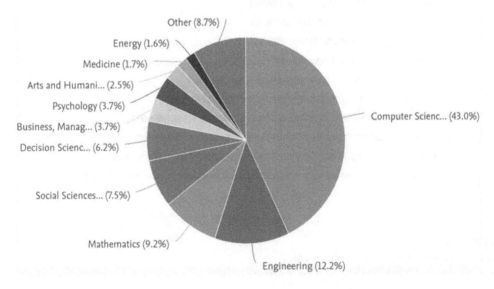

FIGURE 14.3

Extracted publications by subject area.

Source: Accessed on 30 July 2021 with the assistance of www.scopus.com.

research in disciplines including decision sciences, business, management, psychology, and the arts and humanities.

14.4.1.3 Statistics on Affiliation

Figure 14.4 depicts the contribution made by universities in terms of affiliations in publications. Four institutions from China, two from Italy, one from the United States, one from Austria, one from Brazil, and one from Indonesia are among the top ten universities.

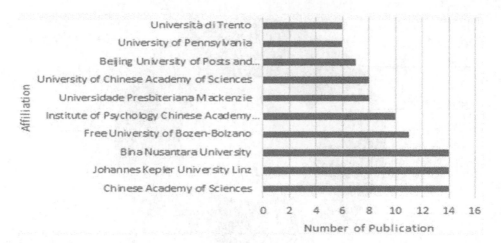

FIGURE 14.4
Extracted publications by affiliation.
Source: Accessed on 30 July 2021 with the assistance of www.scopus.com.

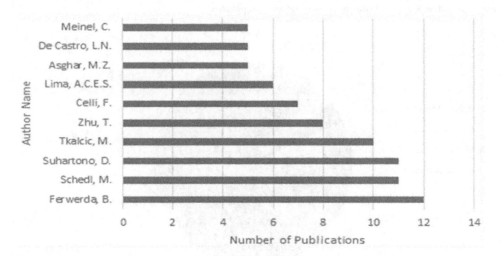

FIGURE 14.5
Author contributions in extracted publications.
Source: Accessed on 30 July 2021 with the assistance of www.scopus.com.

In this field of research, the Chinese Academy of Sciences, Johannes Kepler University Linz, and Bina Nusantara University have all made significant contributions.

14.4.1.4 Most Copious Author Statistics

Figure 14.5 displays the comparison among the top 10 copious authors with the most number of publications. B. Fewerda and M. Schedl, and D. Suhartono have contributed significantly in this research area with 12 and 11 publications, respectively.

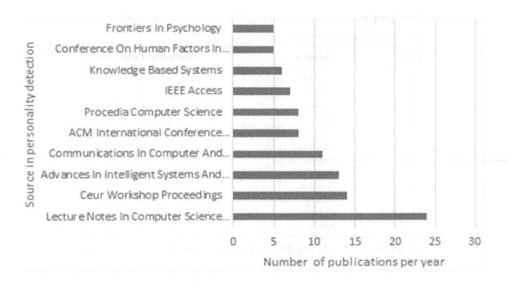

FIGURE 14.6
Yearly publication by source.
Source: Accessed on 30 July 2021 with the assistance of www.scopus.com.

14.4.1.5 Statistics from the Sources

The graph of publications each year employing artificial intelligence sources in resume filtration is shown in Figure 14.6. Some of the most widely cited publications in this field are *Lecture Notes in Computer Science*, Ceur Workshops, and Advances in Intelligent Systems and Computing, which produce 14–24 articles every year.

14.4.2 Analytical Techniques

The data retrieved from Scopus in specific categories were analyzed using these search results and are visualized in the following sections.

14.4.2.1 Analysis of Geographical Regions

Table 14.5 displays the overall publications contributed by numerous countries in this research area. About 12 countries contributed to the personality detection for resume filtration using artificial intelligence research. The majority of the publications were from the United States, with 69 in total, as well as collaborations with other countries.

Figure 14.7 displays the comparability of publications by the major contributing countries during the years 2008–2021. The United States and China have notably contributed to personality detection for resume filtration using artificial intelligence research.

14.4.2.2 Citation Analysis

Table 14.6 offers an outline of the top 11 cited publications annually from 2017 to 2021, alongside the year of publication and their title. The primarily ranked publication is "the impact of the COVID-19 epidemic declaration on psychological consequences: A study on

TABLE 14.5

Country-wise Documents

S. No.	Country	Number of Publications
1	United States	69
2	China	67
3	India	47
4	Italy	35
5	United Kingdom	28
6	Germany	26
7	Indonesia	23
8	Australia	15
9	Austria	15
10	Brazil	12
11	Canada	12
12	Spain	12

Source: Accessed on 30 July 2021 with the assistance of www.scopus.com

FIGURE 14.7

Geographic locations extracted publications.

active Weibo users," with 444 citations. Out of 444 recorded citations, 205 are from the year 2020 and 239 from 2021.

14.4.2.3 Network Analysis

The relationship between the different authors and keywords is represented using nodes and edges in the network diagram. Figure 14.8 shows the network analysis of co-occurrence or author keywords. A total of 817 unique author's keywords are identified

TABLE 14.6
Top 11 Cited Publications

Sr. No.	Publication Year	Document Title	<2017	2017	2018	2019	2020	2021	Sub Total
1	2020	The impact of COVID-19 epidemic declaration on psychological consequences: A study on active Weibo users	0	0	0	0	205	239	444
2	2014	A survey of personality computing	48	46	41	37	54	23	201
3	2013	Predicting personality using novel mobile phone-based metrics	59	26	24	25	26	17	118
4	2017	Beyond binary labels: Political ideology prediction of Twitter users	0	1	46	29	28	16	120
5	2018	Predicting the Big 5 personality traits from digital footprints on social media: A meta-analysis	0	0	5	31	39	35	110
6	2016	Analyzing personality through social media profile picture choice	4	10	16	26	30	10	92
7	2018	Current challenges and visions in music recommender systems research	0	0	20	18	33	20	91
8	2016	Computational personality recognition in social media	8	6	21	26	18	12	83
9	2016	Understanding the impact of personality traits on mobile app adoption – Insights from a large-scale field study	1	6	10	24	24	18	82
10	2015	Selection and transmission processes for information in the emerging media environment: psychological motives and message characteristics	9	9	13	16	24	8	70
11	2011	The effect of the author set size and data size in authorship attribution	35	10	7	9	12	2	40

Source: Accessed on 30 July 2021 with the assistance of www.scopus.com

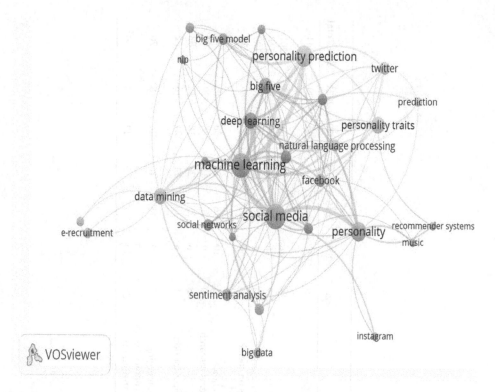

FIGURE 14.8
Network analysis of co-occurrence of author's keywords.

from extracted Scopus records. Furthermore, 30 nodes meet a threshold with a minimum of five occurrences of keywords. Thirty threshold meeting keywords are categorized in six different clusters with purple, green, yellow, blue, cyan, and red.

Figure 14.9 represents the relationship between citation and the documents with the help of a network diagram. At the time of formation of the network, the document must have at least one citation criteria. With the stated criteria, 214 documents got selected from extracted records and grouped into 16 different clusters. From the network diagram, observations are noted as follows:

> "A Survey of Personality Computing" by Vinciarelli A. has 248 citations and 17 links, followed by "Computational Personality Recognition in Social Media" by Farnadi G. having 91 citations and 15 links, whereas "Predicting the Big Five Personality Traits from Digital Footprints on Social Media: A Meta-Analysis" has 109 citations and nine links.
>
> The relationship between bibliographic coupling and sources is presented in Figure 14.10. A total of 220 sources with bibliographic coupling were identified from extracted relevant records from Scopus. Out of 220, eight sources are meeting the threshold with a minimum of five documents benchmark. After analysis, the network was depicted with the assistance of eight nodes majorly divided into two clusters: one represented in red and another in green.

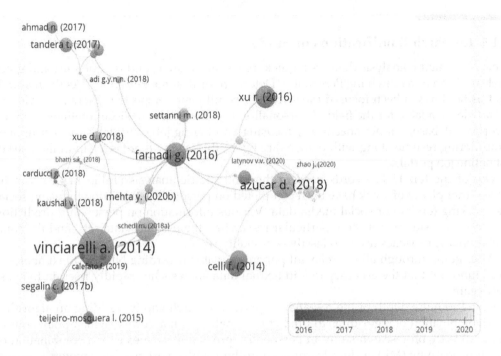

FIGURE 14.9
Relation between document and citations.

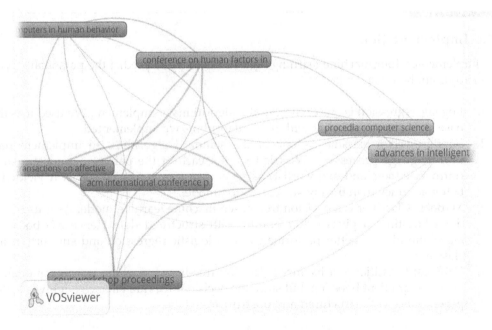

FIGURE 14.10
Relation between bibliographic coupling and sources.

14.5 Research Ramifications of Study

This bibliometric analysis delivers a quick, practical, creative, and unique idea and gives a clear vision of research in "Personality Detection for Resume Filtration." As the research in this field hasn't been focused more from a recruitment perspective, there are a variety of articles available for the field of personality detection using artificial intelligence in the Scopus database, but not specifically focusing on filtering job candidates for recruitment considering resume along with personality types; this is why there is a gap in the market of online job portals.

Out of the top 11 keywords used in the bibliometric analysis (Table 14.4), it can be stated that plenty of work have been completed on personality prediction by using social networking (online) or social media data. Various information on personality prediction models is considered for these particular researches, the usage of data sets, and the computational approaches used to classify personality types.

After going through all the relevant papers available regarding NLP and text analysis, we found out that the accuracy rate in textual data analysis has rapidly risen in the past few years.

Going to more depth of the research displays a research gap in deciding an algorithm or a combination of algorithms to predict personality with accuracy, which points out to focus directly on research study in personality prediction by means of a combination of machine learning (ML) or deep learning algorithms with a variety of parameters.

14.6 Implementation

We implemented four machine learning algorithms to try to predict the personality type of an applicant based on text:

1. Logistic regression is one of the simpler algorithms to implement. We used it as the base algorithm to compare with other algorithms we implemented.
2. Support vector classifier is one of the standard algorithms to implement natural language processing. We tried to plot each of the pair of parameters such (introvertedness and extrovertist) as a point in n-dimensional space. It yielded a better accuracy than the logistic regression model.
3. XGBoost Classifier is a decision tree-based machine learning mode. As it uses gradient boosting, it gives better output with structured data Hence XG boosting algorithm gives a better performance than logistic regression and support vector classifier.
4. CatBoost Classifier is a balanced decision tree-based machine learning model. It also uses gradient boosting, but since the decision trees are balanced, it gives better performance with structured and unstructured data.

After implementing machine learning algorithms, desired accuracy is not obtained. We decided to apply the based uncased distilled version of the BERT model. BERT uses bidirectional training of transformer to perform language modeling. This results in the machine learning model being able to understand the language from left to right and right to left. We trained our BERT model with 16 batch sizes and for 20 epochs.

Hence, we decided to move forward with the CatBoost classification model.

For our research implementation, we decided to develop and test machine learning and deep learning algorithms. For the machine learning approach, the cat boost classifier gives the best result at 68% accuracy while testing our model, as the CatBoost classifier is a gradient boosting approach suited to deal with unstructured data and categorical variables. For our deep learning approach, we decided to develop and test a BERT-based uncased-distilled version of the BERT base model. It gave us 40% accuracy while testing our model.

The reason for low accuracy is due to the lack of data available of some personality types as some personality types are rare, for example, "ESTJ," "ESFJ," "ESFP," and "ESTP". This led to an unbalanced dataset, which led to an over fitted model.

14.7 Conclusion

Our bibliometric analysis provides contributions made by worldwide researchers in personality detection for resume filtration using artificial intelligence. It concludes that the majority of articles were issued in English language, and after that in the Chinese language. Also, the majority of the publications from the conference were issued in the United States, which then followed by China. This study shows that the majority of research is conducted under Computer Science, Engineering, and Math as a subject area. The majority of contributions have been made from the Chinese Academy of Sciences, Johannes Kepler University Linz, and Bina Nusantara University in the research on personality detection for resume filtration using artificial intelligence.

For our research implementation, we preferred machine learning algorithm over deep learning algorithm. The reason behind it is its accuracy. For the machine learning approach, the CatBoost classifier gives the best result at 68% accuracy. For our deep learning approach, BERT-based uncased-distilled version of the BERT base model was used, which gave us 40% accuracy.

As in the future, the formats for applications, resumes, and such are ever-changing and evolving. Therefore, it can be a bit blindsighting for the aspirant and the company to determine the de facto format and procedure to streamline the process. Our proposed solution is an integrated platform that performs a personality test to provide the most favorable categorization for that aspirant.

References

1. D. A. Bhanage and A. V. Pawar, "Bibliometric survey of IT infrastructure management to avoid failure conditions," *Inf. Discov. Deliv.*, June 2020, doi:10.1108/IDD-06-2020-0060
2. F. Ahmad et al., "A deep learning architecture for psychometric natural language processing," *ACM Trans. Inf. Syst.*, vol. 38, no. 1, pp. 1–29, 2020, doi:10.1145/3365211

3. O. Mazni, S. L. Syed-Abdullah, and N. M. Hussin, "Analyzing personality types to predict team performance," *CSSR 2010 – 2010 Int. Conf. Sci. Soc. Res.*, December 2013, pp. 624–628, 2010, doi: 10.1109/CSSR.2010.5773856

4. Z. Chen, X. Shi, W. Zhang, and L. Qu, "Understanding the complexity of teacher emotions from online forums: A computational text analysis approach," *Front. Psychol.*, vol. 11, 2020, doi: 10.3389/fpsyg.2020.00921

5. R. Moraes, L. L. Pinto, M. Pilankar, and P. Rane, "Personality assessment using social media for hiring candidates," *2020 3rd Int. Conf. Commun. Syst. Comput. IT Appl. CSCITA 2020 - Proc.*, pp. 192–197, 2020, doi: 10.1109/CSCITA47329.2020.9137818

6. F. Piedboeuf, P. Langlais, and L. Bourg, "Personality extraction through LinkedIn," *Lecture Notes in Computer Science (including Subseries of Lecture Notes in Artificial Intelligence and Lecture Notes in Bioinformatics)*, vol. 11489 LNAI, pp. 55–67, 2019, doi: 10.1007/978-3-030-183059_5

7. X. Yan et al., "Social skill validation at LinkedIn," *Proc. ACM SIGKDD Int. Conf.Knowl. Discov. Data Min.*, pp. 2943–2951, 2019, doi: 10.1145/3292500.3330752

8. M. Krommyda, A. Rigos, K. Bouklas, and A. Amditis, "An experimental analysis of data annotation methodologies for emotion detection in short text posted on social media," *Informatics*, vol. 8, no. 1, 2021, doi: 10.3390/informatics8010019

9. M. H. Amirhosseini and H. Kazemian, "Machine learning approach to personality type prediction based on the Myers–Briggs type indicator®," *Multimodal Technol. Interact.*, vol. 4, no. 1, 2020, doi: 10.3390/mti4010009

10. S. S. Keh and I.-T. Cheng, "Myers-Briggs personality classification and personality-specific language generation using pre-trained language models," 2019, Online]. Available: http://arxiv.org/abs/1907.06333

11. S. A. Salloum, M. Al-Emran, A. A. Monem, and K. Shaalan, "Using text mining techniques for extracting information from research articles," *Stud. Comput. Intell.*, vol. 740, no. November, pp. 373–397, 2018, doi: 10.1007/978-3-319-67056-0_18

12. R. Putri, N. Puji, and A. Razaq, "Learning style of MBTI personality types in history learning at higher education," vol. 3, no. 6, pp. 289–295, 2016, doi: 10.27512/sjppiukm/ses/a13122016

13. K. Makwana and G. Dave, "A study of identification of personality profiles of undergraduate management students using Myers Briggs type indicator (MBTI) test," *Pacific Bus. Rev. Int.*, vol. 12, no. 8, pp. 26–34, 2020 [Online]. Available: https://papers.ssrn.com/sol3/papers.cfm?abstract_id=3722380

14. A. S. Khan, H. Ahmad, M. Z. Asghar, F. K. Saddozai, A. Arif, and H. A. Khalid, "Personality classification from online text using machine learning approach," *Int. J. Adv. Comput. Sci. Appl.*, vol. 11, no. 3, pp. 460–476, 2020, doi:10.14569/ijacsa.2020.0110358

15. J. Salminen, R. G. Rao, S. gyo Jung, S. A. Chowdhury, and B. J. Jansen, "Enriching social media personas with personality traits: A deep learning approach using the big five classes," *Lect. Notes Comput. Sci. (including Subser. Lect. Notes Artif. Intell. Lect. Notes Bioinformatics)*, vol. 12217 LNCS, pp. 101–120, 2020, doi: 10.1007/978-3-03050334-5_7

16. C. Stachl et al., "Personality research and assessment in the era of machine learning," *Eur. J. Pers.*, vol. 34, no. 5, pp. 613–631, 2020, doi: 10.1002/per.2257

17. H. Ahmad, M. Z. Asghar, A. S. Khan, and A. Habib, "A systematic literature review of personality trait classification from textual content," *Open Comput. Sci.*, vol. 10, no. 1, pp. 175–193, 2020, doi: 10.1515/comp-2020-0188

18. Y. Li, A. Kazameini, Y. Mehta, and E. Cambria, "Multitask learning for emotion and personality detection," vol. 1, no. 1, pp. 1–8, 2021 [Online]. Available: http://arxiv.org/abs/2101.02346

19. L. Alexander, E. Mulfinger, and F. L. Oswald, "Using big data and machine learning in personality measurement: opportunities and challenges," *Eur. J. Pers.*, vol. 34, no. 5, pp. 632–648, 2020, doi: 10.1002/per.2305

15

A Brief Bibliometric Survey of Alphabets Recognition Using Hand Gesture in Sign Language

Sarita Deshpande and Deepali Nilesh Naik

CONTENTS

15.1 Introduction

Sign language is a combination of gestures, movements, postures, and facial expressions equivalent to alphabets and words in familiar languages. Sign languages have their dictionary, along with their syntax and grammar. Sign language is the only approach for hard of hearing people to communicate among themselves and with the regular hearing

DOI: 10.1201/9781003342755-18

community. A collection of gestures is used to perform communication. Gesture recognition plays a vital role in sign language recognition (SLR). The gestures are also a combination of the movements of body parts such as facial expression and hand actions used to communicate thoughts. This communication process is confined to a broad vocabulary and grammar and verbal languages within different means. Visual actions and expressions can only be performed in a sign language. SLR required specific preprocessing of the images of the sign language. Gesture recognition is the initial phase in sign language recognition (Oliveira et al., 2018). Various sign languages are available worldwide, just as various spoken languages and each sign language has a different structure. The ASL (American Sign Language) and BSL (British Sign Language) are diverse but cooperatively incomprehensible languages. The American and British deaf societies were not connected as two languages developed independently. Thai sign language, Brazilian sign language, French sign language, Taiwan sign language, and lots of rest have advanced in societies of hard of hearing individuals. On the other hand, each sign language has different techniques of recognition. Several challenges occurred while working on efficient automated Indian sign language (ISL) recognition. The first challenge is the lack of a standard ISL dataset and consequently creating a dataset based upon any sign language. In the literature, most of the algorithms were evaluated based on the digits dataset, that is, 0–9, and the alphabets dataset, that is, A–Z. Each sign language has created its dataset for research experimentation. Preprocessing, segmentation, and feature extraction are the various phases needed in sign language recognition. Multiple algorithms can be used to implement sign language recognition, such as convolutional neural network (CNN), hidden Markov model (HMM), multidimensional HMM and artificial neural network (ANN). The feature extraction technique is applied to acquire peculiarities out of the images captured by the camera or any other capturing device. In the literature, rotation, scaling, background removal, and illumination operations were considered for the feature extraction (Ghosh & Ari, 2011). Gestures are used consciously and unconsciously in almost all communication perspectives between human beings that form the base of the language exercised by hard of hearing people termed sign language. The stated approach is a natural means by which hard of hearing individuals express their feelings. Studies on gestures and languages specify that vocal languages and gestures are two different representations of a single system if the human mind is considered. Gesture-based communication is the critical strategy between the hard-of-hearing and unable-to-speak individuals. Phonetic analysis on ISL started around the year 1978. It was observed that ISL is a full-fledged regular language for the hard of hearing and the mute people in India and possesses its specific phonology, morphology, grammar, and syntax. The assessment on ISL linguistics and phonological research get congested due to the absence of phonetical explanation. Deep learning-based classification is one of the popular techniques used in sign language translation (Park et al., 2020).

15.1.1 Motivation to Conduct Bibliometric Analysis

The bibliometric investigation methods are quite favorable for further investigators to procure selected research domain's insights (Bhanage & Pawar, 2020). Several scholars have commenced a bibliometric analysis to estimate the selected study field's influence and review distinct researchers, regions, affiliations, and acquaintance with global research. The study was conducted on the statistical data of publications and pulled out of the database. The examination can impede existing research progress, eminent keywords utilized by authors, authors' endowment, source expansion, and affiliation involvement in support through statistical information. Furthermore, it serves in pursuing the scientific developments in a sign language recognition field over a period of time. This chapter performed a bibliometric analysis of "sign language recognition". As per the author's knowledge, this is the first bibliometric analysis proposed in the selected domain. This chapter will provide the overall idea about work done in the literature on the topic of sign language recognition. Details about the demanding subject area, funding agencies, and top contributing authors and university will definitely help forthcoming researchers to plan the track of their research.

15.1.2 Contribution of the Work

The bibliometric analysis is conducted on the topic of "sign language recognition", which covers analysis of various factors and represented it in tabular and diagrammatic format. The authors conducted analysis based on following key parameters:

1. Collection of relevant literature from Scopus database by selecting adequate keywords.
2. Carried out statistical analysis of extracted literature and distributed the records based on language of publication, source type, and year of publication. This analysis helps to track the growth of the publications in stated area.
3. Conduction bibliometric analysis based on keywords used in the extracted articles, subject domains, affiliation, author's contribution, and funding agencies.
4. Diagrammatic representation of citation analysis, growth of keywords, and geographical locations to identify the upcoming opportunities in the field of "sign language recognition".

15.2 Review of Literature

The authors (Park et al., 2020) contributed to the design of a mobile gadget-based sign language interpretation approach by utilizing depth-only images. The authors developed a dataset consisting of 1,394 word samples and translated it to 26,486 frames in the study. The researchers (Barbhuiya et al., 2021) conducted their research to identify pros and cons in the use of convolutional neural networks (CNN) for hand gesture segmentation and recognition (HGR); for this purpose, authors applied deep learning-based CNNs for vigorous modeling of immobile symbols in the connection of SLR. In the research of Ali et al. (2020), the authors proposed a technique for converting Arabic words into voice. Additionally, the authors used different machine learning algorithms like K-mean, K-Medoid algorithms, and artificial neural networks (ANN) to achieve the highest accuracy, data acquisition, preprocessing, and segmentation. The authors (Sharma et al., 2020) developed a D-talk system in the research, which helps people who cannot talk and hear. In the experimentation, authors (Sharma et al., 2020), applied oriented fast and rotated brief (ORB) technique for feature extraction against different preprocessing methods such as histogram of gradients, local binary pattern (LBP), and principal component analysis (PCA) on a similar dataset (Ahuja et al., 2019). The researchers aimed to establish a trustworthy communication rendering algorithm by translating ISL and generating understandable results. The research work was practiced with a combination of image processing and machine learning. According to Dasl et al. (2018), image classification and machine learning can support computer recognizing sign language with the help of the CNN technique.

The research demonstrated a user-friendly technique for converting Bangla sign language to text through the customized region of interest (ROI). In the study (Ahuja et al., 2019), a CNN was applied on 24 hand gestures of American sign language to boost communication mitigation. In addition to that, the author claims, CNN has an accuracy of 99.7% by validating the results.

The authors (Oliveira et al., 2019) have developed a dataset of frames withdrawn through Irish sign language (ISL) videos for SLR. The dataset has been composed by transcription of human actions, also performing ISL hand gestures. Dabre and Dholay's (2014) proposed work was based on the plan and execution of an Android application that can be used anywhere and anytime and converts American sign language to text. Panwar (2012) proposed recognizing Arabic alphabets for sign language based on the K-mean algorithm's clustering approaches.

The authors (Ravi et al., 2018) developed a new segmentation algorithm using features based on the discrete wavelet transform (DWT) and local binary pattern (LBP) to resolve the many complex problems, which are approaches with ISL videos. Apart from this, the authors authenticate the intended feature extraction technique employing sophisticated features such as histogram of oriented gradients (HOG), scale-invariant feature transform (SIFT), and speeded up robust features (SURF) for each sign video.

Loke et al. (2017) presented a sign language converter approach by employing hand gesture recognition features to identify the gestures in ISL and transform them into a natural language. The offered system utilizes hue, saturation, and intensity (HSV) color model for hand tracking and segmentation. Bhowmick et al. (2015) focused their work to facilitate the AI-based technique to read, write, and learn English by recognizing the isolated and continuous English alphabet's hand gestures. Das et al. (2015) introduced a vision-based method to identify facial gestures (lip movement, eyebrow pattern, etc.) to communicate in another way with abnormal individuals from the less investigated domain. To improve their productiveness also to include same in some sign language or vision-based gesture recognition actions in favor of accurate adoption of decisions, the proposed research discovered methods to classify facial gestures. Dabre and Dholay (2014) proposed a methodology for visual ISL recognition by applying image processing, computer vision, and neural network practices to distinguish the hand's features in images engaged out of a video through a web camera. The suggested methodology applied to translate video of day-to-day regularly used complete sentences gesture into text and followed by conversion to audio. Bhowmick et al. (2015) established the computer-vision-based hand gesture recognition technique by applying background subtraction to display targeted gesture motion images. Panwar (2012) proposed an algorithm that is straightforward and self-sufficient for user feature identification; further, there is no need for data training, such as in HMM or neural networks. The developed method has been experimented with 360 images that provide nearly 94% recognition. According to Deora and Bajaj (2012), the steps used in implementing sign language recognition are first segmentation and then applying the fingertip finding algorithm followed by PCA recognition. The arrangement of the chapter is as follows. The following section discusses different views of authors, followed by studying all the research papers from 2011 to 2020 using the Scopus database, final remarks, and related references.

15.3 Primary Data Collection

15.3.1 Methodology

Figure 15.1 shows the methodology used for bibliometric analysis of scholarly articles related to "sign language recognition". In the methodology, the first step is the identification of essential keywords associated with the selected domain. Verification of chosen keywords from experts and finalizing the list of specific keywords to design the search query is done next. Relevant scholarly articles are extracted with the help of executing search queries on the Scopus database. Systematic bibliometric analysis was conducted on the extracted scholarly articles. This bibliometric study is organized as statistical value tables, analysis graphs as well as network diagrams.

15.3.2 Significant Keywords

Table 15.1 presents the significant keywords used in the extracted publication related to "sign language recognition".

15.3.3 Findings from the Primary Study

The Scopus repository was utilized to carry out a bibliometric analysis. With the help of selected keywords, a preliminary investigation is led in all 472 publications, which is then limited to five languages worldwide. In the retrieved 472 articles, 461 articles are in English, five are in Chinese, three are in Turkish, two are in Japanese, and one is in Spanish publication (Table 15.2).

In the retrieved articles, different six types of publications are found. With reference to Table 15.3, 58.47% are conference papers, 29.66% are articles, 9.32% are conference reviews, 1.69% are book chapters, 0.63% are review papers, and 0.21% editorials. Among all the distributions given in Table 15.3, several articles are present under the conference

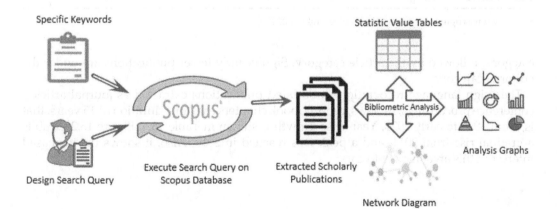

FIGURE 15.1
Methodology followed for bibliometric analysis.

TABLE 15.1
Significant Keywords

Domain keywords	Sign language, Indian sign language
Methodology keywords	Static recognition, dynamic recognition, image processing, pattern recognition, feature extraction, segmentation
Technique keywords	Neural network, machine learning, deep learning
Search query	(("sign language" or "Indian sign language") or ("static recognition" or "dynamic recognition") and ("neural network" or "machine learning" or "deep learning") and ("image processing" or "pattern recognition" or "feature extraction" or "segmentation"))

TABLE 15.2
Division of Extracted Publications According to Language

S. No.	Article Language	No. of Articles
1	English	461
2	Chinese	5
3	Turkish	3
4	Japanese	2
5	Spanish	1
Total Count:		**472**

Source: www.scopus.com (accessed on 12 December 2020).

TABLE 15.3
Division of Extracted Publications According to Source Type

S. No.	Article Type	No. of Articles	Percentage
1.	Conference Paper	276	58.47 %
2.	Article	140	29.66 %
3.	Conference Review	44	9.32 %
4.	Book Chapter	8	1.69 %
5.	Review	3	0.63 %
6.	Editorial	1	0.21 %
Total Count and Percentage:		**472**	**100 %**

Source: www.scopus.com (accessed on 12 December 2020)

category, followed by the article category. Significantly fewer publications are under the editorial category.

The "sign language recognition" associated publications extracted as journal articles, conference proceedings, reviews, reports, book chapters etc., for a duration of 15 years, that is, from 1993 to early 2021. Year-wise growth is shown in Table 15.4. Figure 15.2 exhibits a gradual rise from 2011, and a peak was reached in 2019. Also, it shows the increased interest in this area in recent years.

TABLE 15.4
Year-wise Augmentation in Extracted Publications

Year of Publication	Count	Year of Publication	Count
2021	7	2006	4
2020	70	2005	2
2019	101	2004	8
2018	60	2003	3
2017	41	2002	5
2016	27	2001	2
2015	23	2000	4
2014	19	1999	3
2013	14	1998	2
2012	16	1997	3
2011	14	1996	5
2010	7	1995	3
2009	7	1994	1
2008	7	1993	4
2007	10		
Total:			**472**

Source: www.scopus.com (accessed on 12 December 2020).

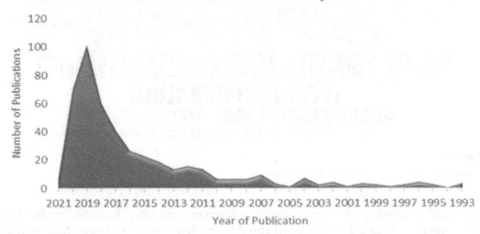

FIGURE 15.2
Year-wise augmentation in extracted publications.

15.4 Bibliometric Analysis

15.4.1 Statistical Techniques

15.4.1.1 Keyword Statistics

The researcher always wants to search relevant articles with the help of keywords. From considered publications in "sign language recognition", the first 10 keywords are selected and listed in Table 15.5. The neural network technique is primarily used in "sign language

TABLE 15.5

Most Used Keywords in Extracted Publication

Keywords	No of times Appearance
Neural networks	199
Sign language recognition	159
Sign language	158
Gesture recognition	124
Feature extraction	122
Pattern recognition	113
Image processing	99
Learning systems	89
Audition	84
Deep learning	81

Source: www.scopus.com (accessed on 12 December 2020).

FIGURE 15.3

Most used keywords in the extracted publications.

recognition" research even though machine learning and deep learning are the future research areas. In Figure 15.3, the word cloud is another way of representation to display relevant keywords. The word cloud is designed using Biblioshiny open-source tool.

15.4.1.2 Subject Domain

Figure 15.4 shows the distribution of withdrawing articles by subject domain. "Sign language recognition" mostly leads to automatic recognition; thus, most of the publications are discovered in engineering and computer science. Statistics show that 41.8% are from the computer science area and 22.4% are from engineering.

15.4.1.3 Affiliation Statistics

The best performing organization contributes to "sign language recognition" for hard of hearing and mute people specified in Figure 15.5. Considerable research is going on in

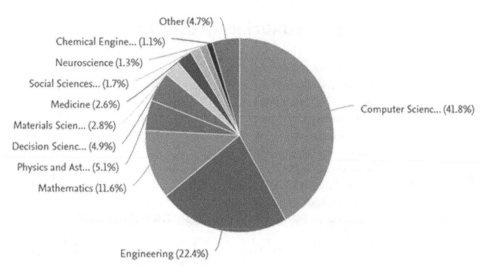

FIGURE 15.4
Division of the extracted publications according to subject area.
Source: www.scopus.com (accessed on 12 December 2020).

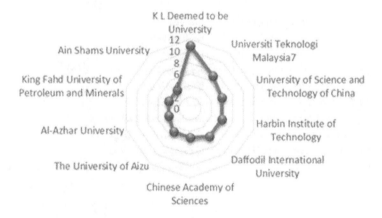

FIGURE 15.5
Presentation of top 10 affiliations from extracted publications.
Source: www.scopus.com (accessed on 12 December 2020).

the Asian region, particularly on ISL. Top Indian universities contributing significantly to Indian sign language recognition are shown in Figure 15.5.

15.4.1.4 Extremely Productive Author's Statistics

The authors' contribution and their influence in the "sign language recognition" domain can be understood easily with the help of Figure 15.6. It indicates the top ten authors contributing to this area. P.V.V. Kishore has published a maximum number, that is, ten papers, under a selected domain.

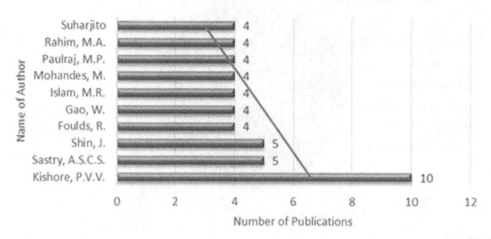

FIGURE 15.6
The endowment of authors in the extracted publications.
Source: www.scopus.com (accessed on 12 December 2020).

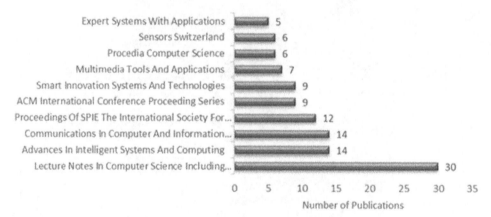

FIGURE 15.7
Division of the extracted publications according to publication year by source.
Source: www.scopus.com (accessed on 12 December 2020).

15.4.1.5 Source Statistics

The statistics for publication per year by a source (Figure 15.7) show that the maximum number of articles are from Lecture Notes in Computer Science (LNCS) and afterwards from Advances in Intelligent Systems and Computing. On the other hand, minimum publications are available in expert systems with applications source.

Publications by Funding Sponsor

- National Natural Science Foundation of China14
- Fundamental Research Funds for the Central Universities7
- National Science Foundation5
- European Regional Development Fund3
- National Research Foundation of Korea3
- Science Foundation Ireland3
- Türkiye Bilimsel ve Teknolojik Araştırma Kurumu3
- Conselho Nacional de Desenvolvimento Científico e Tecnológico2
- Fundação para a Ciência e a Tecnologia2
- King Fahd University of Petroleum and Minerals2

FIGURE 15.8
Publications by funding sponsor.
Source: www.scopus.com (accessed on 12 December 2020).

15.4.1.6 Funding Statistics

Figure 15.8 shows the publications by funding sponsors for the "sign language recognition" domain research. The National Natural Science Foundation of China is supported by capitalization for research as well as publications. The maximum count of 14 publications is from this same agency.

15.4.2 Analytical Techniques

15.4.2.1 Keyword Analysis

Figure 15.9 depicts a connection between the co-appearance of authors and keywords used by authors in the extracted articles. While generating the network diagram, a minimum number of occurrence of author keywords considered is five. The initial layout depicts 99 nodes and 62 edges. Observation reveals that "sign language recognition", "image processing", and "convolutional neural network" are the primary author keywords utilized widely within the selected research domain. Moreover, keyword analysis illustrates applications of sign language recognition techniques in the research work of hand gesture recognition, pattern recognition, computer vision, artificial neural networks, and machine learning.

The research transition takes place from pattern recognition, feature extraction to convolutional neural network, and now in the machine learning (ML) and deep learning (DL) approach. The growth of the author's keyword over the years is depicted in Figure 15.10. It shows the splendid increase in the use of keywords from pattern recognition to deep learning. The graph is drawn with the help of the Biblioshiny open-source tool.

15.4.2.2 Geographical Region Analysis

Table 15.6 provides the list of the top ten countries contributing a significant amount of publications in "sign language recognition" research. Without a doubt, India leads with nearly 101 publications; after that, China about 45 and the United States about 38 articles.

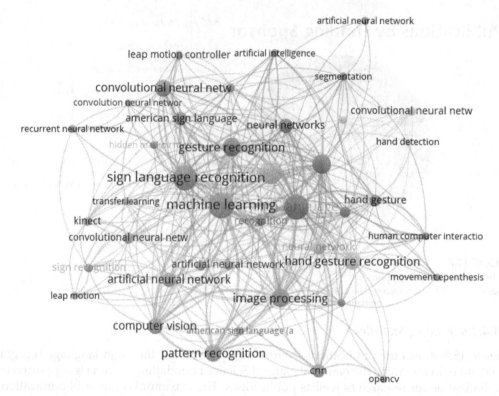

FIGURE 15.9
Network representation of co-occurrence of authors and author's keywords in the extracted publications.

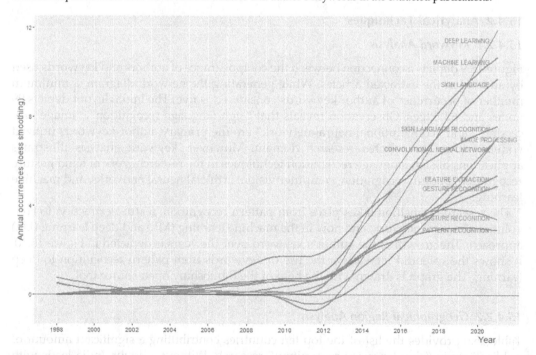

FIGURE 15.10
Growth of author's keywords over the years.

TABLE 15.6

Number of Publications from Top Ten Countries

Country	No. of Publications
India	101
China	45
United States	38
Malaysia	22
Japan	21
Bangladesh	19
Brazil	16
Indonesia	15
Turkey	14
Egypt	13

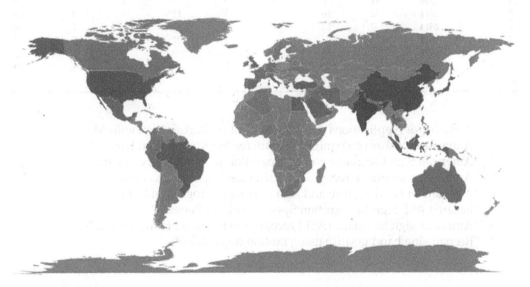

FIGURE 15.11

Geographical places of the extracted publications.

Figure 15.11 exhibits the geography of published articles region-wise, and this figure is drawn using Biblioshiny open-source tool. The engrossment of the source relies upon the dimensions and density of the color. The map shows that the majority of the researchers are located in India.

15.4.2.3 Citation Analysis

Citations were achieved year by year from publications extracted in the "sign language recognition" are presented in Table 15.7. The entire citation number of articles is 4,121. Table 15.8 shows the records of the top ten articles and their citations until the documents' extracted date for the selected research area.

1. "Extraction of 2D motion trajectories and its application to ..."
2. "Max-pooling convolutional neural networks for vision-based h..."

TABLE 15.7

Summary of Citations from Extracted Articles

Year	<2016	2016	2017	2018	2019	2020	Subtotal	>2020	Total
Citations	1200	320	324	436	801	964	2845	76	4121

TABLE 15.8

Top Ten Cited Articles

Article No.	Year	<2016	2016	2017	2018	2019	2020	>2020	Total
1	2002	185	19	15	17	16	9	0	261
2	2011	24	19	32	41	64	59	5	244
3	2015	2	15	27	23	34	31	1	133
4	1996	81	8	1	10	6	4	0	110
5	2011	42	16	7	12	15	14	2	108
6	2014	7	13	13	16	14	16	1	80
7	2019				1	27	46	3	77
8	1995	63	6	2		3	2		76
9	2007	42	10	2	3	8	8	1	74
10	1999	72	1						73

3. "A Survey of Applications and Human Motion Recognition with M..."
4. "A dynamic gesture recognition system for the Korean Sign Lan..."
5. "American Sign Language word recognition with a sensory glove..."
6. "Arabic sign language recognition using the leap motion contr..."
7. "A review of hand gesture and sign language recognition techn..."
8. "Isolated ASL Sign Recognition System for Deaf Persons"
9. "American sign language (ASL) recognition based on Hough tran..."
10. "Recognising hand gesture using motion trajectories"

15.5 Research Implications of the Study

The world is looking for inserting technology to help disabled people. Hard of hearing and mute is a significant community of them. The research work on sign language is taking place around the world and continuously evolving. This study gives comprehensive analytics about keywords, publications, geo locations, and technologies used. It will provide a guiding path for innovative and creative ideas for sign language recognition, specifically Indian sign language, to bring change through technological improvement in the life of disabled people.

As per the bibliometric analysis, the bottom level keywords in Table 15.5 for "sign language recognition" research are machine learning, deep learning, image processing, pattern recognition, and feature extraction. The observation says that the appearance of these keywords will increase in the upcoming years. The more research will be conducted to analyze the gesture images using artificial intelligence to get smart and automated solutions. The study suggests significant research gaps, accordingly furnishing essential scope to experts worldwide to focus on machine learning, deep learning, image processing, pattern recognition, and feature extraction. Listed domains have an additional eminent space and are thus necessary to be researched.

Research on ISL is taking place significantly in the Asian territory, particularly in India, Pakistan, and Bangladesh. Top institutions and universities of these countries contribute to the recognition and application of the Indian sign language. In the existing literature, only three review papers out of 472 are found in the area of "sign language recognition". This bibliometric study will help upcoming researchers to get overall idea about the existing literature. Indian researchers can explore this area as the increasing demand for research for disabled communities, which has been unnoticed in the past. No single standardized sign language is available worldwide, as sign languages are developed in different countries in different periods. Thus, there is huge scope to explore this research area irrespective of specific geographical location. As a future scope in the sign language recognition, authors are suggesting the need of generalize solution that will be able to understand any type of gesture. The contribution of funding agencies is less for this research, particularly in India, as shown in Figure 15.8. Improvement in funding contribution may push the research in upcoming years.

15.6 Constraints of the Research

This research conducted a bibliometric study of the articles retrieved from the Scopus database by applying significant keywords. The analysis is undertaken upon the accessible publications from the Scopus repository till January 2021, and recently published articles are not integrated. Some documents and journal papers were not accessible in the Scopus repository in the literature data analysis; hence, they have not been included in this bibliometric analysis. Research work published in the English language is utilized for the examination. The conducted analysis limits publications in sign language only.

15.7 Conclusion

The bibliometric analysis conducted on sign language recognition (SL), a growing field from 1993 to early 2021, reveals the increase in the accuracy of sign language recognition with the help of recent techniques such as artificial intelligence, machine learning, and deep learning. The publications in this field are available in English, Chinese, Turkish, Japanese, and Spanish, but leading the research is the English language. Considerable research is going on in the Asian region, particularly on the Indian sign language. Top Indian universities are contributing significantly to Indian sign language recognition research. The National Natural Science Foundation of China agency actively supports research and publications in the selected area.

In the existing literature on sign language recognition, the research focuses mainly on hand symbol gestures. Apart from hand gestures, facial expressions, and other body parts, actions can be considered to articulate an idea. Forthcoming researchers can emphasize their work to design the generalized framework by making use of the above-listed parameters. The utilization of research and recent technology will definitely help hard of hearing and mute people to survive in society. In the existing literature on sign language recognition, the research focuses mainly on hand symbols of gestures. The study can be further extended to facial expressions and other body parts to encode sentences' meaning. Considering the features in artificial intelligence, machine learning, and deep learning, these techniques can play a vital role in this research. Furthermore, emphasizing the design of a generalized combined framework for English and other languages can be the future work area in the sign language recognition domain.

References

Ahuja, R., Jain, D., Sachdeva, D., Garg, A., & Rajput, C. (2019). Convolutional neural network based American sign language static hand gesture recognition. *International Journal of Ambient Computing and Intelligence*, 10(3), 60–73. https://doi.org/10.4018/IJACI.2019070104

Ali, S. K., Al-Sherbaz, A., & Aydam, Z. M. (2020). Convert gestures of Arabic words into voice. *Journal of Physics: Conference Series*, 1591(1), 1–10. https://doi.org/10.1088/1742-6596/1591/1/012023

Barbhuiya, A. A., Karsh, R. K., & Jain, R. (2021). CNN based feature extraction and classification for sign language. *Multimedia Tools and Applications*, 80(2), 3051–3069. https://doi.org/10.1007/s11042-020-09829-y

Bhanage, D. A., & Pawar, A. V. (2020). Bibliometric survey of IT infrastructure management to avoid failure conditions. *Information Discovery and Delivery*, June. https://doi.org/10.1108/IDD-06-2020-0060

Bhowmick, S., Kumar, S., & Kumar, A. (2015). Hand gesture recognition of English alphabets using artificial neural network. 2015 IEEE 2nd International Conference on Recent Trends in Information Systems, ReTIS 2015 – Proceedings, 405–410. https://doi.org/10.1109/ReTIS.2015.7232913

Dabre, K., & Dholay, S. (2014). Machine learning model for sign language interpretation using webcam images. 2014 International Conference on Circuits, Systems, Communication and Information Technology Applications, CSCITA 2014, 317–321. https://doi.org/10.1109/CSCITA.2014.6839279

Das, S. P., Talukdar, A. K., & Sarma, K. K. (2015). Sign language recognition using facial expression. *Procedia Computer Science*, 58, 210–216. https://doi.org/10.1016/j.procs.2015.08.056

Dasl, A., Gawde, S., Suratwala, K., & Kalbande, D. (2018). Sign language recognition using deep learning on custom processed static gesture images. 2018 International Conference on Smart City and Emerging Technology, ICSCET 2018. https://doi.org/10.1109/ICSCET.2018.8537248

Deora, D., & Bajaj, N. (2012). Indian sign language recognition. Proceedings on 2012 1st International Conference on Emerging Technology Trends in Electronics, Communication and Networking, ET2ECN 2012. https://doi.org/10.1109/ET2ECN.2012.6470093

Ghosh, D. K., & Ari, S. (2011). A static hand gesture recognition algorithm using k-mean based radial basis function neural network. ICICS 2011 – 8th International Conference on Information, Communications and Signal Processing, I. https://doi.org/10.1109/ICICS.2011.6174264

Loke, P., Paranjpe, J., Bhabal, S., & Kanere, K. (2017). Indian sign language converter system using an android app. Proceedings of the International Conference on Electronics, Communication and Aerospace Technology, ICECA 2017, 2017-Janua, 436–439. https://doi.org/10.1109/ICECA.2017.8212852

Oliveira, M., Chatbri, H., Little, S., O'Connor, N. E., & Sutherland, A. (2018). A comparison between end-to-end approaches and feature extraction based approaches for Sign Language recognition. International Conference Image and Vision Computing New Zealand, 2017 December, 1–6. https://doi.org/10.1109/IVCNZ.2017.8402478

Oliveira, M., Chatbri, H., Yarlapati, N., O'Connor, N. E., & Sutherland, A. (2019). Hand orientation redundancy filter applied to hand-shapes dataset. *ACM International Conference Proceeding Series*. https://doi.org/10.1145/3309772.3309794

Panwar, M. (2012). Hand gesture based interface for aiding visually impaired. Proceedings of the 2012 International Conference on Recent Advances in Computing and Software Systems, RACSS 2012, 80–85. https://doi.org/10.1109/RACSS.2012.6212702

Park, H. J., Lee, J. S., & Ko, J. G. (2020). Achieving real-time sign language translation using a smartphone's true depth images. 2020 International Conference on COMmunication Systems and NETworkS (COMSNETS) 2020, 622–625. https://doi.org/10.1109/COMSNETS48 256.2020.9027420

Ravi, S., Maloji, S., Polurie, V. V. K., & Eepuri, K. K. (2018). Sign language recognition with multi feature fusion and ANN classifier. *Turkish Journal of Electrical Engineering and Computer Sciences*, 26(6), 2871–2885. https://doi.org/10.3906/elk-1711-139

Sharma, A., Mittal, A., Singh, S., & Awatramani, V. (2020). Hand gesture recognition using image processing and feature extraction techniques. *Procedia Computer Science*, 173(2019), 181–190. https://doi.org/10.1016/j.procs.2020.06.022

16

Oxyportal: Oxygen Demand Forecasting with Data Analytics

Sachin S. Sawant, Chandrashekhar B. Dongre, and Animesh D. Dolas

CONTENTS

16.1 Introduction

The COVID-19 disease mainly attacks the lungs and makes it tough to breathe for its victims. Therefore, timely availability and supply of medical oxygen are crucial while treating COVID-19 patients. During the COVID 19 pandemic, the peak of the first wave struck us around September 2020 while that of the second wave around April and May 2021. It's a well-known fact that various hospitals suffered an acute shortage of medical oxygen during this period. Hence, according to newspaper reports, 512 people lost their lives due to oxygen shortage [1]. Lack of proper resource management and logistics of the available oxygen at the manufacturers was the main reason for these fatalities. Logistics related to oxygen supply involve supplying tankers to large hospitals directly from manufacturers and for small hospitals, there are intermediaries. However, owing to the unexpected shoot-up in the medical oxygen requirement across the country, the existing multilevel logistics got severely disturbed. The daily oxygen demand of 3,842 Metric Tonnes (MT) as of 12 April 2021 rose to 8,400 MT on a daily basis till 25 April 2021, and it further shot up drastically to 11,000 MT per day at the beginning of May 2021. But sooner, owing to the decline in the fresh cases, the oxygen demand got decreased progressively [2]. Therefore, it becomes necessary to predict oxygen demand to handle such disruption of the supply chain in the future.

Various methods have been implemented to forecast the number of COVID-19 patients and also to analyze COVID-19 trends. COVID-19 trend analysis has been done using machine learning techniques; there are also various parameters on which COVID-19 spread can be predicted. A dashboard can be developed to showcase the results. A. Jaglan et al. [3] have reported the use of frequency-inverse document frequency (TFIDF) vectorization and a machine learning model based on Polynomial Regression analysis. The use of polynomial regression gives good accuracy to the model. The use of the SIR model and estimating its parameters has also been useful in predicting the peak of infection while considering various parameters like the lockdown. This has been applied to India's data and the results are promising [4]. SIR model-based research done in Algeria predicted that 1.91% of the entire population will be affected and there will remain around 35.23% of vulnerable people after the end of the infection [5]. This shows that the SIR model can give quantitative results. Forecasting oxygen demand can aid the oxygen supply chain in the future. The study done on the method of predictive Big Data applications (BDA) can identify gaps and provide insight for future research [6]. To manage data collected, to use it again for prediction, and to aid the supply chain, a web dashboard can be very helpful. This can be done using HTML, CSS, JavaScript, and MySQL database [7]. However, to the best of our knowledge, no literature has ever reported the oxygen demand prediction with reasonable accuracy. Earlier works [1–7] have reported only the peak of infection for a particular region, but the results aren't used to predict the required medical oxygen demand, which is crucial in managing the supply chain of oxygen during the COVID-19 infection peak period to save lives. This was the motivation behind the present work reported here. This chapter reports a method to obtain oxygen quantity in MT based on future demand by calculating oxygen demand for a region by using Polynomial Regression and the SIR model to forecast the peak of COVID infections. Combining the results of the SIR model and the Polynomial Regression machine learning model, several active cases for N number of days can be predicted. These patients are then divided into critical, severe, and moderate cases as per World Health Organization (WHO) guidelines [8]. Based on this calculation, oxygen demand for a defined patient group in a region can be predicted. In addition, a web portal was designed with HTML, CSS, and JavaScript to manage the data collected and its appropriate and effective utilization for the end-user and hospitals. They can create accounts on this web portal and seek the required useful information.

16.2 Methodology

Handling oxygen data and predicting its demand form the crucial part of this work. A flowchart depicting the same is given in Figure 16.1. The methodology is divided into two parts:

1. Predictive models – Designing of the model to predict data related to COVID-19 cases.
2. Web portal – Accessing the model data and results for public use.

16.2.1 Data Collection

First, the collected data is cleaned, so that it can be used for data analysis. Different data analytic approaches have been implemented on COVID datasets. Figure 16.2 shows various graphs for a visualization based on data collected from various sources, including Kaggle and WHO [8–11]. In Figure 16.2, the data of current active cases starting from January 2020

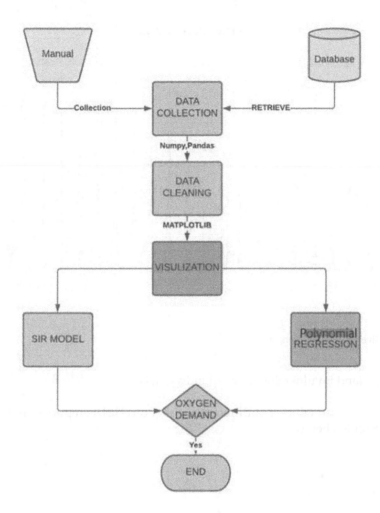

FIGURE 16.1
Flowchart of handling oxygen data and predicting oxygen demand.

to July 2021 is plotted. The figure shows Maharashtra had the highest active cases. The graph also shows the peaks of infections. The stress on the supply chain was very high mainly during these peaks. It can be observed that peaks show a variation for different states.

16.2.2 SIR Model (Susceptible, Infectious, and Recovered)

SIR model is used to model COVID-19 trends from the beginning of infection to the current date. For a quantitative analysis of the infectious disease, compartmental models are used. In this model, populations are labeled as S, I, or R (Susceptible, Infectious, and Recovered). The model used to predict oxygen demand is the simplest model and has three compartments. They are described below:

S: Susceptible individuals
I: infectious individuals

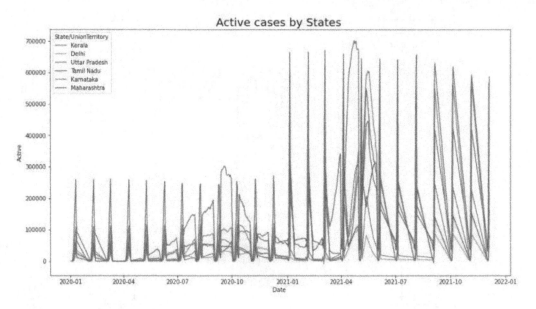

FIGURE 16.2
Plot showing active cases by different states.

R: Removed (and invulnerable) or dead individuals.

The SIR model is based on a set of differential equations [12] as reported in the literature, which is represented below:

$$(t) = (t)/N \tag{16.1}$$

$$(t) = (t)/N \tag{16.2}$$

$$(t) = (t)/N \tag{16.3}$$

$$\mathrm{d}s/\mathrm{d}t = -bs(t)l(t) \tag{16.4}$$

$$\mathrm{d}s/\mathrm{d}t = -bs(t)i(t) \tag{16.5}$$

$$\mathrm{d}r/\mathrm{d}t = ki(t) \tag{16.6}$$

$$\mathrm{d}s/\mathrm{d}t + \mathrm{d}i/\mathrm{d}t + \mathrm{d}r/\mathrm{d}t = 0 \tag{16.7}$$

$$\mathrm{d}i/\mathrm{d}t = bs(t)i(t) - ki(t) \tag{16.8}$$

These equations generate the following graph based on the Kaggle dataset [11] given in Figure 16.3 for given parameters. It shows a yellow line representing the number of susceptible individuals, a maroon line representing infectious individuals, and the teal-colored line gives recovered individuals [13].

The progression of the population within pandemic regions [14] is represented as a flowchart in Figure 16.4. In this, β represents the infectious rate and γ represents the recovery rate. The results are shown in various compartments in the SIR model.

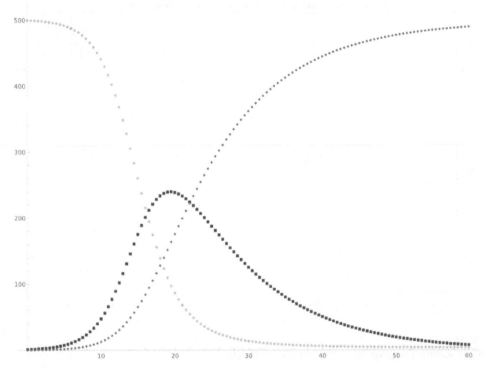

FIGURE 16.3
SIR model with its parameters [13].

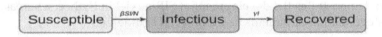

FIGURE 16.4
SIR model and its compartments.

The present model derives the initial parameters such as infection rate and susceptible individuals from the actual data. With this, we obtain the COVID-19 model for given parameters as shown in Figure 16.5. Here, the blue line represents a number of individuals actually infected, and the orange line shows number of individuals actually recovered. Based on actual data, the model was developed further. The red line presents the prediction for infected individuals and violet line shows the prediction for recovered individuals. As we can see in Figure 16.5, the number of susceptible individuals decrease as model progresses through days. Figure 16.5 gives us the peak of infections between June and July 2021. However, the actual peak was observed at the end of May 2021. So, we can say that model's prediction is reasonably good for our application of oxygen demand forecasting.

To develop the SIR model and to implement its calculations for oxygen demand prediction, we have used Python and Numpy. SIR model has been developed and written in Python. Infection rate is derived from previous data of China and Europe [18]. The initial population is considered 108,000 to simplify the model. At the end, an array is obtained containing the number of infected individuals or active cases. After obtaining the number of patients, they are categorized in severe, moderate, and critical as defined by WHO [8].

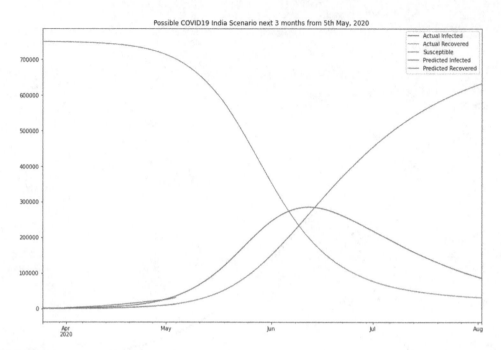

FIGURE 16.5
COVID 19 scenario predicted through plots from actual data.

This model combined with oxygen requirement parameters defined by WHO is reasonably predictive of oxygen demand due to COVID-19 infections in each region.

Figure 16.6 demonstrates the development of SIR model in Python whereas Figure 16.7 shows the categorization of patients based on WHO guidelines.

16.2.3 Polynomial Regression Machine Learning Model

To get the accurate number of patients; Polynomial regression machine learning model was implemented. Polynomial regression works on polynomial equation [15] as given below:

$$y = b_0 + b_1 x_1 + b_2 x_{12} + b_2 x_{13} + \ldots \ldots + b_n x 1_n \tag{16.9}$$

If the data point arrangement shows a nonlinear trend, then polynomial regression model is preferred. This model gives the best fit line through actual COVID data as can be seen in Figure 16.8.

16.3 Predicting Oxygen Demand

To predict the oxygen demand, we have used data from WHO dashboard. Here patients are divided into three categories, namely severe, moderate, and critical. Oxygen demand for each category is gauged through WHO data [8]. This data is then used with number

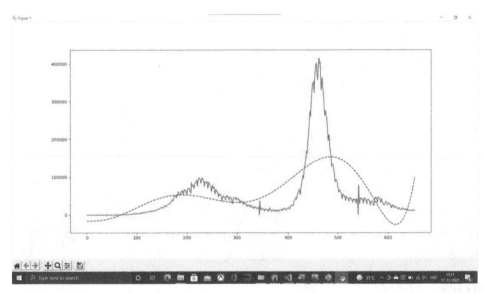

FIGURE 16.6
Polynomial Regression Machine learning model.

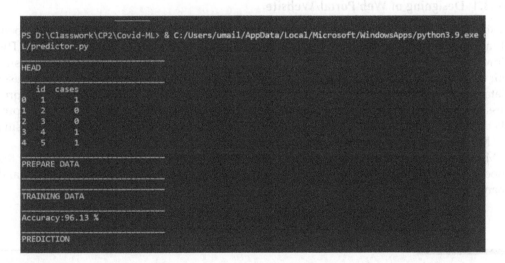

FIGURE 16.7
Polynomial Regression Machine learning model output.

of patients predicted from SIR model and Polynomial Regression to get oxygen demand. Oxygen demand for each of the category, namely critical, severe, and moderate, is different. We presented a simple calculation to determine the total oxygen demand. In order to make it easy to access medical oxygen data for hospitals and end users, a web portal called "Oxyportal" has been developed. The flow of the procedure is shown in Figure 16.8.

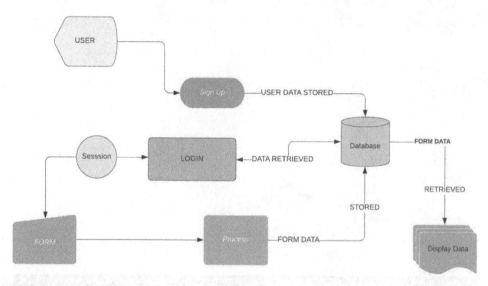

FIGURE 16.8
Design of Web Dashboard.

16.3.1 Designing of Web Portal/Website

A simple website, which has a simple interface for login and signup, has been developed. It makes it easy for public to navigate through site and use data to their advantage. The flow of website is shown in Figure 16.9. HTML and CSS is used for frontend of the website. For the backend, PHP and MySQL is implemented to create a database, which collects user data as well as hospital data. The same website is used to gather data for future data processing from hospitals and other related service providers so that it can give real-time prediction of oxygen demand to the user. The user interface of the website developed using HTML, CSS and JavaScript is shown in Figure 16.9.

MySQL database is used to store data collected from hospitals. The output data of the model was used to predict oxygen demand. This database makes it easy to retrieve and manage data.

16.4 Results and Discussion

The first data is visualized as to get general trend of the disease. In Figure 16.10, it is clearly seen that Maharashtra had the greatest number of cured cases as well as the greatest number of infected cases. This can be one of parameters while managing oxygen supply chain. To get more quantitative results, we have used SIR model and polynomial regression. The SIR model shows that at the peak of infection, we would require around 5300 MT of oxygen. Figure 16.11 is close to actual oxygen required on 18 April 2021, which was around 6,300 MT [8]. That gives an estimated model accuracy of around 84% for our model. The accuracy could have been more if data related to oxygen was available. The peak predicted with our model is around start of June 2021 whereas actual peak was around May 2021. By comparing our results with WHO novel coronavirus (COVID-19)

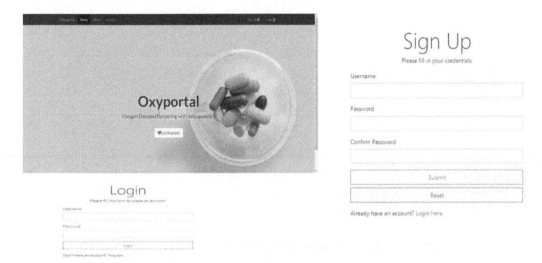

FIGURE 16.9
User Interface of Web Dashboard.

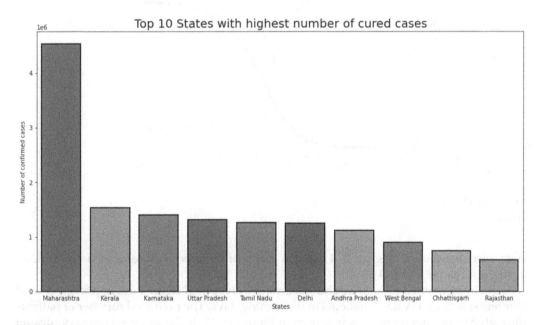

FIGURE 16.10
Visualization of data of state-wise confirmed cases through bar charts.

dashboard of cumulative confirmed cases, the proposed model was able to get the number of active cases of 80%, which is accurate [8] with the SIR model. Further, the SIR model and WHO data of per patient oxygen for different categories model was able to predict the peak oxygen demand for a particular region in India successfully.

The visualization of the number of patients was obtained through various visualization techniques. The successfully implemented SIR model, which can model COVID-19 disease, can be seen in Figure 16.12 and Figure 16.11 shows data of oxygen demand from

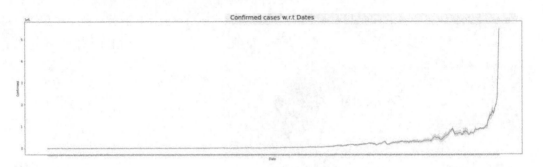

FIGURE 16.11
Plot of confirmed cases versus date.

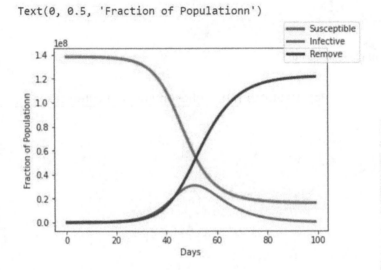

FIGURE 16.12
SIR model.

state-wise distribution. Figure 16.11 shows graph of number of patients vs dates to demonstrate spread of COVID-19

In the implemented model, machine learning Polynomial Regression approach is used to forecast active COVID-19 patients in the coming days. The predicted number of patients through polynomial regression is shown in Figure 16.13. It shows an accuracy of around 97% for short datasets. This prediction gives the number of active cases for future, which can be a good indicator of oxygen demand.

16.5 Conclusion

The SIR model for the COVID-19 epidemic in India was successfully implemented based on the daily confirmed, cured, and expired cases from 30 January 2020 to 6 July 2021.

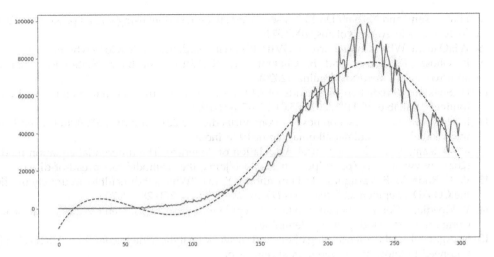

FIGURE 16.13
ML polynomial regression result.

For the estimated period of the study, the peak of the epidemic was seen to be reached in 495 days from beginning of the epidemic. It also predicted the vulnerable population percentage after the end of the infection. Besides, Polynomial Regression can provide the number of patients close to actual data. Similarly, SIR model has predicted oxygen demand in MT for 30 days, which will be useful for hospitals and COVID care centers to plan their resources. All the results obtained are showcased on web dashboard, accessed through the Oxyportal, could be useful for end users.

References

1. Ranjani Madhavan, "India reported 512 oxygen-related deaths during second wave of Covid: Open data tracker", *The Indian Express*, www.newindianexpress.com/nation/2021/may/19/india-reported-512-oxygen-related-deaths-during-second-wave-of-covid-open-data-tracker-2304596.html, {2021}
2. WHO Team, Assessment of the COVID-19 Supply Chain System: Full Report Slide Deck: www.who.int/publications/m/item/assessment-of-the-covid-19-supply-chain-system-full-report-slide-deck, (2021)
3. Abhishek Jaglan, Daksh Trehan, Priyansh Singhal, and Megha, "COVID-19 Trend analysis using machine learning techniques", *International Journal of Scientific & Engineering Research*, 11(12): 1162–1167 (2020).
4. Dilip Kumar Bagal, Arati Rath, Abhishek Barua, and Dulu Patnaik, "Estimating the parameters of susceptible-infected-recovered model of COVID-19 cases in India during lockdown periods", *Chaos, Solitons and Fractals*, 1–12 (2020).
5. Mohamed Lounis and Dilip Kumar Bagal, "Estimation of SIR model's parameters of COVID-19 in Algeria", Published online, pp. 1–6 (2020).
6. Mahya Seyedan and Fereshteh Mafakheri, "Predictive big data analytics for supply chain demand forecasting: methods, applications, and research opportunities", *Journal of Big Data* 7(53): 1–22 (2020).

7. Bhavin Tanti and Nishant Doshi, "A secure email login system using virtual password", 2019 (2010) @article, ArXiv, vol abs/1009.5729.

8. WHO team, WHO Coronavirus (COVID-19) Dashboard: https://covid19.who.int/

9. P. Ghosh, R. Ghosh, and B. Chakraborty, "COVID-19 in India: State-wise Analysis andPrediction", medRxiv, [online] (2020).

10. H. Shekhar, "Prediction of spreads of COVID-19 in India from current trend", medRxiv, [online] Available: 10.1101/2020.05.01.20087460 (2020).

11. K. P Devakumar, Dataset on novel corona virus disease 2019 in India (2019). Retrieved from www.kaggle.com/sudalairajkumar/covid19-in-india,

12. MAA team, MAA (Mathematical Association of America), The differential equation model (2021). www.maa.org/press/periodicals/loci/joma/the-sir-model-for-spread-of-disease-

13. W. C. Roda, M. B. Varughese, D. Han, and M. Y. Lia, "Why is it difficult to accurately predict the COVID-19 epidemic?", *Infectious Disease Modelling*, 5: 271–281 (2020).

14. Wikipedia, "Compartmental models in epidemiology", https://en.wikipedia.org/wiki/Compartmental_models_in_epidemiology

15. R. Agrawal, Data Science Blogathon (2021), www.analyticsvidhya.com/blog/2021/07/all-you-need-to-know-about-polynomial-regression/.

16. A. Alsayed, H. Sadir, R. Kamil, and H. Sari, "Prediction of epidemic peak and infected cases for COVID-19 disease in Malaysia," *Int. J. Environ. Res. Public Health* 17: 4076 (2020).

17. N. Huang, F. Qiao, "A data driven time-dependent transmission rate for tracking an epidemic: a case study of 2019-nCoV", *Sci. Bull.* 65(6): 425–427 (2020).

18. M. Lounis, "A descriptive study of the current situation of COVID-19 in Algeria". *Electron. J. Gen. Med.* 17(6): 253 (2020).

19. Y. Zou, S. Pan, P. Zhao, L. Han, X. Wang, L. Hemerik, J. Knops, and W. van der Werf, "Outbreak analysis with a logistic growth model shows COVID-19 suppression dynamics in China." *PLoS ONE* 15(6): e0235247 (2020).

20. E. Gambhir, R. Jain, A. Gupta, and U. Tomar, "Regression Analysis of COVID-19 Using Machine Learning Algorithms", International Conference on Smart Electronics and Communication (ICOSEC), pp. 65–71 (2020).

21. M. Cascella, M. Rajnik, A. Aleem, S. Dulebohn, and R. Di Napoli "Features Evaluation and Treatment Coronavirus (COVID-19)", StatPearls [Internet]. Treasure Island (FL): StatPearls Publishing, 2020 [online] Available from: www.ncbi.nlm.nih.gov/books/NBK554776/.

22. N. Punn, S. Sonbhadra, and S. Agarwal, "COVID-19 epidemic analysis using machine learning and deep learning algorithms", medRxiv, [online] Available: https://doi.org/ 10.1101/2020.04.08.20057679, (2020).

23. S. F. Ardabili, A. Mosavi, P. Ghamisi, F. Ferdinand, A. R. VarkonyiKoczy, U. Reuter, T. Rabczuk, and P. Atkinson, "COVID-19 Outbreak prediction with machine learning algorithms", 13: 249 (2020), doi:10.3390/a13100249.

24. H. Shekhar, "Prediction of spreads of COVID-19 in India from current trend", medRxiv [online] (2020) available: 10.1101/2020.05.01.20087460.

25. L. Yan, H. Zhang, J. Goncalves, Y. Xiao, M. Wang, Y. Guo, C. Sun, X. Tang, L. Jing, M. Zhang, X. Huang, Y. Xiao, H. Cao, Y. Chen, T. Ren, F. Wang, Y. Xiao, S. Huang, X. Tan, N. Huang, B. Jiao, C. Cheng, Y. Zhang, A. Luo, L. Mombaerts, J. Jin, Z. Cao, S. Li, H. Xu, and Y. Yuan, "An interpretable mortality prediction model for COVID-19 patients", *Nature Machine Intelligence* 2: 283–288 (2020) [online] Available: https://doi.org/10.1038/ s42256-020-0180-7

26. L. Li, Z. Yang, Z. Dang, C. Meng, J. Huang, H. Meng, D. Wanga, G. Chena, J. Zhanga, H. Penga, and Y. Shaob, "Propagation analysis and prediction of the COVID-19", *Infectious Disease Modelling* 5: 282–292 (2020) [online] Available: https:// doi.org/10.1016/ j.idm.2020.03.002, 2029

27. S. Zhao and H. Chen, "Modeling the epidemic dynamics and control of COVID-19 outbreak in China", *Quan. Biol.* 8(1): 11–19 (2020).

28. J. A. Chu, "A statistical analysis of the novel coronavirus (COVID-19) in Italy and Spain." *PLoS ONE*, 16(3): e0249037 (2021).

17

Review on Text-to-Speech Synthesis System for Hindi Language

Shaikh Naziya Sultana and R.R. Deshmukh

CONTENTS

17.1 Introduction

As air is pushed out of the lips and nose, speech sounds are recordings of air pressure waves created by exhaled lungs, modulated and shaped by glottal cord motions and vocal tract resonance. Speech is the ability to express ideas and feelings through vocal cord waves that provide a unified voice. Acoustics (sample), phonetics (phone), phonology (phoneme), morphology (morpheme), and syntax are the seven parts (word). Our goal is to transform arbitrary input text into understandable and natural-sounding synthetic speech in order to relay information from the machine to human user. Text is fed into the text-to-speech (TTS) system, which produces synthetic language [1]. Text analysis (to establish the abstract underlying linguistic representation of the voice) and speech synthesis are the two basic processes conducted by all TTS programmes (to produce the speech sounds corresponding to the text input).

DOI: 10.1201/9781003342755-20

Machine learning of human behaviours such as blogging, reading, and answering questions has been a pipe dream for a long time. In the last few decades, however, document reading by computers has progressed from a pipe dream to practice [2]. Text can be found in everyday life in the form of records (newspapers, magazines, e-mails, journals, and so on) or natural scenes (signs, walls, and schedules) that anybody can read and chat about. Unfortunately, this task is impossible for a blind or visually impaired person to complete. As a result, text-to-speech (TTS) conversion programmes were developed. The optical character recognition (OCR) method has two parts: training and testing. Pre-processing is the responsibility of the training section. Binarisation, morphological processes, and segmentation are all performed in the per-processing state. OCR-based voice synthesis systems have greatly increased the ability of the visually impaired to interact with their surroundings in the same way as sighted people do [3].

17.2 Literature Review

The invention of reading aids for the blind is another area of application. According to a survey by the National Center for Health Statistics [2], about 1.4 million Americans are severely visually impaired and need glasses to read ordinary newsprint. Machines that can scan printed material and produce speech would be extremely beneficial to this community. Personal reading machines are the main dream, but the current price of the best performing device, Kurzweil's, at more than $30,000, is a long way off. Since automatic setup and consumers have access to a huge text library, a blind person does not need to buy a high price text reader anymore. A variety of data collection standards can be met by adding a text-to-speech interface to a personal computer connected to a wide network. In Sweden, a curious experiment uses an FM broadcast overnight to load the daily in the machine of a blind person with indexing software that can scan subjects [3,4]. Other attempts have been made in this field in order to provide speech books for blind people in due course. Currently, Recording for the Blind in Princeton, New Jersey, produces several tape records for blind books.

A method of text for speech (TTS) translates the text into language. The selection unit and the hidden Markov model (HMM) are two of the well-known and commonly used speech synthesis techniques. A suitable pre-recorded units are combined to obtain the corresponding speech for the specified text in the speech collection unit synthesis. For concatenation, the units (word or sub-word) are chosen with optimum concatenation and joining cost. The naturalness of the synthesised speech is based on the scale, sense of the speech unit and number of concatenation points, that is, the naturalness of long units and fewer concatenation points are retained. Each speech unit should be present in the speech database several times in all contexts, ideally for more natural speech. Developing a suitable speech corpus for a synthesis based on unit selection is time-consuming and laborious. The HMM speech synthesis can be used to reduce the speaker's barrier. The synthesis based on the HMM is a technique of mathematical parametric language. In order to construct a parametric representation of speech [4], the defined text is converted to speech using this parametric representation, and spectral and excitation features are extracted from speech corpus. The key benefits of these parametric representations are that only data are processed, which results in a limited footprint, rather than initial speech waveforms.

Previously, the Urdu language HMM language synthesiser has been created by Nawaz and Habib [5] and uses 30 minutes of speech input. As much as 92.5 percent terms were correctly understood during the contextual testing of the device. This HMM-based synthesiser has been trained with speech data of only 30 minutes and is not incorporated into speech text scheme. For the creation of HMM-based Urdu speech synthesiser, 10 hours of manually annotated spoken data is used in the present job. In addition, a unit-based voice synthesiser is built with the same data, as well as evaluating the output of synthesised speech. For the objective intelligibility evaluation of the produced voice, automatic speech recognition technology is used. During the assessment, Hindi language recogniser is also created. Table 17.1 provides the summary of different methods text-to-speech approaches [6–22].

TABLE 17.1
Summary of Different Methods Text-to-Speech Approaches

S. No.	Method/ Techniques Used	Description
1	HMM, ANN, DWT	TTS systems are the best converter for formant synthesis using parallel syntheses and cascade syntheses. Due to its inculcation in benefits of both statistical and rule-based computer technology for translation, hybrid machine translation is used widely. The framework ensures that text is syntactically and grammatically corrected even by ensuring the smoothness of a text, rapid retrieval and acquisition of data.
2	TTS	Suggest the use of the English TTS synthesis. To translate text data to speech, a speech synthesiser is needed. A TTS framework has two essential processes: first, the management of text and, second, the production of expression.
3	Machine learning, ANN ASR, cuck search algorithm	The article outlines the fundamental processes of an ASR architecture covering the STT mechanism (automated speech recognition). The primary emphasis is on the ASR, SVM, ANN and Cuckoo search algorithms of machine learning along with ANN.
4	ANN and HMM	STT conversion can be done best by combining different methods and achieving better text accuracy. The aim is to build an ongoing STT framework with much broader vocabulary, individual speaker, capable of precisely detecting voices of various speakers. A mixture of ANN and HMM is used for the creation of such a method.
5	MFCC and HMM	Traditional HMM MFCC alternative STT method. In extracting features from the voice signals, the traditional MFCC solution was less effective and hence a new approach using HMM was proposed. The functionality transmitted to the HMM network improves the functionality of the input audio as opposed to the MFCC procedure.
6	TTS, STT conversions and IVR	The interface is designed to provide users with a user-friendly application. Interactive voice response technology is used by this method. A pre-registered voice tells users to perform those tasks to access certain services in this framework.
7	MFCC, dynamic time wrapping (DTW)	The study showed, relative to every other language, that speaking acceptance rates are highest for English. It is due to their phonetic form that the poor comprehension rate of Indian languages is found.
8	Speech synthesis, syllabification, concatenation	This is designed to build a TTS for local languages such as Hindi. The method consists of two main steps: preprocessing of text and generation of speech. For the speech from the text, a concatenative synthesis technique is considered. A Spellchecker module is also used to check for native languages such as Hindi the accuracy of words.

(continued)

TABLE 17.1 (Continued)
Summary of Different Methods Text-to-Speech Approaches

S. No.	Method/ Techniques Used	Description
9	Linear predictive coding (LPC)	The principle of LPC is that the voice sample should be used as a linear combination of previous voice recordings, voice signal is broken into N frames and then these framed windows are transformed into texting. The LPC is a static method for function extraction.
10	Mel-frequency cestrum coefficient (MFCC)	The technique extends to STT conversion measures such as framing, windowing and discrete Fourier transform.
11	Dynamic time wrapping	The DTW algorithm serves to locate the analogy of two-time, dynamically programmable events that differ in speed.
12	Hidden Markov model	HMM displays its own self-learning and structure, which makes it very useful for STT conversion.
13	Neural network	Relation values and connection strengths for state transactions are used by neural nets

17.3 Proposed Methodology

17.3.1 Hindi Speech Corpus

Speech corpora for Indian languages (Hindi, Marathi, and Punjabi) were created by C-DAC (Center for Development of Advance Computing), Noida [23]. Three languages were registered in India: Hindi by first language speakers, Hindi by second language speakers, and Indian English in the LILA Hindi L1 database and the LILA Hindi Belt database. The EMILLE/CIIL Corpus was established in the United Kingdom by EMILLE (Enabling Minority Language Engineering) in partnership with CIIL (Central Institute of Indian Languages) [24]. The Utkal University's Department of Computer Science and Application in Bhubaneswar is working on text-to-speech synthesis systems for four Indian languages: Hindi, Odiya, Bengali, and Telugu [25]. Multi-speaker, continuous speech corpora for Hindi have been developed by TIFR (Tata Institute of Fundamental Research), Mumbai, and CDAC Noida. The Indian Institute of Technology (IIT) Kharagpur has developed a Hindi speech database for general use [26].

The TTS for Hindi is focused on an open-source tech Festival. The execution of several modules, as seen in Figure 17.1, translates into expression due to Hindi text. The module for text analysis processes text information in the first step, converting all non-standard terms to standard words before translating to grapheme using the written data. The text analysis method is discussed in detail in the following section. Prosody modelling incorporates the process's intonation and duration models. Speech synthesiser for the selection unit or HMM language synthesiser are two transcription engines that can be used to synthesise phonemes. The different versions of these speech synthesisers are generated using a phonetically balanced Hindi speech corpus [6].

17.3.2 Text Preprocessing

The Hindi text is converted into the corresponding pronunciation, resulting in voice generation. The Festival text analysis module has been upgraded to complete this project.

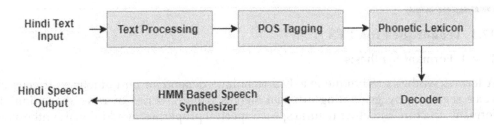

FIGURE 17.1
Hindi TTS architecture.

The text processing module has been upgraded to include Hindi text and converted to CISAMPA transcription of the transcript: (1) term segmentation; (2) word boundary marking; (3) grouping of numbers, dates, and symbols based on context; and (4) text production based on the previous study [27].

17.3.3 Parts of Speech Tagging

Using the parts of speech (POS) lexicon and the trigram language model apply POS tags to the words in the text. A trigram language model generates some of the speech tags, and the odds of words receiving their share of speech tags are calculated, which involves the POS lexicon [28].

17.3.4 Phonetic Lexicon

Since it is used to allocate the word phonemic transcript, the lexicon of pronunciation is an important component in the transmission of natural languages. The Hindi lexicon is divided into three parts: one is the Hindi word, the second is the POS tag, and the third is CISAMPA's phonemic transcription [29].

17.3.5 HMM-Based Speech Synthesiser

In addition to unit compilation speech synthesis, the Hindi TTS method supports HMM-based speech synthesis. HMM-based speech synthesis is a statistical parametric synthesis method that uses recorded speech to train parameters. Since these parameters are used for synthetic purposes after the synthesis parameters have been trained, it has a smaller footprint than unit selection. During the training period, arousal and spectral parameters are calculated as feature vectors. These feature vectors are represented by the HMM structure. In the synthesis part, the history takes a series of phones as input and generates excitation and spectral parameters using a parameter generation algorithm.

In order to reconstruct the waveform signal, these parameters are applied to the synthesiser filter. The HTS toolkit is used to create mathematical templates for speech synthesis. Ten hours of speech data was used to train the models. Wave files are used for the extraction parameter during the training process, along with structure files of utterances (derived from Festival), and training is done according to the procedure previously mentioned. Waveforms are generated at the overview level by choosing appropriate models from the Festival utterance context. These models, along with the excitement parameters, establish the synthesis filter and final waveform [30].

17.4 Techniques for TTS

17.4.1 Formant Synthesis

A format synthesis technique is a TTS technique dependent on guidelines. It generates voice segments by generating artificial signals using a series of rules that mimic the formant structure and other natural speech spectral properties. A additional synthesis and an acoustic model are used to create the synthesised voice. Speech, simple pitch, noise, and other parameters are used in the acoustic model. With the help of a few techniques for prosodic and intonational modelling, formant instruments can track any aspect of the output sound and include a wide variety of emotions and tone voices [31].

17.4.2 Parametric TTS

To address the limitations of concatenative TTS, a more statistical approach has been established. The idea was that by comparing the parameters that makeup the speak, we could train a model to generate various types of speech. Parameters such as fundamental frequency, magnitude spectrum, and others are used in the parametric method. The text's linguistic characteristics, such as phonemes and length, are extracted in the first step. The second stage entails obtaining features unique to human language, such as cepstra, spectrogram, and fundamental frequency.

Audio synthesis may also benefit from these functions. These manual characteristics, along with the linguistic capabilities, are fed into a mathematical model called a vocoder. When generating waveform, the vocoder transforms features and measures speech parameters such as phase, voice rate, intonation, and other parameters. Hidden semi-Markov models are used in the technology; there are still transitions between states, and the model is Markov, although the explicit duration pattern in any state is not [32].

17.4.3 Hybrid (Deep Learning) Approaches

Another version of the computational synthesis technique used in HMMs to model dynamic context dependence is deep neural networks (DNN) based on the DNN approach. Letting the construction of computers without human intervention was a step ahead and a possible milestone. Our interpretation of voice, although it is not strictly accurate, are the features designed by humans. The relationship between input texts and their acoustic performances is modelled on a DNN in DNN techniques. Acoustic characteristics are generated using trajectory smoothing with maximum probability parameter generation. The information gathered by Deep Learning cannot be interpreted by humans, but it can be read by algorithm and represents information that is required for a model [33].

17.5 Toolkit for TTS

17.5.1 Festival

Festival offers a general framework with examples of various modules for designing speech synthesis systems. From the shell level, it offers full text for speech using a variety of APIs: a Scheme command, a C++ library, Java, and an Emacs GUI. The Festival is multi-lingual, but English (British, American), and Spanish are the most advanced languages. Other parties release new languages for the framework. FestVox, a Carnegie Mellon project, contains all of the necessary resources and documentation for creating new vocals. The code is written in C++ for low-level architecture, and it makes use of the Edinburgh Speech Tools Library and a scheme-based control order interpreter (SIOD). The documentation is given in FSF Texinfo format, with a printing manual, info folders, and HTML. The required paperwork is available [34].

17.5.2 MaryTTS

The objective of the MaryTTS language portion is to enable the device to extract language features from spelled text by means of natural language processing (NLP). This involves at least the phonemes sequence, that is, the pronunciation, but usually also other phonological characteristics and used for acoustic parameter prediction including the section length and the basic frequency (F0). The MaryTTS pronunciation prediction consists of a basic module "Phonemiser", which searches any token in a lexicon, and returns the phonemes series. The module will fall back on the G2P prediction rules for any out-of-vocabulary (OOV) tokens. MaryTTS' development has taken on various important paradigms that in the years since the project was initiated have become best practice in software engineering rooted in Java.

17.5.3 ESPNET-TTS

The updated ESPnet-TTS, an extension of the open-source speech processing kit ESPnet, has been added to this end-to-end text to speech (E2E-TTS). Table 17.2 shows the comparison with other open-source TTS toolkits.

The toolkit supports cutting-edge E2E-TTS versions, including Tacotron 2, Transformer TTS and Fast Speech, and also offers Kaldi automatic spoken recognition (ASR) toolkit recipes. The receptes are designed to have a high reproducibility, unified with the ESPnet ASR recettes. The toolkit includes all of the recettes with pre-trained templates and prototypes so that users can use this as a base. The single architecture also allows ASR functions to be integrated into the TTS system [35]. ESPnet-TTS offers three cutting-edge

TABLE 17.2
Comparison with Other Open-Source TTS Toolkits

	Rayhane	NVIDIA	Mozilla	OpenSeq 2Seq	ESPnet-TTS	Mary-TTS	Festival
Multi Speaker	Yes	Yes	Yes	Yes	Yes	Yes	Yes
Adaptation				Yes	Yes	Yes	
Neural Network				Yes	Yes		
Vocoder					Yes		
Deep Voice 3		Yes	Yes		Yes	Yes	Yes
TTS		Yes			Yes		
Fast Speech					Yes		
No. of Datasets	2	1	6	2	11	2	3
No. of. Language	8	1	8	8	11	2	4
Input	Char	Char	Char / Phn	Char	Char / Phn	Char	Char
Backend	Tensor Flow	PyTorch	PyTorch	TensorFlow	PyTorch	Java-based	C++

E2E-TTS versions, including Mozilla, Transformer TTS, and FastSpeech compared to other toolkits. In addition, a variety of reproducible recipes with multi-speaker TTS support and speaker adaptation techniques are provided for more than ten languages. While the other toolkits have only a small number of previously trained models and experiments, we provide all the recipes to the researchers, allowing them to play on TTS demos as a baseline for their study.

17.6 Conclusion

We discussed the Festival, MaryTTS and ESPnet-TTS toolkit open domain Hindi text. This report contains the following information. The Festival modules have been revised to handle Hindi text. In addition, HMM-based speech synthesisers and selection unit construction are employed. The speech signal is manually annotated at the phoneme, word, and syllable levels. An automatic speech recognition system based on HMM and a unit selection-based synthesis engine analyses Hindi synthesised speech. HMM speech accuracy is increased by unit array discourse, according to objective assessment results. This demonstrates that HMM-derived speech is more understandable than speech generated by a unit-dependent synthesiser.

References

1. Zhang, Z. (2016). Mechanics of human voice production and control. *The Journal of the Acoustical Society of America, 140*(4), 2614–2635.
2. Delić, V., Perić, Z., Sečujski, M., Jakovljević, N., Nikolić, J., Mišković, D., & Delić, T. (2019). Speech technology progress based on new machine learning paradigm. *Computational Intelligence and Neuroscience*, 2019.
3. Cylke, F. K. (Ed.). (2016). *Library service for the blind and physically handicapped: An international approach* (Vol. 16). Walter de Gruyter GmbH & Co KG.
4. National Academies of Sciences, Engineering, and Medicine. (2017). *Making eye health a population health imperative: Vision for tomorrow*. National Academies Press.
5. Technical Devices and Special Equipment for the Blind, Future Reflections Winter 1986, Vol. 5 No. 1, https://nfb.org//sites/default/files/ images/nfb/ publications/fr/fr5/issue1/ f050113.html
6. Isewon, I., Oyelade, O. J., & Oladipupo, O. O. (2012). Design and implementation of text to speech conversion for visually impaired people. *International Journal of Applied* Information *Systems, 7*(2), 26–30.
7. Guennec, D. (2016). *Study of unit selection text-to-speech synthesis algorithms* (Doctoral dissertation, Université Rennes 1).
8. Godambe, T., Rallabandi, S. K., Gangashetty, S. V., Alkhairy, A., & Jafri, A. (2016). Developing a unit selection voice given audio without corresponding text. *EURASIP Journal on Audio, Speech, and Music Processing, 2016*(1), 1–11.
9. Jain, S., & Paul, S. (Eds.). (2020). *Recent trends in image and signal processing in computer vision* (Vol. 1124). Springer Nature.

10. Kanojia, D., Jyothi, P., & Bhattacharyya, P. (2018, January). Synthesizing Audio for Hindi WordNet. In *Proceedings of the 9th Global Wordnet Conference* (pp. 388–393).

11. Rao, K. S. (2011). Role of neural network models for developing speech systems. *Sadhana*, 36(5), 783–836.

12. Mendiratta, S., Turk, N., & Bansal, D. (2019). A robust isolated automatic speech recognition system using machine learning techniques, *International Journal of Innovative Technology and Exploring Engineering (IJITEE)*, 8(10), 2278–3075.

13. Singh, S. K. "Features and techniques for speaker recognition", Electronic Systems Group, November 2003, www.ee.iitb.ac.in/~esgroup/es_mtech03_sem/sem03_paper_03307409.pdf.

14. Alim, S. A., & Rashid, N. K. A. (2018). *Some commonly used speech feature extraction algorithms* (pp. 2–19). IntechOpen.

15. Kumar, A., & Niranjan, S. (2012). Design, development and implementation of an automated IVR system with feature based TTS using open source tools. *Automation and Autonomous Systems*, 4(6), 218–221.

16. Coupé, C., Oh, Y. M., Dediu, D., & Pellegrino, F. (2019). Different languages, similar encoding efficiency: Comparable information rates across the human communicative niche. *Science Advances*, 5(9), eaaw2594.

17. Alam, F., Habib, S. M., Sultana, D. A., & Khan, M. (2010). Development of annotated Bangla speech corpora.

18. Graf, S., Herbig, T., Buck, M., & Schmidt, G. (2015). Features for voice activity detection: a comparative analysis. *EURASIP Journal on Advances in Signal Processing*, 2015(1), 1–15.

19. Michael Cerna and Audrey F. Harvey, The Fundamentals of FFT-Based Signal Analysis and Measurement, July 2000, www.sjsu.edu/people/burford.furman/docs/me120/FFT_tutorial_NI.pdf.

20. Jiang, Y., Qi, Y., Wang, W. K., Bent, B., Avram, R., Olgin, J., & Dunn, J. (2020). Event DTW: An improved dynamic time warping algorithm for aligning biomedical signals of nonuniform sampling frequencies. *Sensors*, 20(9), 2700.

21. Whoriskey, K., AugerMéthé, M., Albertsen, C. M., Whoriskey, F. G., Binder, T. R., Krueger, C. C., & Mills Flemming, J. (2017). A hidden Markov movement model for rapidly identifying behavioral states from animal tracks. *Ecology and Evolution*, 7(7), 2112–2121.

22. Zhou, J., Cui, G., Zhang, Z., Yang, C., Liu, Z., Wang, L., & Sun, M. (2020). Graph neural networks: A review of methods and applications. *AI Open*, 1(2020), 57–81.

23. C-DAC: Centre for Development of Advanced Computing, India, www.cdac.in/index.aspx?id=mc_ilf

24. The EMILLE Corpus, December 2003, www.lancaster.ac.uk/fass/projects/corpus/emille/

25. Mohanty, S. (2011). Syllable based Indian language text to speech system. *International Journal of Advances in Engineering & Technology*, 1(2), 138.

26. Aarti, B., & Kopparapu, S. K. (2018). Spoken Indian language identification: a review of features and databases. *Sādhanā*, 43(4), 1–14.

27. Raj, A. A., Sarkar, T., Pammi, S. C., Yuvaraj, S., Bansal, M., Prahallad, K., & Black, A. W. (2007, August). *Text processing for text-to-speech systems in Indian languages.* (pp. 188–193).

28. Marquez, L., Padro, L., & Rodriguez, H. (2000). A machine learning approach to POS tagging. *Machine Learning*, 39(1), 59–91.

29. Kirchner, R., Phonetics and phonology: understanding the sounds of speech, https://nptel.ac.in/content/storage2/courses/109106085/downloads/03-%20Phonetics%20and%20Phonology-%20week%203.pdf.

30. King, S. (2011). An introduction to statistical parametric speech synthesis. *Sadhana*, 36(5), 837–852.

31. Carlson, R. (1995). Models of speech synthesis. *Proceedings of the National Academy of Sciences*, 92(22), 9932–9937.

32. Räsänen, O., Statistical parametric speech synthesis, https://wiki.aalto.fi/display/ITSP/Statistical+parametric+speech+synthesis

33. Dahl, G. E., Yu, D., Deng, L., & Acero, A. (2011). Context-dependent pre-trained deep neural networks for large-vocabulary speech recognition. *IEEE Transactions on Audio, Speech, and Language Processing, 20*(1), 30–42.

34. SynSIG, www.synsig.org/index.php/Software

35. Hayashi, T., Yamamoto, R., Inoue, K., Yoshimura, T., Watanabe, S., Toda, T., & Tan, X. (2020, May). ESPnet-TTS: Unified, reproducible, and integratable open source end-to-end text-to-speech toolkit. In *ICASSP 2020–2020 IEEE international conference on acoustics, speech and signal processing (ICASSP)* (pp. 7654–7658). IEEE.

18

Weibull Distribution Parameters Estimation Using Computer Software

Sarfraz Ali Quadri, Dhananjay R. Dolas, and Varsha D. Jadhav

CONTENTS

18.1 Introduction

The effectiveness of the industries closely depends on many factors such as the availability of the individual machines and controlled maintenance of their critical components, reliability of its outcomes produced and a safe working environment. The improved reliability, productivity and availability of the manufacturing system can be achieved through the utilization of the proper maintenance strategies. Therefore, the forecast of the most critical sub-system or machines or their most critical components becomes an essential activity for improved maintenance management system in the manufacturing industry. The important parameters, like reliability, availability and maintainability, of the industries are evaluated with special selections and combinations of repair, failure rates of the individual machines, and their components. Almost every major item that consumers purchased has a warranty period. One of the best and most suited methodologies is Weibull analysis, which is used for performing life data analysis of complex mechanical systems. Life data basically is statistical data of failure iterations of a product's life. The Weibull distribution is frequently used in lifetime data analysis mainly not only because of its flexibility of analyzing diverse types of phenomena, but also its simple and straightforward mathematical forms compared with other distributions as it can model failures caused by fatigue, corrosion, or such mechanical processes. In case of two-parameter Weibull analysis, the two parameters are characteristic life (η) and shape values (β) where β decides the shape of the distribution under study. If shape parameter is greater than 1, the failure rate is increasing. If shape parameter is less than 1, the failure rate is decreasing. If shape parameter is equal to 1, the failure rate is constant. There are several ways to check whether data follows a Weibull distribution. The best

DOI: 10.1201/9781003342755-21

choice is to use a Weibull analysis software product. The data can be graphically plotted on a Weibull probability distribution plot to check if it follows a straight line. The straight line on the probability distribution plot showcases that the data is following a Weibull distribution. Weibull analysis can be performed graphically as well as analytically.

18.2 Literature Review

Jinghuan Ma et al. [1] presented a reliability assessment method for manufacturing process by using the Weibull analysis. In this assessment method, the system reliability is calculated by analyzing the failures of manufacturing system and later the correlation model of reliability is created for further study. With the help of the correlation model, the study proposes a reliability estimation method based on Weibull analysis technology. The study also validates the assessment method by a case study. Bruno Zberg et al. [2] investigates the mechanical properties of magnesium wires and their reliability with the help of Weibull analysis. Their study concentrates mostly on the compression data of wires with rectangular cross-sections beyond the plastic zone. They also investigated the effect of small dimensions and round cross-section samples for tensile strength, the behavior of deformation and their reliability. Milan Ambrozic [3] performed extensive Monte-Carlo computer simulations with the help of the two-parameter Weibull distribution. The study uses the maximum-likelihood approach to evaluate the effect of Weibull modulus and the scale parameter on different input values. Researchers have also considered the influence of the measurement uncertainty on the determination of the statistical parameters. For the experimental evidence, they used bend strength data for alumina test samples from serial production in this year.

Zhu et al. [4] developed a hierarchical assessment model for reliability estimation. The study focused on a comparison of Bayes method and maximum-likelihood method with the help of extensive simulations. The study also incorporates a case study to showcase the effectiveness of the model. Reliability analysis of turbo-generator engine fans was done [5–7] using Weibull and log-normal models for suspended samples. This method can be conveniently operated [8] in MS Excel. The two-parameter Weibull and Gamma distributions are used for reliability estimations and predictions [9]. Data analysis has been done with support of computer-aided reliability software Essay fit, with the application of the Weibull and Gamma distributions. A comparison between the two important distribution functions showcase that the Weibull method has performed well for decision making. Two-parameter Weibull distribution theory and its parameters shape and scale [10] using Weibull probability distribution plot was used for estimation of the reliabilities of Bulldozers, The Weibull Parameters are calculated [11, 12] using Microsoft Excel 2010. The Weibull analysis was also used [13–16] for reliability analysis of railway diesel locomotive engine.

18.3 Research Gap

From the above literature, it is clear that studies on system analysis of complex industrial systems gives clear results when done using reliability, availability, and maintainability

(RAM) Approach. Although many researchers have used various approaches for reliability analyses like the Weibull distribution, log-normal model, gamma distribution, and Markov modeling, it is noted that the Weibull distribution, that too two-parameter Weibull distribution, is more suited for complex repairable industrial systems, because the failures rates of such systems are not constant. Different research studies show that most of methods use the analytical and graphical method for Weibull parameters estimation, some studies parameters are estimated using the different available statistics software. This study uses Minitab 16.1R, MS Excel and Windchill Quality Solution 10.1 Try Out software with least regression method for parameters estimation.

18.4 Methods and Materials

18.4.1 Weibull Distribution Estimation Using Least Square Method

The least square method (LSM) is extensively used in reliability engineering, mathematical problems, and the estimation of Weibull parameters. The method provides a linear relation between the two parameters.

The cumulative density function (CDF) is

$$F(t) = 1 - e^{-\left(\frac{t}{\cdot}\right)^{\beta}}$$

where
β = Shape parameters.
η = Scale parameters.

To get a linear relation between the two parameters taking the logarithm of above equation as follows:

$$\ln[1 - F(t)] = -\left(\frac{t}{\eta}\right)^{\beta}$$

$$\ln\{-\ln[1 - F(t)]\} = \beta \ln\left(\frac{t}{\eta}\right)$$

$$\ln\{-\ln[1 - F(t)]\} = -\beta \ln \eta + \beta \ln(t)$$

$$\ln\{-\ln[R(t)]\} = -\beta \ln \cdot + \beta \ln(t)$$

$X = \ln t$, $Y = \ln\{-\ln[1 - F(t)]\}$
where $t = 1, 2\ldots n$ and n is the sample size.
The linear approximation of this $Y = \beta X + c$

Performing rank regression on Y requires that a straight line to be a set of data points so that the sum of the squares of the deviation from the points to the line is minimized. Both β and η parameters can be evaluated from the coefficient of polynomial linear fitting using a simple linear regression:

$$\text{Shape parameters} = \beta$$

$$\text{Scale parameters} = \eta = e^{\frac{c}{\beta}}$$

$$\text{Reliability} = R(t) = e^{-\left(\frac{t}{\eta}\right)^{\beta}}$$

18.5 Case Study

Time to failure data of repairable system is given as 88, 117, 345, 385, 514, 887, 981, 1073, 1141, and 1306 hours. Using this data, find the system reliability.

Solution: To estimate the reliability of system using the two-parameter Weibull distribution, least square method is performed in MS Excel in Table 18.1 and also Figure 18.1.

As given time to failure data is used in Minitab 16.1R least square estimator, estimate the Weibull parameters as per different plots in Figure 18.2.

Similarly, Windchill quality solution 10.1 tryout-software is used to estimate the Weibull parameters and the graphs of probability, reliability, failure rate, unreliability probability density function and contour plot has been plotted (Figure 18.3).

The comparative results of MS Excel, Minitab 16.1R and Windchill Quality Solution 10.1 Tryout is listed in Table 18.2.

TABLE 18.1

Failure Data Arranged in Ascending Order and Weibull Analysis

Failure Number	Time to failure Hours	Median Rank	1/1-M R	ln(ln(1/1-MR)))	ln(time to failure)
1	88	0.067307692	1.072165	-2.663843085	4.477336814
2	117	0.163461538	1.195402	-1.72326315	4.762173935
3	345	0.259615385	1.350649	-1.202023115	5.843544417
4	385	0.355769231	1.552239	-0.821666515	5.953243334
5	514	0.451923077	1.824561	-0.508595394	6.242223265
6	887	0.548076923	2.212766	-0.230365445	6.787844982
7	981	0.644230769	2.810811	0.032924962	6.88857246
8	1073	0.740384615	3.851852	0.299032932	6.978213743
9	1141	0.836538462	6.117647	0.593977217	7.03966035
10	1306	0.932692308	14.85714	0.992688929	7.17472431

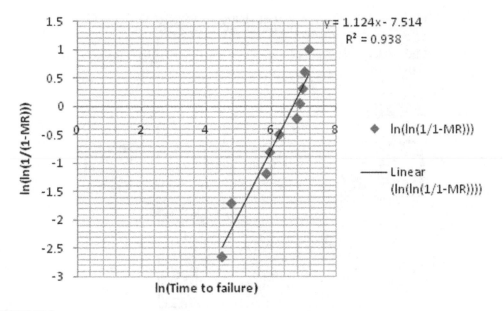

FIGURE 18.1
ln (ln(1/(1 − Median Rank))) × ln (time) Hours.
Parameter = β = 1.124 and scale parameter = η is calculated as follow Scale parameters = $\eta = e^{\frac{c}{\beta}} = \eta = e^{\frac{7.514}{1..124}} = e^{6.68}$
η = 796.3 Hours.

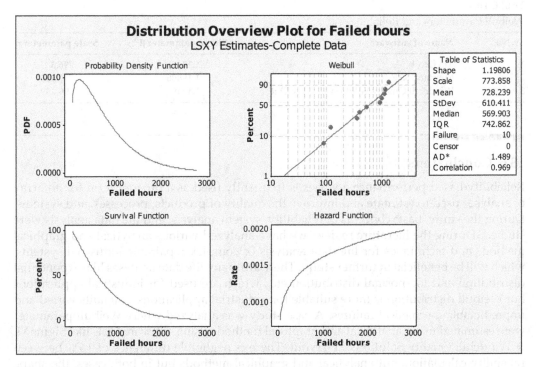

FIGURE 18.2
Weibull parameters using Minitab 16.1R software.

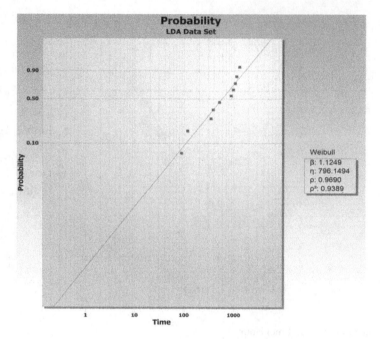

FIGURE 18.3
Weibull parameters using Windchill Quality Solution 10.1 Try Out.

TABLE 18.2
Weibull Parameters and Reliability

Sr. No.	Name of software	Shape parameter β	Scale parameter η
1	MS Excel	1.124	796.3
2	Minitab 16.1R	1.19806	773.858
3	Windchill Quality Solution 10.1 Try Out	1.1249	796.149

18.6 Conclusions

Reliability-based performance analysis is frequently used as a broader term for an array of analyses used to estimate and improve the quality of products, processes, and systems. During the study, basic concepts of reliability, system analysis, and life data analysis were studied. During the literature review, we have analyzed various analytical and graphical methods and techniques for life data analysis of complex repairable industrial systems, which will be beneficial in further study. There are many life data analyses like exponential distribution and log-normal distribution etc., which are used for industrial applications but Weibull distribution is more suitable for industrial applications as it suits varied and unpredictable mechanical failures. A case study was analyzed where Weibull parameter were estimated using analytical and graphical methods using software tools like SigmaXL & Windchill Quality Solutions 11 Tryout. There is negligible difference of 1.7% between reliability calculation, but analytical and graphical methods but in both cases, the shape parameter is more than 1. As **β > 1**, that is, the failure rate is likely to increase over time, this could be an indication of premature wear issues or lack of proper maintenance as it lies in early life phase of bath tub curve.

References

1. Jinghuan Ma, Yihai He, and Chunhui Wu (2012). Research on Reliability Estimation for Mechanical Manufacturing Process Based on Weibull Analysis Technology, Prognostics and System Health Management Conference, 978-1-4577-1911-0/12 ©2012 IEEE
2. Bruno Zberg, Edward R. Arata, and Peter J. Uggowitzer (2009) Tensile properties of glassy MgZnCa wires and reliability analysis using Weibull, *Acta Materialia.* doi:10.1016/j.actamat.2009.03.028
3. Milan Ambrožič and Lovro Gorjan (2011) Reliability of a Weibull analysis using the maximum-likelihood method, *J Mater Sci* 46: 1862–1869.
4. Tiefeng Zhu (2007) Reliability estimation for two-parameter Weibull distribution under block censoring, *Reliability Engineering and System Safety*, 203(C). doi: 10.1016/j.ress.2020.107071
5. N. V. R. Naidu (2011) Optimal preventive maintenance policy in a steel industry: six sigma approach, *International Journal for Quality Research*, 5(3): 179–185.
6. C. E. Ebeling (1997) *An Introduction to Reliability and Maintainability Engineering*, McGraw-Hill (Asia), p. 5.
7. G. R. Pasha, M. Shuaib Khan , and Ahmed Hesham Pasha (2007) Reliability analysis of fans, *Journal of Research (Science)*, Bahauddin Zakariya University, Multan, Pakistan, 18(1): 19–33.
8. Jinlei Qin, Yuguang Niu, and Zheng Li (2014) Data analysis method and its applications in Excel, *Journal of Software*, 9(12): 299–300.
9. Amal El-Berry and Afrah Al-Bossly (2013) Application of computer model to estimate the consistency of air conditioning systems engineering. *International Journal of Engineering and Technology (IJET)* 5(2): 659–668.
10. Dascar Secara Monia Camelia, Nan Marin Silviu, and Dascar Emil (2015) Study of reliability modeling and performance analysis of haul trucks in quarries, *Advances in Information Science and Computer Engineering*, pp. 143–150.
11. Chetan Deka and Somnath Chattopadhaya (2013) A comparative reliability analysis of bulldozers arriving at workshop in Eastern India: a case study. *IOSR Journal of Mechanical and Civil Engineering (IOSR-JMCE)* 10(2): 47–52.
12. Saurabh Kumar, Gopi Chattopadhyay, and Uday Kumar (2007) Reliability improvement through alternative designs – A case study, *Reliability Engineering and System Safety*, 92: 983–991.
13. D. Bose, G. Ghosh, K. Mandal, S.P. Sau, and S. Kunar (2013) Measurement and evaluation of reliability, availability and maintainability of a diesel locomotive engine, *International Journal of Engineering Research and Technology*, 6(4): 515–534.
14. Suresh Kumara and Bijan Sarkara (2013) Design for reliability with Weibull analysis for photovoltaic modules, *International Journal of Current Engineering and Technology*, 3(1): 129–135.
15. Muhammad Abid, Suleman Ayub, Humza Wali, and Muhammad Najam Tariq (2014) Reliability centered maintenance plan for the utility section of a fertilizer industry: A case study. *International Journal of Science and Advanced Technology*, 4(3): 9–16.
16. Seung-Wook Eom, Min-Kyu Kim, and Ick-Jun Kim (2007) Life prediction and reliability assessment of lithium secondary batteries, *Journal of Power Sources*, 174: 954–958.

19

Navigation Systems of Indoor Automated Guided Vehicle

Rahul Pol

CONTENTS

19.1 Introduction: Navigation Systems of Indoor Automated Guided Vehicle

As versatile machine-driven production instrumentation, automated guided vehicles (AGVs) are often used, and their performance and accuracy of navigation are vital. Conventional AGV navigation strategies are commonly on one sensing element. Along the development of sensing element technology, multiple-sensor fusion methods are being devolved for navigation. Detection of the hurdles and mapping are key for AGV. Environments where safety of AGV and surrounding is very important [1,2]. Technical developments associated with the AGV navigation methodology are planned in the analysis field. In general, these approaches utilize vision sensors like camera or optical device vary sensors for noticing and matching the landmarks that are already provided in the map data for localizing itself [3]. Robot navigation strategies are often differentiated into two categories: the first is global and local path strategy, where the global methods assume that the surrounding data is totally known and utilize all information to search the best path to a fixed goal whereas the local path planning methods only take into account the steps for the robot according to information of neighborhood environment [4]. This chapter provides a broad overview of guided vehicle navigation systems. Different navigation

DOI: 10.1201/9781003342755-22

systems are discussed in Section 19.2, the major variety of literature work is discussed in Section 19.3, and finally in Section 19.4, conclusions are given.

19.2 An Overview of Different AGV Navigation Systems

19.2.1 Sensor Fusion

Multi-sensor AGV navigation was used by vesting Kalman filter. Using the fusion of acceleration and encoder sensors with Kalman filter, the location of AGV was obtained [1]. Altitude was obtained by combining acceleration and gyro sensors together with Kalman filter. Another sensor fusion method was proposed, which combines the positioning measures from ultrawide band (UWB) based indoor-SLAM systems along with the ones from inertial navigation systems (INS), which is based on the Kalman filter [5]. The proposed method-based vehicle navigation accomplishes self-navigation while its trajectory is observed in real time. The vehicle accommodates few sensors such as accelerometers on the both sides, as well as gyroscope at the center, and two UWB tags on both sides of the vehicle. Implementing multi-sensor fusion methods in AGV can improve the system's endurance, dependability, and sturdiness [1,5] (Table 19.1).

19.2.2 Vision Sensors

Detection of obstacles and mapping are of importance for indoor navigation. This can be very important for an automated guided vehicle (AGV) that operates within the known and unknown environments where the protection of surroundings along with the vehicle is primary concern. The three-dimensional range camera depends on the time of flight (TOF) concept; also it can produce pictures and range data of the elements in the surroundings simultaneously. This varying camera is good for hurdle detection in various applications since it is comparatively cheaper than the other sensors and it can produce data on the given pictures at a rate of 30 Hz with an active span of 7.5 m [2]. In this study, the author has enforced a driving algorithm based on vision sensor that permits the AGV to go after a predefined path that was the signs that are put in on the ground, which gave high dependability and fast execution. This technique only needs a couple of modifications to make changes to be used with any given configuration. Using two cameras, the position errors were reduced and it permits the AGV to alter the steering function smoothly while going after the described route [6]. ACCD camera is provided on the ceiling for overlooks working space of the AGVs. To ascertain AGVs simply, all of them have IR units, and that area unit is not visible for humans. The module incorporate multiple infrared LEDs to

TABLE 19.1

Comparison between the One Sensor and Multisensory Method

Criteria	IPS	INS
Short-term accuracy	Less accuracy	More accuracy
Long-term precision	More precision	Less precision
Update rate	Less rate	More rate
Path delay	More Path delay	Less Path delay

transmit enough concentrated optical rays. The infrared rays passing through the filter, which bypasses spectrum of visible ray, is attached with the camera placed over the walls and ceiling for improving the detective work [3]. The obstacle detection and fractionalization function combine range pictures and their intensity from the camera to find the hurdle and predict the space between the object and the robot. A closed-circuit device (CCD) camera is provided on the roof to observe the working space of the robots. For locating the AGVs simply, all of them have IR units on them, and those units are not visible for humans. The process is made up of three submodules such as SLAM for indoor, the customize user interaction block, with standalone AGV arrangement [3].

The author has two steps to calibrate the camera: starting from image to the work arena floor, after that from the working arena floor to the autonomous robot. While doing primary calibration task, the camera takes a picture of a fixed dimension calibration object. As the author does not want to use the traditional least squares method, which requires precise measures in world coordinates, the author has used all the points of the calibration object to be on the floor for the object such as a white square with a width of 21 cm. The coordinates of its vertex are computed. Using least squares, M is estimated for the first picture and trying to match the reference square. Using the Newton method, the initial estimates are improved [7].

19.2.3 Passive RFID

The author has planned a technique for assessing both the locations with positions of an autonomous navigating robot, that is, AGV by utilizing nothing but passive radiofrequency identification. Furthermore, the radiofrequency ID (RFID) is utilized to predict the AGV position along with its placement accurately by the basic trigonometric functions and the RFID tags over the Cartesian coordinates in this algorithm. Using the given method, robust environmental data can be acquired. The author has prepared an upgraded algorithm, which predicts AGV posture run time using received database and SLAM information. Thus to appear at its rationality, the author enforced it on AGV [8]. The automaton has three parts to it: the laptop as a servo system, to acquire the positioning information of RFID system, in addition with platform for AGV steering systems. It is designed according to electric wheelchair as a base device. The laptop attached to the electrical wheelchair works as a servo control that operates data of RFID tag system and gives orders to the AGV base for achieving the set goal. The system scans the tags of the ICs on the ground, which permits the laptop to approximately predict the position and posture of the robot based on the given algorithms [8].

19.2.4 Probabilistic Tracking of People

This chapter contains an indoor robot system that will be used for transportation works within the indoor surroundings. It is going to be connected to a wireless sensor network (WSN). This network consists of many nodes and every single node has a PIR sensor attached, that is, to discover objects in motion (i.e., personnel). A particle filter is employed for proceeding the information obtained online to trace the location of the personnel. The information of the filter is utilized for adapting the top speed is possible for the robot by doing so. The system forever stays in a risk-free state while minimizing conveyance time [9]. The tracking of targets using probably disturbance and inaccurate sensor knowledge is a major domain of analysis with applications in several fields that don't seem to be restricted to the field of robotics. An answer for the personnel-tracking issue in a WSN depends on the algorithm of Bayesian filtering obtained gradually. To deal with the tracing issues, the Bayesian filter is needed. Widespread options are the Kalman filter and the particle filter. A tracker continuously operates on some state variable, which narrates all the positions that the objects which are to be traced might take on. To integrate the measurements, every filter uses an alleged detector model. This program determines however sensors events result in the change in state of the filter [9]. A small wireless network has been implemented for tracking an individual smoothly and low-cost sensors. The output of the following task is used on a AGV to enhance its speed. The probabilistic data has been later worked on and has resulted to modify the most possible speeds of the mobile robot, consistent with the state of the system. Taken into account on its own, the tracing of one personnel using PIR sensor among a wireless sensing element network works efficiently [9].

19.2.5 Wireless Sensor Networks

A sensor network embedded in the surroundings can take control of sensing, processing, communicating, and providing route information, whereas a mobile robot is simply responsible for the action. For example, the interaction of mobile robots and static sensor networks enhances each other's capability in a scenario in which the mobile robot is allotted a particular task like moving to the region of interest. For example, this approach doesn't need a predefined map of the surroundings [10]. The method proposed is a navigation and localization technique for mobile robots working on wireless sensor networks. In our navigation system, a robot will navigate autonomously without the necessity for a map by getting the data of pre-set radio emission sensors deployed in indoor surroundings and their relative distance [11]. Localization basically depends on getting a location and posture of an AGV depending upon surroundings, previous locations, and detector information. The positioning method of a AGV is obtained by censoring detectors like camera and odometer. Laser localization methods include two classes: tracing and global localization [12]. In the given paper, a localization array depending on an ultrasonic web is produced for mobile robots. The triangle localization principle is examined and a digital filter method is acquired in the localization process. In the proposed navigation function for robots, detecting nodes will perform as signposts and simultaneously they update the bot for the successive nodes to go accordingly, while the robot traces every detector node on the trajectory line and interchange location data with every detector node for determining the space precisely. The detector junctions are spared surrounding the bot's operating zone and makes the complete ad hoc detecting system, and their locations are identified. The radio transmission equipment is placed on each detecting junction, which will give the electromagnetic wave with a unique frequency [11]. The automaton is provided with a rotational receiver, which is utilized for getting the radio frequencies from the detecting junction and naming every detector by getting the frequency database. Triangulation technique is used to predict the location of an AGV utilizing the data of radio frequency detectors within the cluster Ni in subclass Ej, containing a priori points in system and administration with relevance to the automaton. For improving the productivity of automaton localization, an extended Kalman filter is used [11].

19.2.6 Using DWA*

In this paper, a brand-new navigation method, dynamic window approach (DAW) is presented [4]. It integrates a local method DWA, which is one of the most widely known local strategies today, and an A* tree search algorithm. DWA improves the path quality by taking into account many steps ahead for the robot and might still recompute quickly for dynamic environments [4]. The primary objective of the global path planning is to find the shortest path that joins the current location of the robots to the final goal location. The previous methods for finding global path planning strategies are visibility graph, where the present hindrances are replaced with polygons with their vertices stored as a vertex set V, an edge set E is developed through interconnecting each vertices pair V. The final estimated route of the robot is then explored using various topological techniques. However, though the path explored using visibility graph method starting from the goal position through connecting each vertices of in path obstacles is not appealing one [4]. Most widespread local reactive strategies these days are identified as velocity space and directional way approaches. The directional ways method divides the navigation disadvantage into a two sections. However, due to the kinematic and dynamic limitations, the automaton is unable travel to the destined way smoothly. Therefore the velocity space technique is introduced to tackle this shortcomings. In the velocity space approach, the earliest one is that the curvature velocity method (CVM). After that, the dynamic window approach (DWA) was developed. DWA inherits the idea of CVM and becomes the most popular velocity space approach today. Thus directional ways method such as VFH with ND perform better for exploring inherent least problems compared velocity space technique [4]. For finishing the safe navigation of autonomous mobile robot, each local and global technique is required. Through combining both NF1 and DWA, and therefore, the integration of D* algorithm with DWA algorithm is experimented, using which the author designed a function for avoiding the path dynamic obstacle. For modified DWA first [4], the environmental data is accomplished as an interval configuration in velocity space. Then the intervals are analyzed to search out passable regions. For every region, a candidate velocity is found. Finally, the rate for the robot is chosen among the candidate velocities using the A* search algorithm. Velocity space is realized as a group of intervals: an interval is created by two lines within the velocity space, which is nothing but the region among the two polygon robot paths over the workspace. According to DWA* algorithm, the robot velocity is divided into intervals; even the approval of each interval is further processed individually [4]. During the interval analysis of DWA* algorithm, the author mentioned two perks in which initially it improves the overall computational time. Whereas in basic DWA, clearance values inside the specific dynamic window for each obstacle is verified for all the possible velocity vectors. If the scale of the dynamic window is n and the variety of obstacles is o, the computation complexity is $O(o * n)$. In addition to this, the other advantage is the utilization of directional approach creation of vector field histogram [4].

19.3 Design of AGV System

The major objective of this chapter is to introduce show the design of structural chassis and compartment for the automated guided vehicle considering the accurate dimensions and research along with complete structural analysis of the chassis structure while considering suitable loads on AGV. It is to introduce the complete control system for AGV with optimized performance. The robot is in the form of an automated guided vehicle (AGV), which will transport various components to their respective stations within industrial hours. This takes a lot of effort to implement successfully. But in a long-term scenario,

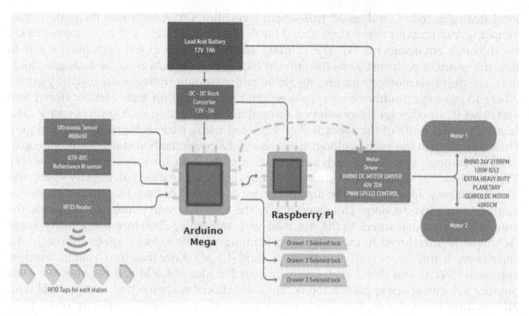

FIGURE 19.1
Electronic circuitry and power distribution block diagram.

automating this function will improve efficiency. For example, transporting components can be done by humans, but it is very tiring work and a wastage of human potential. By automating this function, there will be fewer interruptions and humans will be available wherever they are truly needed. When it comes to actual work being done in industries, it will be difficult to remove the human element. Artificial intelligence simply has not reached human level competency. We cannot yet have robots interacting with humans and listening and reacting to our complaints. In the meantime, however, we can automate the peripheral functions currently being done by humans. Besides, the ultimate goal of an industrialized society is to reduce its dependency on human labor and improve efficiency. This is our ultimate motivation to try and let a robot take over this task.

Figure 19.1 is the block diagram of the embedded system used in AGV; Raspberry Pi is the main central processing unit, which will hold the OS for the automated ground vehicle. The Arduino Mega is connected to a Raspberry Pi. The Arduino Mega will control the DC motor via motor driver module, which has PWM speed control. The input components are ultrasonic sensor, IR sensor, and RFID reader for object detection, and line path following and RFID tag recognition tasks, respectively. Respective of the inputs from the sensors the outputs/actuation is done through DC motors and electronic solenoid lock for automated guided vehicle movement and drawer unlocking, respectively. The Raspberry Pi updates all tasks through Wi-Fi and Bluetooth connectivity on the server to communicate with the custom-designed application.

Figure 19.2 describes the application for the said AGV. The material handling and delivery AGV continuously receives command and order for components from central store to which it receives the specific material delivery order from each workstation. There might be many workstations as per the production line. Here in Figure 19.3, we included three such workstations requesting the required material through central store and accepts the delivery from the delivering AGV. Upon receiving many requests from

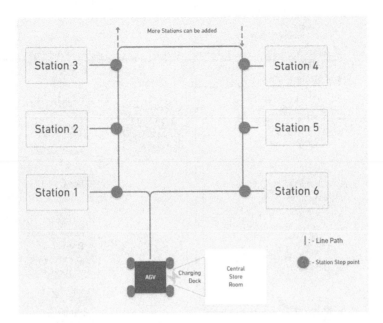

FIGURE 19.2
Electronic circuitry and power distribution block diagram.

multiple stations, the central store computes the number of AGVs required according to the payload (delivery material). Thus, the number of AGVs sent to delivery is according to the requirement of material at any particular instance. In addition to this, the central store decides the type and quantity to be loaded over each AGV. the material is loaded into the respective compartment of the AGV at the central store. To perform the said operation, AGVs were synchronized and instructed by central storeroom. Moving the AGV throughout the working arena, a well-shaped paths were formed, which can be easily detected through IR-based line sensor. The path following method used by AGV and to maintain distance between two moving AGV sharp sensor are used. While moving into work arena for delivery, these AGVs will detect the destinations workstation place by the reading the RFID tags placed closed to the respective station. Thus, on reaching the destined workstation, these AGV will unlock its respective drawer compartment to unload or deliver the material through manual procedure. The worker from that particular station unloads the material and presses the unload completion button to acknowledge the AGV for moving further. Thus, the AGV delivers the all-loaded materials to its respective workstation one by one. On completing the order, the AGV finally marches back to the charging dock if its battery level is low or central store for attaining the next delivery.

19.4 Operation Flow Chart

The automated guided vehicle (AGV) is a line following bot, which delivers the goods from source to destination. Figure 19.3 depicts the flow of operation for AGV for executing the task. The description is as follows:

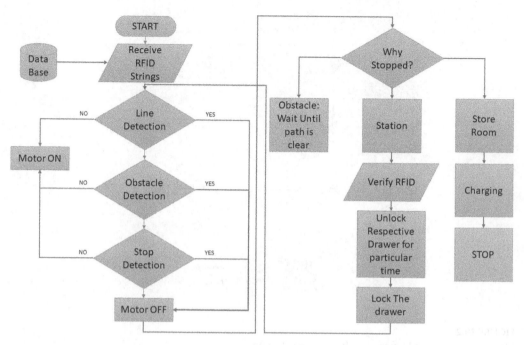

FIGURE 19.3
Flowchart for AGV operation.

1. The AGV will get ready to deliver the goods by getting the information from the database. The RFID numbers, stations numbers, and other data are received by the AGV. Once this transfer is completed, it will start following the line and reach the stations.

2. The line detection is done simultaneously with obstacle detection and stop detection. Let's take some examples to understand the flow if one of the three conditions occurred:
   (i) Line detection
   (ii) Obstacle detection
   (iii) Stop detection conditions
      (a) If the line is detected, then it will follow the line. To have motor ON, there should not be any obstacle and any stop if all these conditions are satisfied then motor will be ON and AGV will follow the line and it will remain in that loop unless any of condition is not satisfied.
      (b) If obstacle is detected, then motors are OFF and will remain OFF unless the obstacle is being cleared.
      (c) If stop/station is being detected, then the motor will be OFF. The condition will be check why motors are OFF. Once confirmed, there is a station in the next step for verification and goods delivery will be performed.
      (d) If stop/station is being detected, then the motor will be OFF. The condition will be check why motors are OFF. Once confirmed, there is stop and then the AGV will get to charging.

When AGV is at station, the verification process will start. The AGV will verify the identity by the RFID tags. Once confirmed, the respective drawer will be unlocked.

The verified person can pull the drawer to get his goods/materials. Again, he will scan the RFID and lock the drawer.

3. The location of AGV and the delivered material notification will be sent to database and the mobile applications.

4. This process continues until it will detect the stop; once detected, it will get back to the charging.

19.5 Experimentation and Simulation

The AGV CAD model was imported in V-REP software, where it was simulated as shown in Figure 19.4: V-REP simulation interface performs the following tasks.

1. To perform line following.
2. To identify the station stops.
3. To lock and unlock the drawer compartments whenever and wherever required.
4. To respond to multiple orders and deliver efficiently.

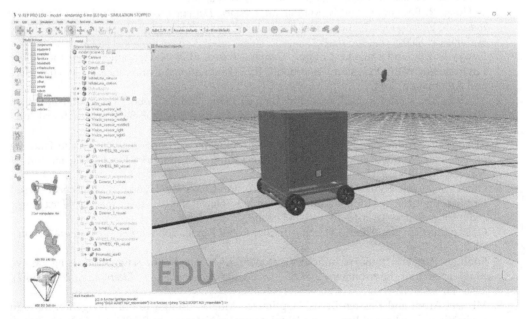

FIGURE 19.4
V-REP Simulation interface.

19.6 Experimentation and Simulation

Software still plays the largest role in the evolution of the industry, even with these individual pieces of technology contributing to the future of AGVs. It often serves as the backbone of an AGV system. By coordinating functions like vehicle communication, order generation, and traffic control, software distinguishes the "good" systems from the "bad" ones. Even in stand-alone systems, the software programmed into the AGVs dictates the efficacy of the system.

As such, the application knowledge of software development and engineering teams holds the greatest potential to transform the AGV industry. Their abilities can solve the unique challenges of individual facilities and can implement specific pieces of technology to best suit certain applications. This power translates into AGV systems that provide solutions, rather than simply vehicles, for those that implement driverless units. Improving technology combined with ever-advancing application knowledge means that the issues typically encountered in these types of AGVs may soon disappear. As forklift manufacturers begin to cooperate with AGV experts, a viable solution to the pitfalls of prior iterations of dual-mode vehicles could soon emerge.

References

1. Ti-chun Wang, Chang-sheng Tong, and Ben-ling Xu, *AGV Navigation Analysis based on Multi-Sensor Data Fusion*, Springer Science + Business Media, 2018.
2. T. Hong, R. Bostelman, and R. Madhavan, *Obstacle Detection using a TOF Range Camera for Indoor AGV Navigation*. National inst of standards and technology gaithersburg md intelligent systems div, 2004.
3. Naoya Isozaki and Daisuke Chugo, "Camera- based AGV Navigation System for Indoor Environment with Occlusion Condition", IEEE International Conference on Mechatronics and Automation, 2011.
4. Yi-Chun Lin, Chih-Chung Chou, and Feng-Li Lian, "Indoor Robot Navigation Based on DWA*: Velocity Space Approach with Region Analysis", ICROS-SICE International Joint Conference, 2009.
5. Risang Gatot Yudanto and Frederik Petré, "Sensor Fusion for Indoor Navigation and Tracking of Automated Guided Vehicles", International Conference on Indoor Positioning and Indoor Navigation (IPIN), 2015.
6. Quan V. Nguyen, Hyuk-Min Eum, Jeisung Lee, and Chang-Ho Hyun, "Vision Sensor- Based Driving Algorithm for Indoor Automatic Guided Vehicles", *International Journal of Fuzzy Logic and Intelligent Systems*, 2013, 13, 140–146.
7. Giuseppina Gini and Alberto Marchi, "Indoor Robot Navigation with Single Camera Vision", 2002. *PRIS*, 2, 67–76.
8. Sunhong Park and Shuji Hashimoto, "Autonomous Mobile Robot Navigation Using Passive RFID in Indoor Environment", *IEEE Transactions on Industrial Electronics*, 2009, 56(7), 2366–2373.
9. Michael Arndt and Karsten Berns, "Optimized Mobile" Indoor Robot Navigation through Probabilistic Tracking of People in a Wireless Sensor Network. In *ROBOTIK 2012; 7th German Conference on Robotics* (pp. 1–6). VDE, 2012.

10. Woo-Yong Lee, Kyeong Hur, Kwang-ilHwang, Doo-Seop Eom, and Jong-Ok Kim, *Mobile Robot Navigation Using Wireless Sensor Networks Without Localization Procedure*, Springer Science + Business Media, 2010.
11. Siyao Fu, Zeng-Guang Hou, and GuoshengYang, "An Indoor Navigation System for Autonomous Mobile Robot using Wireless Sensor Network", IEEE International Conference on Networking, Sensing and Control, 2009.
12. Jia Qian, Niu Weiqiang, Wang Mulan, Liu Shuqing, and Ge Jianjing, "Design of Localization System for Indoor Mobile Robots Based on Ultrasonic Net", 27th Chinese Control and Decision Conference (CCDC), 2015.

Index

A

AdaBoost 159
artificial intelligence 4
artificial neural network 36
automated guided vehicles 221

B

blockchain technology 4
body mass index 39

C

cloud computing 7
convolution neural networks 41, 175
curvature velocity method 225

D

deep neural network 48
discrete wavelet transform 176
distributed denial of service 75
dynamic time wrapping 205
dynamic window approach 224

E

electrocardiogram 36
electrocardiography 36
electroencephalography 36
Euclidean distance 38

F

F1 score 128
first order logic 36

G

Gaussian mixture modelling 122
gradient boosting classifier 32
GSM module 14

H

hidden Markov model 122, 174

I

Indian Council of Medical Research 137
internet of things 35

K

K-means clustering 38

L

least square method 215
least square support vector machine 37
linear predictive coding 206
local area networking 75
logistic regression 32
long short-term memory 159

M

MediaPipe 29
mel frequency cepstral coefficients 122
Middle East respiratory syndrome 59
MobileNetv2 49
multi-input and multi-output 139
multilayer perceptron 36
Myers Briggs type indicator 158

N

naive Bayes 159
National Dairy Research Institute (NDRI) 138
natural language processing 150
novel coronavirus pneumonia 60

O

Opencv 49
optical character recognition 203

P

precision 128
Precision Recall F1 Score Support 128
principal component analysis 175
proportional integral derivative 140

Q

quality of service 84

R

radiofrequency Id 223
random forest classifier 32
Recurrent Neural Network 84, 175